*Experience
and
Expression*

Experience and Expression

Wittgenstein's Philosophy of Psychology

JOACHIM SCHULTE

CLARENDON PRESS · OXFORD
1993

Oxford University Press, Walton Street, Oxford OX2 6DP
Oxford New York Toronto
Delhi Bombay Calcutta Madras Karachi
Kuala Lumpur Singapore Hong Kong Tokyo
Nairobi Dar es Salaam Cape Town
Melbourne Auckland Madrid
and associated companies in
Berlin Ibadan

Oxford is a trade mark of Oxford University Press

Published in the United States
by Oxford University Press, New York

This English edition has been translated by Joachim Schulte
from the original German publication Erlebnis und Ausdruck:
Wittgensteins Philosophie der Psychologie
© Philosophia Verlag GmbH, München 1987
Translation © Oxford University Press 1993

British Library Cataloguing in Publication Data
Data available

Library of Congress Cataloging in Publication Data
Schulte, Joachim.
[Erlebnis und Ausdruck. English]
Experience and expression: Wittgenstein's philosophy
of psychology / Joachim Schulte.
p. cm.
Includes bibliographical references and index.
1. Psychology—Philosophy—History—20th century.
2. Wittgenstein, Ludwig, 1889–1951—Contributions in psychology.
3. Experience—History—20th century. 4. Psycholinguistics—
History. I. Title.
BF38.S3513 1992 150'.1—dc20 92–20322
ISBN 0–19–824255–7

Typeset by Pentacor PLC, High Wycombe, Bucks
Printed in Great Britain by
Biddles Ltd., Guildford & King's Lynn

Preface

THE way this book has been written has been influenced by an experience I have had again and again, the experience of hearing people use expressions like 'concept X in Wittgenstein's sense' or 'this concept is to be understood in the sense in which Wittgenstein employs it in the *Investigations*', and so forth. When I hear this kind of formulation I am generally at a loss and often wonder what the speaker could possibly mean; for normally there is not *one* sense in which Wittgenstein uses the term in question, nor does there seem to be much agreement among his readers as to what he wanted to say. I am equally surprised whenever people mention *the* private-language argument, *the* concept of a rule, or *the* notion of a criterion advocated by Wittgenstein. I simply cannot find these allegedly definite ideas in Wittgenstein's writings. To be sure, it sometimes looks as if he wanted to defend a certain thought in a clear-cut and definitive way, but in most cases it suffices to read on for a while to see that he has changed his attitude and is now looking at the relevant question in an entirely different light.

This is not meant to discredit the philosophical ideals of simplicity, straightforwardness, and clarity. But whether or not one will succeed in realizing them depends on the way one tries to reach them. The question is whether one wishes to cover as much ground as possible in as short a time as possible or whether one intends to follow every turn of the road without succumbing to the temptation of taking short cuts wherever they look promising. In my opinion Wittgenstein clearly belongs to the second group of travellers, and for this reason I believe that in trying to find an interpretation it will be advisable to follow the slow road; for otherwise there would be a great risk of leaving the author behind and ending up in a completely different place from him. If the reader wants to keep his eye on Wittgenstein, he will do well if he decides to walk the same way he does, and even that is not always easy. The contrast I wish to bring out has been vividly described by Walter Benjamin in the following passage from his *One Way Street:*

The power of a country road is different when one is walking along it from when one is flying over it by airplane. In the same way, the power of a text is different when it is read from when it is copied out. The airplane passenger sees only how the road pushes through the landscape, how it unfolds according to the same laws as the terrain surrounding it. Only he who walks the road on foot learns of the power it commands, and of how, from the very scenery that for the flier is only the unfurled plain, it calls forth distances, belvederes, clearings, prospects at each of its turns like a commander deploying soldiers at a front. Only the copied text thus commands the soul of him who is occupied with it, whereas the mere reader never discovers the new aspects of his inner self that are opened by the text, that road cut through the interior jungle forever closing behind it: because the reader follows the movement of his mind in the free flight of day-dreaming, whereas the copier submits it to command.[1]

I really walked the road, that is, before setting out to write the present study I actually copied out the relevant manuscripts by Wittgenstein. At the time, during the second half of the seventies, I was busy producing transcriptions of those manuscripts for the Wittgenstein archive at the University of Tübingen, which has long since become defunct. Even the experience of learning what kind of mistake one tends to make in copying out Wittgenstein's manuscripts has been useful—it often happens that short cuts appear tempting. Moreover, in copying out a text one can hardly help developing a certain feeling for the pace, the peculiar tempo, and the individual irregularities of the thinking of the author one strives to follow. And this sort of feeling can be a great help in giving an exegesis of writings by that author, or so I imagine.

Starting from my transcriptions and from what I learned in producing them I have tried to become clearer about some central concepts of Wittgenstein's later philosophy of psychology. In those cases where I feel I have reached a certain degree of clarity I have attempted to trace the road Wittgenstein follows in developing his ideas. In addition, I try to give some information which is more easily or more straightforwardly acquired from the manuscripts than from the published texts. I hope I have not lost my way too often and have succeeded in sketching a serviceable hiking map. I wish I were sure that in this field tramping will get you further than using an aeroplane.

I am grateful to the Thyssen Foundation and to the Deutsche Forschungsgemeinschaft for making part of my work possible; to my former colleagues at the Wittgenstein archive for their help; to

[1] Walter Benjamin, *One-Way Street and Other Writings* (London, 1979), 50.

Wittgenstein's literary executors (G. E. M. Anscombe, the late R. Rhees, and G. H. von Wright) and to Peter Winch for their permission to quote unpublished material from Wittgenstein's manuscripts.

In the autumn of 1985 I enjoyed the opportunity of presenting some of the ideas of this book in a seminar which I gave at the University of Graz. I wish to thank all those who took part in that seminar; I learned a good deal from discussing my material with them. I am indebted to Hannes Marek for his help and many comments on my work, and to Rudolf Haller for his unforgettable hospitality and for making those discussions possible.

I am grateful to Hans Jürgen Heringer and Rüdiger Bubner for their active support; to Christoph Nyíri for nudging me on; to Georg Henrik von Wright for his critical comments on Chapter 9; to Brian McGuinness for encouragement and advice. Of especial help was a certain frown Eva Picardi gave me. Many thanks.

The greater part of the English version of this book is a very free translation of the German original. Exceptions are Chapters 1, 8, and 10. The Introduction (Chapter 1) and the Epilogue (Chapter 10) have been largely rewritten; Chapter 8 on emotion is new and has been added to round off my account of Wittgenstein's philosophy of psychology. Besides these there are many small changes which I hope will contribute to making this book a useful one.

Quotations from unpublished manuscripts have been translated by myself. Quotations from published translations containing mistakes or infelicities have been amended tacitly.

I am extremely grateful to my friend John Baker, who went through my English manuscript, made many helpful comments on it, and patiently discussed a great number of questions with me.

Contents

Abbreviations

(*for further details, see Bibliography*)

Bl Bk	Wittgenstein, *Blue Book*
BrBk	—— *Brown Book*
C&V	—— *Culture and Value*
LPP	—— *Lectures on Philosophical Psychology*
LW	—— *Last Writings on the Philosophy of Psychology*
OC	—— *On Certainty*
PG	—— *Philosophical Grammar*
PI	—— *Philosophical Investigations*
RFM	—— *Remarks on the Foundations of Mathematics*
RPP	—— *Remarks on the Philosophy of Psychology*
WVC	Waismann, *Wittgenstein and the Vienna Circle*

Note on Unpublished Sources

Wittgenstein's manuscripts and typescripts are referred to by their numbers in G. H. von Wright's catalogue. Translations of manuscript passages are my own. Whenever possible, manuscript entries are specified by their dates, otherwise by page number. Dates are throughout given in Wittgenstein's preferred style, e.g. 13.4.47 for 13 April 1947. Occasionally the translations of Wittgenstein's writings mentioned in the Bibliography have been modified so as to make them correspond more closely to the German original. The German versions of the manuscript quotations in the text are given in an Appendix (pp. 167–70), prefaced in each case by the page number for the translation.

1

Introduction

APART from his *Logisch-philosophische Abhandlung* (better known under the title of its English translation, *Tractatus Logico-Philosophicus*) the only philosophical writings by Wittgenstein which appeared during his lifetime were a brief review, which he wrote as a student, and the article 'Some Remarks on Logical Form' of 1929. All the other philosophical writings which have been published under his name are posthumous. They are taken from the vast body of material which he left to his literary executors, who edited them in the years since Wittgenstein's death in 1951.

The present study is mostly concerned with manuscripts that Wittgenstein wrote in the years 1946 to 1949.[1] A sizeable part, but by no means all, of this material has been published since this study was begun. In order to help the reader to get a rough idea of the relative bearing of these writings I shall in the following pages give a sketch of the types of material to be found among Wittgenstein's papers and then indicate in which category the writings forming the basis of this study belong.[2]

Do the typescripts and manuscripts on the philosophy of psychology which Wittgenstein wrote in the years 1946 to 1949 constitute a philosophical work or, perhaps, a series of philosophical works? Or do these typescripts and manuscripts form different versions of one major work? These questions are not at all easy to answer. Not everything which can be, or has been, published can legitimately be called a 'work'. With most well-known authors there are no such problems as arise in the case of Wittgenstein. Of Kant's *Critique of Pure Reason*, for example, we have two versions that differ in various clearly defined respects. Modern editions reproduce both versions and show where they differ. Both versions were published by Kant himself and the later one was intended to supersede the earlier one. In the case of Wittgenstein, the situation is

---

[1] Cf. the list of manuscripts given at the end of this book.
[2] A fuller account is given in my book *Wittgenstein. Eine Einführung* (Stuttgart, 1989), 43–56.

different. It is difficult to speak of 'versions', as it is not clear what they might be regarded as versions of. Because of his failure to publish his writings there is no clear indication of what to consider a complete text which could be taken to represent the author's views on a certain subject at a certain time.

But Wittgenstein's manuscripts do not form an amorphous mass of more or less disconnected remarks. It is often possible to identify breaks and connecting links, different themes and their variations. Take the *Philosophical Remarks*. The typescript of 1930 on which the printed book is based is in its turn derived from a number of manuscript volumes. From these manuscript volumes Wittgenstein selected remarks, which were then incorporated in a typescript. This typescript was cut into little slips containing individual remarks. These remarks were, after another process of revision and selection, arranged in a new order. This revised arrangement was then typed, and the typescript resulting from this arrangement formed the 'final' version of the *Philosophical Remarks*. In the case of this posthumous book we can follow the various stages of development. There can be little doubt that Wittgenstein regarded each later stage as an improvement on the earlier ones, and it seems clearly justified to call the *Remarks* one of Wittgenstein's works.

The manuscripts and the intermediate typescript, on the other hand, are to be regarded neither as separate works nor as different versions of a work. And there are at least three reasons which can be adduced to support this claim. (1) It can be shown that in Wittgenstein's own view these writings represented preliminary stages of something more unified and with a more clearly defined structure. (2) These preliminary stages lack a comprehensive line of argument. (3) Neither in point of style nor regarding their form can these preliminary stages be said to display the degree of organization and finish which the 'final' typescript undeniably possesses. For these reasons the preliminary stages of the *Philosophical Remarks* are not to be counted as earlier versions of this work, any more than Beethoven's sketches for a symphony are to be regarded as earlier versions of that symphony.

But if one looks at the typescript of the *Philosophical Remarks* from a different perspective, it turns out that it is but one of several versions of the one great work which Wittgenstein was trying to write after his return to Cambridge in 1929. For there can be no doubt that virtually everything written by Wittgenstein after that date is part of his attempt at producing one book which was to succeed both in correcting what he regarded as the mistakes of the *Tractatus* and in giving a satisfactory account of his new ideas. The relatively finished typescripts of 1930 and 1933 (on which the published books *Philosophical Remarks* and *Philosophical Grammar* are based) and the first typescript stages of the *Philosophical Investigations* and of the *Remarks on the Foundations of Mathematics* show quite clearly that Wittgenstein wanted to produce a comprehensive work that was to deal with a certain number of subjects, which the printed preface of the *Philosophical Investigations* specifies as follows: 'the concepts of meaning, of understanding, of a proposition, of logic, the foundations of mathematics, states of consciousness, and other things'. Logic and the foundations of mathematics are not treated in the published *Philosophical Investigations*; evidently the plan to include them in this work was abandoned sometime between the first attempts at writing what is now known as *Remarks on the Foundations of Mathematics* and the last revision of the first part of the *Philosophical Investigations*, if it was ever consciously abandoned at all. At any rate, it is surely justified to regard the typescripts of 1930 and 1933 as well as the original plan of *Philosophical Investigations* as different versions of Wittgenstein's intended *summa*.

It will be useful to reformulate the negative criteria mentioned two paragraphs ago in a positive way, so that they may serve to distinguish between relatively accomplished 'works' by Wittgenstein and mere preliminary writings. These criteria are the following. (1) It can be shown that according to Wittgenstein's own judgement the text in question is a fairly complete and independent treatment of its subject-matter. (2) The reader is in a position to recognize and reproduce a certain line of argument involving theses, supporting arguments, objections, helpful considerations, examples, and so on. (3) The text in question is, as regards form and style, sufficiently finished to call it a 'completed' work.

Using these criteria or standards for judging Wittgenstein's manuscripts, we shall arrive at something like the following picture. First, there are a number of notebooks clearly exhibiting the character of first sketches, drafts, or mere jottings. Secondly, there are volumes (Wittgenstein himself called them *Bände* and numbered them consecutively) which in many cases use material from the notebooks of the first category, often improving on the style of the notebook remarks without normally arriving at a more comprehensive line of argument. Thirdly, there are manuscripts and typescripts which are products of a certain amount of sifting and revising material belonging to the first two categories but do not yet exhibit the formal and stylistic features of an at least partially finished work in its own right. And fourthly, there are those writings which satisfy all three of the criteria mentioned, and it will surely be justified to call these—and only these—writings real 'works' by Wittgenstein.

This fairly clear picture is blurred as soon as one recognizes that Wittgenstein was never quite contented with his writings. Whenever he completed one of his 'finished' typescripts, he immediately started to revise it or he turned away from it in disappointment, trying to look at the matter from a different point of view or changing the subject altogether. For this reason it will be appropriate to regard the writings belonging to the fourth category—which, this caveat notwithstanding, I shall continue to call Wittgenstein's 'works'—not as a definitive conclusion of a certain development but rather as a kind of sediment in a river which has at this point come to a temporary standstill and will presently find a new bed in which to continue its course. As soon as Wittgenstein starts revising a work, all his ideas are in flux again; we are no longer confronted with a 'work' in the sense intended here but with constitutive parts of a work in progress.

These considerations show that it is not possible to apply the concept of a work to Wittgenstein's published and unpublished writings without qualification. To the extent that the *Philosophical Remarks*, for instance, represent an early version of a text produced in subsequent years, they are superseded by the later material, for we must not forget that Wittgenstein's belief in the completion of works like his typescripts of 1930 and 1933 or the pre-war version of the *Philosophical Investigations* never lasted very long. Even with the final version of the *Philosophical Investigations* he was contented only inasmuch as he felt that he was not able to do any better. Thus, if we are prepared to call the Philosophical Remarks or the First Part of the *Philosophical Investigations* a 'work' by Wittgenstein, this must not be taken to imply that there was a continuous process of development leading from one work to the next and that draft material and sketches can be said clearly to belong to this or to that work. For the points where sediment accumulates in the river of Wittgenstein's philosophical investigations are at the same time points where the flow of this river is interrupted. Here we are confronted with a caesura or a hiatus. They are points where in view of unresolved problems Wittgenstein decides that he will have to tackle the matter in a new way: points where the river must find a new bed.

The manuscripts on which the present study is based belong to the second category distinguished above. In G. H. von Wright's list of Wittgenstein's papers they bear the numbers 130 to 138.[3] By far the greatest part of this material comes from the time between 26. 5. 1946 and 22. 3. 1949. The first of these dates appears roughly half-way through volume 130, whose first fifty pages or so were probably written earlier, at the beginning of 1945.

These manuscript volumes 130–8 are ledgers of British or Irish make; the last three were bought in Dublin, as is shown by labels inside them. Their sizes vary; some of them are a little smaller and others a little larger than A4. Taken all together these manuscripts contain more than 1,900 written pages. The published part of this material amounts to roughly 450 printed pages, the unpublished part to perhaps two-thirds of that.[4] Generally the remarks are written in ink; occasionally there are pencilled corrections. There are a large number of alternative formulations or stylistic variants, practically always enclosed in parentheses of this kind: // . . . //. Most of the text is quite easy to read.

The material contained in manuscripts 130–8 was revised by Wittgenstein in several respects. First, he cut out or changed certain formulations. Secondly, he selected a number of remarks with which he was satisfied or which he intended to use for some further purpose. He took great pains over this process of selection. His judgement was marked by means of certain symbols in front of the relevant remarks. Not infrequently we find three or four of these symbols in front of a single remark, which shows that the process of selection was repeated several times. The most frequent symbols and their meanings are the following:

/ (rarely //)—sign of satisfaction

S-shaped sign (perhaps for *schlecht* (= 'bad'))—to be suppressed

---

[3] G. H. von Wright, 'The Wittgenstein Papers', in *Wittgenstein* (Oxford, 1982).
[4] The material printed in *Culture and Value* is here left out of account. The remarks written between 1946 and 1949 are there printed on pp. 47–83.

?—throws doubt on the following symbol (e.g. '/') or (rarely) on the relevant remark itself

| . . . |—the remark in question does not belong in this context; many of these remarks are of a general nature (a number of them have been printed in *Culture and Value*)

C-shaped sign—appears from MS 136 onwards and means roughly the same as the S-shaped sign, viz. that the remark in question is to be suppressed

L.L.—from 24. 10. 48 (MSS 137 and 138), additional positive sign indicating that the relevant remark is to be included in MS 144 (a loose-leaf (= L.L.) folder on whose contents Part II of the *Philosophical Investigations* is based)[5]

Most of the selected remarks were included in two typescripts, whose dictation was completed in November 1947 (TS 229) and October 1948 (TS 232), respectively. The selected remarks written between October 1948 and March 1949 were not directly included in a typescript but in MS 144, which was written by Wittgenstein before going to America in July 1949. This manuscript also contains *c*.70 remarks from TS 229 and *c*.40 remarks from TS 232.

Thus the manuscripts we are dealing with belong to the second of our categories. The typescripts belong to the third category, but barely so because for the greatest part they do not attempt any rearrangement of the manuscript material. In this respect, MS 144 is different: it presents the remarks taken from various manuscripts and typescripts of this period in a different order and clearly constructs recognizable arguments. But it still seems to me that MS 144 has remained a fragment of what was intended to be a much more comprehensive enterprise, and even this fragment is incomplete and unfinished compared to the style and form of what was achieved in the first part of the *Philosophical Investigations*.

The value of the manuscript material examined in the present study lies, among other things, in allowing us to investigate the *complete* first stage of the production of a work which remained unfinished. These manuscripts contain virtually all of Wittgenstein's work written in those three years and his attempts at revising and selecting remarks from this material. Trying to understand Witt-

[5] The typescript from which the second part of the *Philosophical Investigations* was printed is lost. Cf. G. H. von Wright, 'The Origin and Composition of the *Philosophical Investigations*', in *Wittgenstein* (Oxford, 1982).

genstein's writings from this time by using only the selected and published texts would put one at a great disadvantage. For in that case one would have to content oneself with a smaller amount of material without enjoying a completed and rounded-off work. This is one of the reasons why in the following chapters I frequently refer to 'suppressed' remarks.

Another advantage of using the manuscripts lies in the fact that they contain a large number of dates and thus permit the reader to make safe inferences as to continuity or discontinuity of Wittgenstein's work. These dates can serve as an independent criterion for deciding what belongs together and what does not.

There is yet another respect in which the manuscripts may help the reader. The formulation of Wittgenstein's revised remarks is often more general than his first versions; that is, the later versions tend to mention fewer examples and allusions to sources than the earlier ones. Thus in a number of cases earlier formulations, which do contain clear hints or allusions, can be used to confirm or disconfirm certain readings of the more polished later versions of some remarks.[6]

As regards their subject-matter, manuscripts 130–8 are fairly unified; they deal with what one may call the 'logic of psychological concepts'. Among the topics treated are the concepts of thinking, sensation, understanding, and perception. In addition to these there are general remarks on the method of doing philosophy and on the possibility of arguing for certain philosophical claims as well as more specific discussions of the analysis of conditional statements and of the 'heterological' paradox. Besides these the manuscripts contain a number of remarks on aesthetic and in a sense ethical subjects.

It is characteristic of Wittgenstein's thinking in general that, even though he may be stimulated by the ideas of other philosophers, he immediately modifies these ideas and makes them tally with his own ways of asking questions and looking for answers. For this reason it

[6] This can be illustrated by means of the first sentence of section xiv on the last page of the *Philosophical Investigations*. This sentence runs as follows: 'The confusion and barrenness of psychology is not to be explained by calling it a "young science".' Here one may *guess* that Wittgenstein alludes to the chapter 'Psychology as a Young Science' of Köhler's book *Gestalt Psychology* (1st US edn., 1929; rev. edn., New York, 1975). This guess is confirmed by looking at the corresponding manuscript passage, where Köhler's name is mentioned in brackets.

is hardly ever possible to speak of a real influence on Wittgenstein—with one exception perhaps, namely that of Frege.
Frege's writings have left more traces on Wittgenstein's thought
than those of any other author, and the impact of Frege's
philosophy can be shown to have had a lasting effect even in
contexts where one would not expect it. Thus Frege's influence can
be felt in manuscripts 130–8 too, in particular in Wittgenstein's
discussion of Moore's paradox ('It is raining but I do not believe it',
cf. Chapter 9, below).

Another author who was important for Wittgenstein at the time
of writing manuscripts 130–8 was Wolfgang Köhler, whose book
Gestalt Psychology Wittgenstein read at that time. It is likely that
Wittgenstein also knew Köhler's earlier book about testing the
intelligence of anthropoid apes, *The Mentality of Apes*.[7] Several of
Köhler's theses are discussed in Wittgenstein's last lectures in
Cambridge, and in manuscripts 130–8 his name is mentioned
relatively frequently. There is no clear evidence of whether
Wittgenstein studied other authors belonging to the gestalt school
of psychology. But we may be confident that at least from
conversations and perhaps also from his own reading he knew a
good deal more about gestalt psychology than can be found in
Köhler's book. (Cf. Chapter 6, below.)

Wittgenstein was also familiar with problems of experimental
psychology. He had already done some work during his first years
in Cambridge at the institute of the well-known psychologist
Charles Samuel Myers and had there 'carried out an investigation at
the psychological laboratory concerning rhythm in music. He had
hoped that the experiments could throw light on some questions of
aesthetics that interested him.'[8]

An unfailing source of new suggestions for Wittgenstein's
thinking was William James's two-volume work on *The Principles
of Psychology* of 1890 (cf. Chapter 8, below). As early as the

---

[7] Cf. G. Hallett, *A Companion to Wittgenstein's 'Philosophical Investigations'*
(Ithaca, NY, 1977), 688 and 769. Hallett cites the following remark from MS 130 (31.
7. 46): 'This [*RPP* i. § 174] reminds me of certain remarks of Köhler, when he is
describing the behaviour of his apes. He makes evidently correct psychological
observations, without however emphasizing that one must attend to the *finer*
differences of behaviour.'

[8] G. H. von Wright, 'A Biographical Sketch', in *Wittgenstein* (Oxford, 1982), 19–
20. Cf. Wittgenstein's letters 2 and 3 to Russell; B. McGuinness, *Wittgenstein: A Life*, i.
Young Ludwig 1889–1921 (London, 1988), 125–8.

beginning of the *Brown Book* (p. 78) Wittgenstein refers to James's idea of specific word feelings. In the *Philosophical Investigations* James is mentioned four times—that is, just as often as Frege—but allusions to his work are much more frequent than that. A large number of remarks in manuscripts 130–8 are due to James, but the source in these cases is not always evident.[9] The importance of James is indicated by the following report:

One of [Wittgenstein's] former pupils, Mr. A. C. Jackson, tells me that Wittgenstein very frequently referred to James in his lectures, even making on one occasion—to everybody's astonishment—a precise reference to a page-number! At one time, furthermore, James's *Principles* was the only philosophical work visible on his bookshelves.[10]

But even though there are a large number of allusions to James, he did not really *influence* Wittgenstein. He stimulated Wittgenstein and provided him with ideas and examples, and Wittgenstein liked his narrative and often non-theoretical style.[11]

When I embarked on my study of Wittgenstein's manuscripts on the philosophy of psychology the entire material was still un-published. In the mean time typescripts 229 and 232 have appeared under the title *Remarks on the Philosophy of Psychology*, and these typescripts reproduce a little more than half of the manuscript material written up to the time the second was dictated. The book published under the title *Last Writings on the Philosophy of Psychology* is of a different character, for it reproduces the entire manuscript material written between October 1948 and May 1949. In reading the *Remarks on the Philosophy of Psychology* one must always remember that one is dealing with a *selection* of remarks taken from manuscripts and mostly copied in chronological order. To be sure, the selection was made by Wittgenstein himself. But he

[9] To be sure, in the cases where Wittgenstein seems to allude to James one cannot always be sure if James *was* his source. An example would be the feeling of unreality discussed in Wittgenstein's remarks on the philosophy of psychology. Was Wittgenstein stimulated by what James says about 'feelings of unreality' in *The Principles of Psychology* (New York, 1950), ii. 298? Cf. *LPP* 75, 205.
[10] Passmore, *A Hundred Years of Philosophy* (Harmondsworth, 1978), 592 n. 4.
[11] An interesting remark is the following, taken from lecture notes and quoted in Hallett, *Companion*, 767: 'Goethe's doctrine on the origin of spectral colours is not a theory which has proved inadequate, but is in fact no theory. It permits no predictions. It is just a vague thought-schema, of the kind one finds in James's psychology. There is no *experimentum crucis* which could decide for or against this doctrine.'

did not finish his work. Had he lived to continue his work on this material, he would have rearranged most of the remarks, he would have made a great number of stylistic changes, and he would have added new remarks and hints necessary to understand the old ones. Such additions and hints are naturally lacking in the published *Remarks on the Philosophy of Psychology*, but some hints can be divined and reconstructed from suppressed manuscript remarks;[12] they will thus help to facilitate our understanding and prevent us from drawing false conclusions.

The following chapters are meant both to clarify hidden or obscure remarks in Wittgenstein's remarks on the philosophy of psychology and to point out certain conceptual connections and developments in his thinking during the late forties. The best-known result of his thinking during that time is the 'Second Part' of the posthumous *Philosophical Investigations*. But most people who have investigated this question will agree that this part, which was added by the editors of that book, is rather awkwardly placed where it stands now. I think that von Wright is *grosso modo* right in saying that 'Part I of the *Investigations* is a complete work and that Wittgenstein's writings from 1946 onwards represent in certain ways departures in *new* directions'.[13] Perhaps the following chapters will help readers to understand the direction in which Wittgenstein's ideas moved in the late forties.

[12] By calling unpublished passages 'suppressed remarks' I do not wish to imply that these passages do not represent Wittgenstein's views. In many cases Wittgenstein's motives for *not* selecting such remarks may have been purely stylistic ones. For us as readers they may be of great importance if they are our only or our best evidence for attributing a certain idea to Wittgenstein.

[13] Von Wright, 'The Origin and Composition of the *Philosophical Investigations*', 136. In view of Wittgenstein's original intention to include material on logic and the foundations of mathematics one may wonder if Part I of the *Investigations* really is to be regarded as a 'complete work'. Nevertheless I should agree that—as regards form, style, and argument—Part I of the *Investigations* is an accomplished and rounded-off work.

2

Language Games

THE concept of a language game is one of the most important and most characteristic of Wittgenstein's later philosophy. This concept refers to the subject-matter of many of Wittgenstein's reflections upon both the meanings and the differences in meaning of linguistic expressions and at the same time marks a feature of his philosophical method. This method is intended to shed light on conceptual connections by means of describing language games.

The general idea on which the concept of a language game is based goes back to an analogy between the function of linguistic expressions and the function of chess-men or similar pieces used in playing games. This analogy comes to the fore in Wittgenstein's many comparisons involving the game of chess, particularly numerous in his writings of the early thirties. These comparisons, however, are merely the starting-point of a development which leads to an increasingly comprehensive and autonomous conception in which the confrontation between games like chess or tennis, on the one hand, and games comprising real or possible uses of linguistic expressions, on the other, loses most of its former significance. It is thus a mistake if in explaining Wittgenstein's notion of a language game too much stress is laid on the existence of *analogies* between games and uses of language, thereby suggesting that the concept 'language game' is largely a metaphorical one. What this concept is really intended to emphasize are the interactive aspects of linguistic and other activities. Wittgenstein does not content himself with pointing out mere similarities between uses of linguistic expressions and uses of chess-men or between following the rules of games and those of language.

It is true that the concept of a language game is closely connected with Wittgenstein's principle that in many cases the meaning of a linguistic expression is its use. It would be a mistake, however, to follow Kenny's strategy of employing this idea of the use of linguistic expressions to construct a connection, or at least a certain continuity, between the conception of meaning which can be found

in the *Tractatus* and Wittgenstein's later notion of language games.[1]
One gets nearer the mark if one sees the development of that notion
in the context of Wittgenstein's gradual rejection of the ideas of the
Tractatus in his writings of the late twenties and early thirties.[2]
According to this view, the first identifiable predecessor of the
concept of a language game is the idea of language as a calculus, an
idea which, in the early thirties, gains more and more importance in
Wittgenstein's writings and is found attractive by him for the reason
that at that time he is basically 'interested in language as a procedure
according to explicit rules' (*PG*, 68). But the closer Wittgenstein
investigates the idea of language as a calculus, the more inadequate it
proves to be; and the clearer the inadequacy of the idea becomes, the
better he grasps the need to turn to an examination of different
features of the use of language.

The first detailed characterization of what Wittgenstein means by
the concept 'language game' is given in the *Blue Book*, which was
dictated in 1933/4:

I shall in the future again and again draw your attention to what I shall call
language games. These are ways of using signs simpler than those in which
we use the signs of our highly complicated everyday language. Language
games are the forms of language with which a child begins to make use of
words. The study of language games is the study of primitive forms of
language or primitive languages. If we want to study the problems of truth
and falsehood, of the agreement and disagreement of propositions with
reality, of the nature of assertion, assumption, and question, we shall with
great adavantage look at primitive forms of language in which these forms
of thinking appear without the confusing background of highly complicated processes of thought. When we look at such simple forms of language
the mental mist which seems to enshroud our ordinary use of language
disappears. We see activities, reactions, which are clear-cut and transparent.
On the other hand we recognize in these simple processes forms of
language not separated by a break from our more complicated ones. We see
that we can build up the complicated forms from the primitive ones by
gradually adding new forms. (*BlBk* 17)

---

[1] A probable influence on Wittgenstein's early notion of a language game is
Frege's discussion of formalist theories of arithmetic in *Grundgesetze der Arithmetik*
(Hildesheim, 1977), ii. 86 ff. There the analogies between games and arithmetical
procedures are considered at length. Wittgenstein knew Frege's discussion well. Cf.
WVC 103 ff.; G. P. Baker and P. M. S. Hacker, *Wittgenstein: Understanding and
Meaning* (Oxford, 1980), 90.
[2] Cf. A. Kenny, *Wittgenstein* (London, 1973), p. 159; Baker and Hacker,
Understanding and Meaning, 90 ff.

Great stress is laid in this passage on the simplicity of the forms which are to be studied; and Wittgenstein expresses his firm belief that consideration of primitive language games—in particular of the techniques employed by children, which often are considerably less complicated than those employed by adults—will facilitate an understanding of our complex ways of using linguistic expressions.

This appeal to the ways children learn and use language is also to be found in the *Brown Book*, which Wittgenstein dictated in the academic year 1934/5, as well as in the German version of this work, which was written in Norway in the summer of 1936. In the *Brown Book* Wittgenstein says that ' "language games" . . . are more or less akin to what in ordinary language we call games. Children are taught their native language by means of such games, and here they even have the entertaining character of games.' But then Wittgenstein goes on to add a new thought:

We are not, however, regarding the language games which we describe as incomplete parts of a language, but as languages complete in themselves, as complete systems of human communication. To keep this point of view in mind, it very often is useful to imagine such a simple language to be the entire system of communication of a tribe in a primitive state of society. (*BrBk* 81)

In this remark Wittgenstein declares that language games are not to be regarded as fragments of a more comprehensive whole, but rather as independent units. And these units are said to be self-sufficient to such an extent that they could be conceived of as complete languages which are used by a community. This radical idea, however, is untenable. If it is construed as a kind of preventive reply to an anticipated objection alleging the incompleteness of a given account,[3] then there may be some point to it. But the claim that a language game like that of the builders, described in § 2 of the *Philosophical Investigations*, is to count as a 'complete primitive language' is simply incredible and, in addition, incompatible with Wittgenstein's mature notion of a language game.[4]

[3] Cf. R. Rhees, 'Wittgenstein's Builders', in *Discussions of Wittgenstein* (London, 1970), 76: 'In this he is warning against the mistaken idea that a language may be found to be "incomplete", and against a view like that of the *Tractatus* that it should be possible to calculate all the possible forms of propositions.'

[4] Baker and Hacker defend Wittgenstein's radical claim in the following way: 'No language is, as it were, incomplete *from within*—it is what it is. If it provides no means for a certain type of discourse, then it is silent' (*Understanding and Meaning*, 66). So far, so good. The real difficulty, however, does not arise for the example Baker and Hacker use to illustrate their case when they explain that it would not

What is more important than the misleading suggestion of the completeness of language games is the recommendation given in the German version of the above-quoted passage from the *Brown Book*. There Wittgenstein advises us to 'draw a more comprehensive picture' and to remember the ways language is used in the life of a community of speakers. This recommendation is meant not only to encourage us to make use of a certain heuristic means, but also to indicate a criterion which can be used to establish the sense of linguistic expressions. Such expressions are, as Wittgenstein keeps reminding us, used in a way similar to that of using tools or instruments (cf. *PI* § 11). In order to grasp what a hammer is, it is necessary to know how it is used; and in order to understand how it is used, it will not be enough to know how it is handled but also what it is used *for*. Similarly with language. And just as it is impossible to indicate *one* purpose served by all tools, so it is also impossible to specify *one* end which could be said to be the end of all uses of linguistic expressions. It would not only be futile but wrong to claim that language serves no purpose but that of communication or that it is the function of *all* linguistic expressions to refer to something. Just as we shall be able to make out the different jobs done by different tools only if we pay attention to the varieties of ways in which they function, so we shall be able to grasp the different types of end served by linguistic expressions only if we investigate their ways of functioning in different contexts of use.

If we wish to discover the sense of an expression, we need not restrict ourselves to looking at those language games which are actually played by speakers of the language in question. We may also examine invented language games and in this way try out, as it were, to what extent it is possible to stretch or telescope the sense of certain expressions and whether it is at all possible to establish their senses.

Wittgenstein's descriptions and discussions of actual and invented language games serve a number of purposes. First of all, a

make much sense to assert that our language was 'incomplete' before the introduction of the terminology of chemistry. Wittgenstein's request to regard the language game of the builders as a complete language is misguided for *this* reason: that it is not compatible with the requirement to describe language games in such a way that they fit the form of life of the community in question. The language game of the builders could count as a complete language only if those builders literally did nothing but work in the way described in § 2 of the *Philosophical Investigations*. But not only is it hard to imagine a society of builders who neither eat, nor procreate, nor know any form of entertainment, but their 'behaviour' would simply shed no light on *our* language games. Cf. Rhees, 'Wittgenstein's Builders', 83.

comparative examination of different language games which succeeds in pointing out similarities and differences, overlappings and
discontinuities, will enable us to arrive at a *conspectus* or *overview*
of the various ways in which our use of linguistic expressions is
determined by rules; it will allow us to estimate the extent to which
that use is determined by rules; and it will make it possible for us to
grasp whether and how these rules can be modified. Here the aim is
to develop a sequence or series of cases by juxtaposing them as
perspicuously as possible and, if necessary, to invent missing
'connecting links', thus giving our use of linguistic expressions a
certain shape—a 'face' or a 'physiognomy', as Wittgenstein
says—in order to render strikingly visible the relevant similarities
and differences.[5]

Secondly, descriptions and examinations of language games serve,
as has already been pointed out, as criteria for determining the sense
of an expression and also as a kind of test for finding out whether
expressions make sense and whether they can—for instance in
invented language games—be given a certain sense.

Thirdly, descriptions of different language games are intended to
indicate points where the surface grammar of our language obscures
differences in depth grammar.[6] This involves trying to distinguish
different *types* of language games, for example the games of
asserting, making assumptions, asking questions, etc. Here it must
be remembered that Wittgenstein recognizes language games of all
kinds of complexity. Not only does he speak of comprehensive
types of game like that of asserting; he also mentions more specific
ones like the games of reporting and recounting dreams. Moreover,
he often uses such locutions as 'the language game with the word
"red"', and of course a language game in this sense will cut across
several types, as 'red' can occur in assertions as well as in questions,
in reports, and in narratives of dreams.[7] In each of these cases
Wittgenstein emphasizes that it must be possible to specify the
relevant context, to indicate the point or purpose of the utterance in

---

[5] Wittgenstein's extremely important concept of *Übersichtlichkeit* (overview,
conspectus, bird's-eye view, synoptic view, see *PI* § 122) is discussed in Baker and
Hacker, *Understanding and Meaning*, 531 ff. Cf. my article 'Chor und Gesetz', in
Chor und Gesetz (Frankfurt, 1990).

[6] An example mentioned by Kenny is the following: 'Wittgenstein would insist
that it is misleading to lump together all indicative sentences' (Kenny, *Wittgenstein*,
167).

[7] The great variety of language games is indicated in *PI* § 23.

question, and to describe the skills needed for mastering the expressions concerned.

In Wittgenstein's writings of the late forties the concept of a language game as it was developed in the thirties retains its importance. It continues to play more or less the same role it plays in the *Philosophical Investigations*, and its use exhibits all the features mentioned above. But a certain tendency can be noticed which is well worth pointing out. In the later writings there occur fewer invented games than in the earlier ones, and frequently Wittgenstein is content to make rough and ready suggestions and to ask the reader simply to look at the language game; for then the sense may become clear to him.

But Wittgenstein's later remarks on the philosophy of psychology contain not only this habitual use of that consolidated notion of a language game; in these writings there also occur reflections upon this notion which are speculative in character and anticipate a number of considerations which are made more explicit in the context of *On Certainty* and, in particular, in his remarks concerning our world picture.[8] In this respect Wittgenstein's remarks of the late forties belong to a period of transition. On the one hand, they constitute a continuous development of thoughts discussed in Part I of the *Philosophical Investigations* and apply some of the central concepts of that period to new or newly conceived subjects; on the other hand, they point forward towards those insights which Wittgenstein articulates in his very last manuscripts.

The speculative reflections which were alluded to in the last paragraph are chiefly concerned with a subject of extreme generality. They deal with questions which may be reformulated in the following way: 'In what kind of context can one statement be said to constitute a reason for another one?' 'What is it that justifies certain conceptual claims?' 'Why should we accept a given justification?' On the one hand, Wittgenstein's answers to these questions express his characteristic belief that philosophical, and hence conceptual, questions are to be discussed as if they were questions regarding the use of the relevant concepts in the context of describable language

[8] Cf. G. H. von Wright, 'Wittgenstein on Certainty', in *Wittgenstein* (Oxford, 1982), 176 ff.; J. Schulte, 'World-picture and Mythology', *Inquiry*, 31 (1988), 323–34.

games. This involves a kind of reduction, and if this reduction succeeds, the original problem will disappear and we shall be satisfied for the reason that we are no longer tormented by that problem. (Alternatively, we may be frustrated for the reason that we have been pursuing a mere phantom—but this alternative is not especially emphasized by Wittgenstein.) On the other hand, Wittgenstein's replies contain polemical points against philosophical attempts to represent certain isolated concepts, and sometimes certain objects or events which are supposed to correspond to those concepts, as fundamental and thus as an ultimate court of appeal. More specifically, in the context of his remarks on the philosophy of psychology Wittgenstein wants to show, if only indirectly, that all attempts at justifying conceptual statements about psychological phenomena by means of purely psychological or introspective evidence are bound to fail.

This becomes particularly clear when Wittgenstein ponders over a temptation which he strongly felt, namely the temptation to assume the concept 'experience' as the basis and cardinal point of his observations on the philosophy of psychology. In this vein he writes:

Here we think we are standing on the hard bedrock, deeper than any special methods and language games. But these extremely general terms have an extremely blurred meaning. They relate in practice to innumerable special cases, but that does not make them any *solider*; no, rather it makes them less tangible. (*RPP* i. § 648)

This is evidently meant to express that something which is extremely general is, precisely because of its generality, not a particularly useful means of justification: it is too diffuse, too evanescent, to serve as a useful basis or to lay the foundations of an important chain of reasoning. But this does not mean that Wittgenstein wishes to defend a claim which could be seen as the opposite of what he is obviously taking exception to. He does not wish to contend that in giving reasons for our statements we should always recur to individual cases or concrete instances, as a particular case can at best serve as an *example* of something. The passage quoted also implies that the 'special methods and language games' themselves can serve as 'the hard bedrock' to which we should, if possible, appeal in our attempts at giving reasons for our statements. The highest or, if we wish to retain the image of 'the hard bedrock', 'deepest' authority is to be found at the point of intersection of acting and speaking, of conduct and use of language: this is the point marked by Wittgenstein's concept of a language game.

Wittgenstein mentions two reasons for ascribing such a fundamental role to language games: (1) 'The primitive language game we originally learned needs no justification' (*RPP* ii. § 453); (2) language games are 'based on' primitive reactions, and these primitive reactions are 'prototypes' of a way of thinking, 'not the result of thought' (*RPP* i. § 916).[9]

The first of these reasons, the one according to which a language game needs no justification, is mentioned in the course of a discussion of the concept 'see'. An early version of the remark in question continues that 'false attempts at justification, which force themselves on us, need to be rejected' (*RPP* ii. § 453) while a later version underlines the point of this statement by generalizing it: 'attempts at justification need to be rejected' (*PI* II. xi, p. 200). Accordingly, not only 'false' attempts at justification, 'which force themselves on us', need to be rejected; now Wittgenstein's judgement concerns *all* attempts at such a justification. This radicalization of Wittgenstein's formulation confirms the tendency indicated above. He is clearly moving in the direction of *On Certainty*, where he will write: 'You must bear in mind that the language game is so to say unpredictable. I mean: it is not based on grounds. It is not reasonable (or unreasonable). / It is there—like our life' (*OC* § 559). And here one might continue that games which

---

[9] In this context a possibly inevitable weakness of Wittgenstein's use of the concept 'language game' becomes apparent. It seems that in some way a distinction needs to be made between primitive or basic language games, on the one hand, and less basic ones, on the other. But Wittgenstein does not have any means at his disposal to draw such a distinction in a systematic fashion. It may of course be that for Wittgenstein's purposes it would be sufficient to be able to indicate a relatively small number of language games—for instance some of those with words like 'pain', 'see', and 'sour'—on whose primitiveness all or most speakers would agree. There is at least one passage, after all, where Wittgenstein explicitly asks the question whether a given language game is to be regarded as more or less fundamental: 'I can play a whole series of language games with a report. One might be: acting according to the report; another one: using the report to test whoever gave it. / But isn't the first language game the more primitive [*ursprünglich*] one, so to speak, the real purpose of a report?' (*RPP* ii. § 278) Unfortunately, Wittgenstein does not answer this question. He does, however, mention cases where the relation between more and less fundamental games becomes fairly clear, for instance: 'To begin by teaching someone "That looks red" makes no sense. For he must say that spontaneously once he has learnt what "red" means, i.e. has learnt the technique of using the word' (*RPP* ii. § 326).

are so inaccessible to attempts at justifying them will in their turn be able to play a special role in other contexts of justification.

The idea that we have no choice but to '*accept* the familiar language game' (*RPP* ii. § 453) can be found in many parts of the manuscripts written in the late forties, even though the formulations tend to be less pronounced than those in *On Certainty*. But this idea, it must be remembered, is of course just as incapable of being established by means of giving reasons for it as is a claim to the effect that primitive language games cannot be justified and should *for this reason* count as the last court of appeal. When Wittgenstein reaches this stage of his discussion he cannot do more than give examples and hope to be able to persuade his interlocutors that his point of view is a helpful one. But if these speculative considerations are to persuade an interlocutor, they will have to support each other and form a coherent and unified view. In his manuscript discussion of the concept 'see' Wittgenstein adduces a further reason why one has to accept this concept—and that means the language game with the word 'see'—'as one finds it' and why one 'must not wish to refine it': 'Because it is not our business to modify it, to introduce (in the way it is done in the sciences) one which is adequate to certain purposes; our business is that of coming to understand it, that is, not to draw a false picture of it' (MS 137, 9. 2. 48). To come to understand our most basic concepts, which in Wittgenstein's view is an important part of the philosopher's task, is possible only if the concepts to be understood are not modified, for otherwise one would no longer be dealing with the concepts originally intended. Now, whether or not this argument will accomplish a great deal, it does at any rate point in the same direction as the other considerations mentioned so far and agrees with Wittgenstein's growing inclination simply to allude to actual language games and to neglect those numerous games which in previous writings were invented, in a spirit of playfulness, to serve as objects of comparison and to test the validity of claims about the limits of our conceptual capacities.

The second reason Wittgenstein gives for holding that in contexts of justification language games play a particularly important role amounts to this: that language games tend to rest on primitive, pre-linguistic behaviour. A well-known example illustrating this claim is the idea that human pain behaviour originates in what one might call the more primitive pain expression of children; the more conventional behaviour of adults is something that *replaces* the more natural behaviour of children (cf. *PI* § 244). Rudiments of natural behaviour appear, as we shall see, when we express our understanding of music, for example, and also in other situations where we are inclined to make characteristic gestures or use forms of expression which force themselves on us. One reason for Wittgenstein's interest in these rudiments of natural behaviour is the fact that they constitute particularly reliable criteria of sincerity and help to shape the pattern of more conventional conduct: the more conventional elements must be in harmony with the more primitive ones if they are to form a recognizable 'physiognomy', an identifiable pattern of behaviour. Our immediate, natural, primitive reactions and forms of behaviour are *instinctive* expressions; there are no reasons that we could give for them. 'Instinct comes first, reasoning second. Not until there is a language game are there reasons' (*RPP* ii. § 689). But language games and instinct do not stand in unmediated juxtaposition; language games *rest on* instinctive forms of behaviour and can partially *replace* them.

Only where there are doubts and questions can there be an interest in learning what reasons could be given for the relevant claims. But even doubt has its basis in instinct:

We must not forget: even our more subtle, more philosophical scruples have an instinctive basis. There is, for example, that 'You can never know . . .', that keeping an open mind for new arguments. People who could not be taught that would appear mentally inferior to us. *Not yet* capable of forming a certain concept. (MS 137, 30. 6. 48)

This conviction of Wittgenstein's, according to which even our doubts rest on an instinctive basis, is turned into an argument which he uses in his discussions of uncertainty about other people's thoughts and feelings. His opponent holds that this uncertainty as to what may be going on in another person is dependent on the asymmetrical fact that, while we are aware of our own inner events, we do not know what is happening in the other person's mind. Wittgenstein attacks this position by availing himself of the 'grammatical' argument that it makes no sense to apply the word 'know' to my own present sensations and inner experiences. In Wittgenstein's view it makes sense to use this word only in contexts where it is also possible to speak of doubt, for example; and as far as one's own inner life is concerned, there is normally no instinctive basis for entertaining any doubts of the kind we may have regarding the sensations or feelings of other people.[10]

In his remarks on the philosophy of psychology Wittgenstein employs a further argument. Our doubts as to whether other people are in pain or whether they have certain sensations are embedded in our instinctive behaviour towards them. Even if I find what another person's conduct and demeanour appear to express clear and convincing, I shall none the less expect him to display behaviour which may not agree with my first impressions. The fact that I have to *find out* what another person thinks and feels forms an essential part of my primitive behaviour. No additional reasons can be given for it, even if I use extremely complicated tests to learn what is going on in another person's mind. While it is possible to give reasons for applying those tests and expecting certain results from their application, I shall soon run out of possible answers to the questions of why I entertain any doubts regarding the utterances of other people and why I wish to learn the truth about them. The only point I may add is that we simply want to know what is going on in the other person's mind; that is part of our lives; we want to be able to form an exact judgement of the other person's character and his likely way of acting. Even though doubts about what appears to be going on in another person's mind can be closely connected with forms of behaviour for whose understanding further reasons can often be given, we shall ultimately appeal to primitive, instinctive reactions and simply describe our general situation: here there is another person; I am looking at him and wondering if he will do this or that, etc. And this basic, instinctive doubt is by no means the reverse—it is independent—of my alleged certainty about my own sensations and thoughts, for this primitive doubt is an immediate expression of my natural attitude towards other people:

Doubt about an inner process is an *expression*. *Doubt*, however, is an instinctive form of behaviour. A form of behaviour toward someone else. And it does not follow from this that I know from my own experience *what* pain, etc. is; or that I know that it is something inward, and can go along with something outward. That's the last thing I know! (*RPP* ii. § 644)

Thus there are not only 'grammatical' reasons for rejecting the appeal to an asymmetry in our knowledge about our own and other

[10] See *PI* II. xi, p. 221. Cf. B. McGuinness, ' "I Know What I Want" ', *Proceedings of the Aristotelian Society* (1957-8), 305-20.

people's inner events for the purpose of accounting for our uncertainty about other people's feelings and thoughts; there are further reasons for rejecting that appeal which are connected with the fact that this uncertainty and our corresponding doubts are anchored in instinct: 'I really want to say that scruples in thinking begin with (have their roots in) instinct. Or again: a language game does not have its origin in *consideration*. Consideration is part of a language game. / And that is why a concept is in its element within the language game' (*RPP* ii. § 632). Giving reasons and adducing arguments for our views are activities which only exist within language games, for these games are the natural habitat of our concepts. It is true that there is a basis on which our concepts rest; this basis, however, is not formed by higher-level concepts but by our ways of acting. (For this reason Wittgenstein refers to Goethe's '*Im Anfang war die Tat*'(*OC*, § 402).) Accordingly Wittgenstein writes in one of his manuscripts:

A concept is not merely a way of *thinking* about something.

It is not only a way of dividing up things, not only a point of view according to which they can be arranged. It is a constitutive part of our acting. (MS 137, 1. 7. 48)

The decisive point is that a concept is a *constitutive part* of our actions. This is the only way acting can become a basis of our use of concepts; for if there were no actual interrelations between concepts and ways of acting, the philosopher would not be in a position to connect them. This, however, does not mean that our concepts cannot produce any effects on the sphere of our actions. On the contrary, Wittgenstein's writings abound with examples of ways in which our concepts may have an impact on our actions. But if we are playing a language game and are from within the game asking for reasons or justifications—and in many cases it is Wittgenstein's first move to arrange his questions in such a way that they are recognizably asked in the context of a language game—then we shall in some cases ultimately reach a point where we can recognize primitive, instinctive, unreflective actions. In such cases, however, we must remember that we should have no conception of such actions if we had not developed both our language games and the concepts which make it possible to see their structure.

There is at least one problem which remains unresolved in this context. Language games can fulfil the function ascribed to them by

Wittgenstein—the function of justifying certain claims about the uses of our concepts—only to the extent that some of them can be seen to be more fundamental than others. Not all language games can in equal measure rest on primitive reactions or instinctive behaviour. Consequently, only if we may speak of a hierarchy of language games or a hierarchy of uses within certain language games will it be possible to assume that more primitive and less primitive moves can be made in these language games. If it were otherwise, Wittgenstein would have no reason to claim that our 'special methods and language games' are the 'hard bedrock' while regarding our most general terms as evanescent and blurred. If no gradation within individual language games as well as between different language games could be appealed to, it would be possible to object to Wittgenstein that, as a matter of fact, both general and less general terms are used in various kinds of language games.

To this objection Wittgenstein will have to reply by admitting a kind of hierarchical ordering of language games or conceding that certain uses of our concepts are more primitive and come closer to instinctive forms of behaviour than other ones. The arrangement of such a hierarchy can of course be decided and justified according to the needs arising in individual cases; our conceptual disputes are after all different in character from our typical discussions of problems within strictly built theoretical systems and do not for instance require anything analogous with a theory of types. A description of specific uses of concepts in language games is a very different matter from giving a characterization of the instances of a scientific hypothesis. Such a description will, if it is well chosen, help us to arrive at a better understanding of our own ways of proceeding and will, if it is adequate, contribute to a conspectus of a large number of techniques and practices. Here, as in the case of many other kinds of philosophical discussion, it will according to Wittgenstein be useful to avoid a 'theoretical attitude':

When one describes simple language games in illustration . . . then more involved cases keep on being held up before one, in order to show that our theory doesn't yet correspond to the facts. Whereas more involved cases are just more involved cases. For if what were in question were a theory, it might indeed be said: It's no use looking at these special cases, they offer no explanation of the most important cases. On the contrary, the simple language games play a quite different role. They are poles of a description, not the resources from which to construct a theory. (*RPP* i. § 633)

3

Classifications of Psychological Concepts

In his manuscript book 134, a volume which appears particularly
discontinuous, Wittgenstein notes down the following comment:
'The genealogical tree of psychological phenomena: It is *not
exactness* which I am striving for, but a perspicuous way of looking
at things [*Übersichtlichkeit*].'[1] But the way of dealing with his
subject-matter does not become more perspicuous after this remark.
The number of daily entries decreases; after a short time only
sporadic remarks are to be found, and these are often unconnected
with the philosophy of psychology. Only towards the end of June
Wittgenstein resumes continuous work on his manuscript and
begins to write relatively systematic remarks discussing Wolfgang
Köhler's ideas (until 3. 8. 47, MS 135; *RPP* i. §§ 964–1125). Then he
makes a selection of remarks from volumes 130–5 and dictates this
selection to a typist. In this way typescript 229 is produced (=
Remarks on the Philosophy of Psychology, volume i). Before the
date '9. 11.' we read in the manuscript: 'Dictated up to this point.'
Then there follow a few entries whose dates are not very clear, and
from 8. 12. 47 until 20. 2. 48 (*RPP* ii. § 483) we can follow a
practically uninterrupted sequence of remarks. After this there is a
gap until March.

   The remarks of this new sequence leave no doubt that Wittgenstein is here struggling to find a more systematic approach to
his subject. He is, among other things, dealing with the concept
'thinking' and trying to get clearer about enumerative descriptions
like 'A man thinks, feels, desires, believes, wills, knows.'[2] A
suppressed remark from 12. 12. 47 reads: 'I feel that I should write

[1] 2. 4. 47. There is a further remark, which was written between 12 and 27 Dec.
1947, where Wittgenstein mentions the possibility of a genealogical tree of
psychological concepts; here he wonders if this would have a similarity to a
genealogical tree of different number concepts (*RPP* i. § 722).
[2] On 11. 12. 47 he notes down the following suppressed remark: 'Consider the
fear, the joy, the thinking, etc. of human beings!' And then he wonders: 'But how is it
possible that here I can say "etc.".?' In this connection, too, what interests him is the
possibility of finding a *general* way of distinguishing various kinds of psychological
phenomena.

about "psychological phenomena" in general. As it were, about the way the different psychological categories come into being.' Then, on 14 December, he returns to the idea of a genealogical tree of psychological phenomena. He observes: 'Once I mentioned a genealogical tree of psychological concepts: I might just as well speak of an order in which one ought to discuss them and explain their connections. This order I am not clear about; especially not about its beginning.' After this remark there is one day (15. 12.) without any entry, and on 16. 12. Wittgenstein makes an attempt at drawing a general distinction between states of consciousness and dispositions. The general distinguishing mark of the former is said to be their having *genuine* duration, whereas in the case of the latter, he adds jokingly, one has to find out by means of spot checks whether they are still going on (*RPP* ii § 57).

Wittgenstein's struggle for a more systematic approach to a resolution of his philosophical problems becomes particularly apparent when on the same day (16. 12. 47) he reminds himself:

But this is still not quite the right way of tackling this problem [of a distinction between states of consciousness and dispositions]. It is as if I *wanted* to paint an impressionist painting but was still too partial towards the old way of painting; and so, in spite of all my efforts, was still painting what one does *not* see. I am striving, for instance, far more than I need to or ought to go into details. (MS 135, 16. 12. 47)

A few days later, on 18 December, he begins to work on his 'plan for the treatment of psychological concepts' (*RPP* ii. § 63), a veritable classification of, and distinction between, various types of sense impression and representations. This plan or list is continued on 24. 12. by systematic statements about emotions and emotional dispositions and the way they differ from sense impressions (*RPP* ii. § 148).

There are small but important differences between the two sets of remarks about a genealogical tree (those of 2. 4. and those of 14. 12. 47): in the first set Wittgenstein speaks of psychological *phenomena*, in the second set he deals with psychological *concepts*. Now one might dismiss this difference as a purely verbal one, pointing out that Wittgenstein will refer to phenomena only in so far as they appear relevant to a better understanding of our concepts, but at this point his choice of words suggests that his thinking is still too close to individual phenomena, that he is not yet sufficiently clear about those factors which are constitutive of our concepts.

That this excessive respect for details may turn out to be an obstacle on his way to a clearer understanding of the decisive constituents of, and the relevant connections between, our concepts is shown by Wittgenstein's simile of the impressionist mode of painting. Wittgenstein, whose aim in philosophy is not explanation but description, wishes to give an unvarnished account of the subjects he tries to deal with. He wishes to draw a picture which represents our everyday impression of these subjects and whose only difference from this impression consists as it were in its having a frame, that is, in its admittedly being a picture. The salient point is this: that such an 'impressionist' picture is in no sense a simple copy of the represented subject; through an extremely complicated technique it strives to make us aware of the fact that our everyday way of seeing works by means of leaving out and adding, by means of distorting and rectifying things. The 'old mode of painting', on the other hand, is not concerned about our everyday way of seeing objects. It focuses on details and emphasizes peculiarities; in this way it constructs something new and makes it difficult to get a clear view of phenomena and to understand our own way of taking in these phenomena. Precisely through underlining details and portraying in a kind of 'explanatory' fashion, the old mode of painting (that is, science or a philosophical theory trying to emulate scientific procedures) presents something which is normally *not* seen. The impressionist painter (that is, Wittgenstein himself) uses complicated techniques which, by leaving certain details out of consideration,[3] attempt to describe phenomena in the way they are normally seen by us and to draw our attention in this indirect manner to the peculiarities of this normal way of seeing things.

This is directly connected with the second parts of the two quoted remarks about a genealogical tree of psychological phenomena or concepts. In his first remark Wittgenstein emphasizes that what he is really concerned about is not exactness but an overview or a perspicuous way of looking at things. In his second manuscript entry he indicates what he means by a perspicuous representation or an overview: it is a representation which renders its objects in such a way that they will appear in an adequate, 'natural' order. Such a representation in accordance with the

---

[3] It is worth noting that on 18. 12. 47 two entries, which are crossed out, are in the margin classified as 'details'.

'natural' order of things is analogous to an impressionist painting. It does not strive to portray the historical genesis of its subject or to make us look at it through the glasses provided by some external conceptual scheme; rather, it wants to give the impression of a natural order which agrees with our everyday concepts. But in order to reach its aim it is just as much as the impressionist mode of painting bound to make use of techniques which are far from 'natural'; on the contrary, its techniques of representation can be extremely complicated and contrived. Accordingly, Wittgenstein's above-quoted resolve to write about, 'as it were', the way 'the different psychological categories come into being' is not to be understood in the sense of a plan to give a historical explanation recording causes and effects. What he means when he speaks of such a seemingly genetic account is a way of 'developing things in accordance with an apparently natural order'. Just as Goethe, who is quoted several times in these manuscripts,[4] tries to 'derive' natural phenomena in the shape of an ordered chain—in a manner which is supposed to be quite different both from a historical account and from a classification in Linnaean terms—so Wittgenstein intends to present psychological concepts (and at the same time psychological phenomena) in a perspicuous order, thus aiming at a method which will allow us to understand the variety of connections, contrasts, and dependencies obtaining between them.

What is extremely unusual by Wittgenstein's standards is that this attempt at developing a more systematic approach to an investigation of psychological concepts finds its expression in a 'plan for the treatment of psychological concepts' (18. 12. 47, *RPP* ii. § 63) and in a 'continuation of the classification of psychological concepts' (24. 12. 47, *RPP* ii. § 148). This classification, which altogether amounts to more than two printed pages, has a predecessor: a remark which was written on 18. 3. 47 (*RPP* ii. § 836), that is, about two weeks earlier than the above-quoted remark on a genealogical tree of psychological phenomena. This early division of the psychological realm shows similarities as well as crucial differences if one

---

[4] It surely is not mere chance that only a few paragraphs before making his remark about a genealogical tree Wittgenstein quotes Goethe: 'Don't look for anything behind the phenomena; they themselves are the theory.' (29. 3. 47, *RPP* i. § 889) A fuller comparison of Goethe's and Wittgenstein's views is given in my article 'Chor und Gesetz: Zur "morphologischen Methode" bei Goethe und Wittgenstein', in *Chor und Gesetz* (Frankfurt, 1990).

compares it with the later classification. Such a comparison will help to show the direction in which Wittgenstein's idea of psychological concepts was developing at that time.

The early attempt at a classification (*RPP* i. § 836) begins with a question: 'Ought I to call the whole field of the psychological that of *"experience"*?' The right answer to this question seems to be yes, for Wittgenstein continues to represent all the other psychological concepts as subclasses or elements of subclasses of the general class of experiential concepts. Altogether Wittgenstein distinguishes three subclasses of experiences, and some of these subclasses are in their turn subdivided into further subclasses. What remains unclear is the exact status of the concept 'thinking', as Wittgenstein's formulation is extremely difficult to understand ('Denken ist Reden unter bestimmten Umständen, und anderes, was ihm entspricht', which G. E. M. Anscombe translates as: 'Talking under particular circumstances, and whatever else corresponds to that, is thinking'). Now we shall have a closer look at the clear part of Wittgenstein's classification.

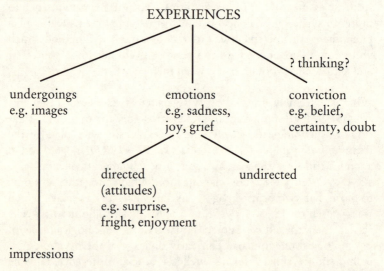

FIG. 1 Early Classification (*RPP* i. § 836)

The characteristic feature of EXPERIENCES is that the third person of the corresponding verbs is used on the basis of observation while their first person is not.

The first subclass of experiences (*Erlebnisse*) is formed by
UNDERGOINGS (*Erfahrungen*). Their characteristic marks are
that they have *duration* and a certain *course*, which may be uniform
or not; they also have *intensity*. A negative characteristic is that they
are 'not characters of thought'. What Wittgenstein presumably
means by that is that undergoings differ from emotions in that they
do not 'colour' our thoughts. The only example of undergoings
given by Wittgenstein is images.[5] The only subclass of undergoings
mentioned is that of *impressions*, whose characteristic features are
their spatial and temporal relations as well as the possibility of
blending (thus there are for example blended impressions of smells,
colours, and sounds).

The second subclass of experiences is constituted by the EMOTIONS.
Their characteristics are *duration*, typical mimetic *expression*, lack of
a *place*,[6] and the fact that they involve characteristic *undergoings*
and *thoughts*. Thoughts are in their turn 'coloured' by emotions;
examples of emotions are sadness, joy, grief, delight. And the
emotions can be subdivided into directed and undirected ones; of
these the former might be called 'attitudes', and include surprise,
fright, admiration, and enjoyment.

[5] This sheds some light on Wittgenstein's use of the term 'Erfahrung' if one
remembers that *Vorstellung* is said to be voluntary (cf. e.g. *RPP* i. § 848). *Vorstellung*
is used by Wittgenstein throughout in the sense of 'imagination', and in this he differs
from Brentano, for instance, who comes closer to the usual *philosophical* use of this
term when he writes: 'We speak of a presentation [*Vorstellung*] whenever something
appears to us. When we see something, a colour is presented; when we hear
something, a sound; when we imagine something, a fantasy image. In view of the
generality with which we use this term it can be said that it is impossible for
conscious activity to refer in any way to something which is not presented' (F.
Brentano, *Psychology from an Empirical Standpoint* (London, 1973), 198). A
narrower concept of *Vorstellung* is employed by Wundt, and this concept, too, is
completely different from Wittgenstein's term. Wundt writes: 'What we mean by a
representation [*Vorstellung*] is, according to common usage, the picture of an object
or an event in the external world generated in our consciousness. To the extent we
know the world it only consists of our representations. These, however, are by an
ingenuous consciousness identified with the objects to which we make them refer,
and it is only scientific reflection which raises the question of how the picture
provided in the representation relates to its object' (W. Wundt, *Grundzüge der
physiologischen Psychologie* (Leipzig, 1893), ii. 1).
[6] Wittgenstein maintains that emotion 'has no place'. What he means by that
statement remains unclear. Does he want to say that, in contrast with the case of
impressions, we do not speak of specific bodily organs (eye, ear, etc.) corresponding
to certain emotions? Or is it that we do not conceive of emotions as standing in
spatial relations? Or does it mean that we do not ascribe a place to them which could
be located either in our minds or in our bodies?

The third subclass mentioned by Wittgenstein comprises forms of CONVICTION. The only things he says about them is that they are not colourings of thoughts and that their *expression* is the expression of thoughts. Examples of forms of conviction are belief, certainty, and doubt.

What remains unclear is the role of the concept of THINKING. Does thinking too form a subclass of experiences? Is it really a part of the psychological realm? Does it constitute a separate psychological domain beside that of experiences?

Several problems arising in connection with this early classification will be discussed below. What can already be said, however, is that among other reasons the obvious inadequacy of several of the formulations contained in this list must have aroused Wittgenstein's immediate dissatisfaction (even though he did include it in his typescript 229). He does not even allude to a possible reason for choosing 'experience' as the highest concept supposed to cover the whole realm of psychological phenomena. And the sheer difficulty (or impossibility) of finding an adequate translation into English shows that distinctions between *Erlebnisse* and *Erfahrungen* will always be extremely precarious.[7] Moreover, the claim that images are to count as *Erfahrungen* or 'undergoings' would surely require a highly elaborate justification.

Wittgenstein's later classification is not an ordering of 'experiences'; the word is not even used in this context. It is a classification of psychological *concepts* or psychological *verbs*. Again they are characterized by pointing out that in the third person their use depends on observation while in the first person it does not. To put it in a nutshell: psychological sentences in the first person present tense are 'utterances' or 'avowals' (*Äußerungen*) while psychological sentences in the third person are 'communications' (*Mitteilungen*). In double brackets Wittgenstein adds the words 'Not quite right', presumably because some psychological sentences in the first person come fairly close to being 'communications', for example by being open to correction, which marks a contrast with paradigmatic 'utterances'.

The new classification, too, is divided into three parts, but its terminology is simpler and more pertinent than that of the earlier one. The concept 'thinking' is not mentioned any more, and the

---

[7] Cf. the translator's note, *RPP* i. 184e.

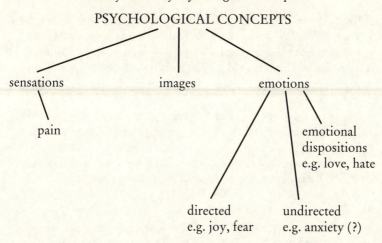

FIG. 2 Later Classification (*RPP* ii. § 63, 148)

forms of conviction are no longer mentioned. Instead, the former category of undergoings (*Erfahrungen*) is divided into two separate classes: that which used to be called impressions now bears the name 'sensations', and images are treated separately. The third class of psychological concepts is again constituted by concepts for emotions. Notwithstanding its greater clarity and more precise terminology this classification, too, is not unproblematic, as we shall see.

The characteristic marks of SENSATIONS are the following: they have *genuine duration*, they admit of degrees and qualitative *mixtures*, and they inform us about the *external world*. This last-mentioned criterion is put in quotation marks, perhaps because it is to be taken with a grain of salt.[8] The characteristic of genuine duration is elucidated by pointing out that it is possible to indicate the beginning and end of sensations and that such sensations can occur absolutely simultaneously. Furthermore, all sensations can be ascribed a degree, which may reach from 'scarcely perceptible' to 'unendurable'. In these respects the class of the so-called sensations of position and movement (that is, kinaesthetic sensations) is

[8] Cf. *RPP* i. § 702: 'What is common to sense-experiences?—The answer that they acquaint us with the outer world is partly wrong and partly right. It is right inasmuch as it is supposed to point to a *logical* criterion.' Even though Wittgenstein is still speaking of sense-*experiences*, he would surely have accepted the content of this remark even after he had changed his terminology.

different from that of the sensations of seeing and hearing, for what is normally called a sensation of position or movement has neither genuine duration nor an ascribable degree, nor does it inform us about the external world. The position of one's own limbs is something one simply knows; here a sensation does not normally come into question.

Sensations proper differ according to whether or not they are felt at a certain part of one's body: seeing and hearing are not normally felt that way, while pressure, temperature, taste, and pain are always felt as occurring at a certain place. Often we *react* to sensations of this kind by touching the relevant part of our bodies.

In addition to the criteria of sensations already mentioned Wittgenstein adduces a further characteristic, which might involve us in difficult questions. He says: 'No local sign about the sensation. Any more than a temporal sign about a memory-image.' Is this perhaps meant to exclude the idea that the bitter taste now sensed by me is felt *as a taste on my tongue*? Does Wittgenstein consequently think that there is, for instance, such a thing as a 'pure' sensation of taste, that is, a sensation which is as it were abstracted from the place where it is felt?

In Wittgenstein's new classification IMAGES are allowed to play a more important role; they are allotted a separate subclass. Alluding to a famous claim made by Hume,[9] Wittgenstein remarks that it is not 'vivacity' which distinguishes imagination from sensation. As criteria of imagination he mentions the facts that, in contrast with sensations, they do not inform us about the *external world* and that they are subject to the *will*. He also emphasizes that seeing and imagining exclude each other; it is never possible to imagine something and see it at the same time. The fact that imagination does not inform us about the external world should not, however, mislead us into thinking that it is a kind of

---

[9] *Treatise* I. i. § 1: 'The first circumstance, that strikes my eye, is the great resemblance betwixt our impressions and ideas in every other particular, except their degree of force and vivacity.' I. i. § 7: 'since all ideas are deriv'd from impressions, and are nothing but copies and representations of them, whatever is true of the one must be acknowledg'd concerning the other. Impressions and ideas differ only in their strength and vivacity.' It is often claimed that Wittgenstein used to boast that he was unfamiliar with Hume's writings (cf. K. Britton, 'Portrait of a Philosopher', in K. T. Fann (ed.), *Ludwig Wittgenstein* (New York, 1967), 61), but even if it is true that he never read a book by Hume he at any rate knew the indicated passages from William James's *Principles of Psychology* (New York, 1950), ii. 45–6, where they are quoted *in extenso*. (Cf. *LPP*, 80, 92.)

hallucination. And even though it is possible to answer a question about what we are imagining in the same way as we can answer a question about what we are seeing, namely by showing or pointing to a picture, an image is by no means a depiction: what I imagine does not depend on whether or not the image is similar to a possible object corresponding to it.

The third group of psychological concepts comprises our concepts for EMOTIONS. These are, on the one hand, to be distinguished from *emotional dispositions* and, on the other hand, they can be divided into *directed* and *undirected* emotions. Their common criteria are the following: genuine *duration*, characteristic *course*, typical *feelings* (*Empfindungen*, here not in the sense of 'sensations'). They, too, do not inform us about the *external world*.

As examples of the characteristic course taken by emotions Wittgenstein mentions the flaring up and abating of rage; similar courses are taken by joy, depression, and fear. A characteristic behaviour is for instance crying when one is sad, and this is accompanied by typical feelings, for example the feeling that one's voice is 'heavy with tears'. A general mark distinguishing emotional dispositions (such as love and hate) from emotions is not mentioned by Wittgenstein. He indicates that the distinction is not always easy to draw; thus fear will normally count as an emotion proper, but it may turn into a disposition. In the former case it is an 'acute' emotion, in the latter it becomes 'chronic'.

Directed emotions differ from undirected ones in having an *object*. Fear and pleasure, for instance, normally have an object; you are afraid *of* someone or something and you are pleased *about* someone or something, and here the object must not be confused with the *cause* of the relevant emotion. Another aspect of emotions which must not be confused with their objects is their *content*, which according to Wittgenstein appears to be something like the typical accompanying imagery, at any rate something that can be pictured. The examples mentioned by Wittgenstein are the flames of anger and the darkness of depression. Thus both directed and undirected emotions may have a content.[10]

What is confusing is Wittgenstein's statement that emotions differ from sensations inasmuch as the former are 'not localized'. This seems to imply that the sensations of hearing and seeing are to be

---

[10] For the concept of content, cf. below, Chapters 7 and 9.

excluded from this comparison, for they, too, have been claimed not to have a place (*RPP* ii. § 63). Thus 'sensations' would here mean those sensations which we feel in a certain part of our bodies, as for instance pain,[11] pressure, heat, and cold. What Wittgenstein may have in mind are sensations of the kind of 'a lump in my throat' or 'an unpleasant feeling in my stomach'.

Apart from the problems already mentioned, the obvious question arises of what possible purposes might be served by these attempts to classify psychological phenomena or concepts. After all, it cannot be denied that Wittgenstein's remarks on the philosophy of psychology, both in manuscript and in their published form, produce the impression of being an unordered, random collection of remarks about a possibly very general but not clearly defined subject. And it is true that these remarks are not really ordered, as Wittgenstein never succeeded in getting near a final revision of this material. But it would not be correct to call them a 'random' collection, as they owe their existence to Wittgenstein's concentrated, sometimes perhaps even desperate efforts to reach a clear understanding of the manifold uses of our psychological concepts; they owe their existence to his quest for the most general criteria defining our uses of these concepts or entire classes of such concepts.

From the start, however, this enterprise presents itself as fairly unpretentious, if one compares it with some attempts made by other philosophers (for example, Franz Brentano and his school). Of

---

[11] In his article 'Wittgenstein's Theory of Knowledge', in G. Vesey, *Understanding Wittgenstein* (London, 1974), 248, Christopher Coope claims that there is a contradiction between the following two Wittgenstein passages: 'One *knows* the position of one's limbs and their movements. One can give them if asked, for example. Just as one also knows the place of a sensation (pain) in the body' (*Zettel* (Oxford, 1981), § 483, *RPP* ii. § 63); and: ' "I know where I am feeling pain", "I know that I feel it *here*" is as wrong as "I know that I am in pain". But "I know where you touched my arm" is right' (*OC* § 41). At first blush there really seems to be a contradiction here, but it disappears as soon as one takes the context of these passages into account. In the first passage 'know' is only used in the sense of 'being able to indicate where', while in the second quotation it is a question of the use of 'know' in the sense of 'finding out and being able to assert with certainty'. But as I *cannot* find out about the position of my own pain for the reason that I am 'immediately aware' of this position, it is not permissible here to use the word 'know'. If one is so inclined, one may say that in the first quotation 'know' is used in an improper or secondary sense. At any rate, here there is no contradiction in the sense that Wittgenstein asserts at one place and denies at another that we are able to *indicate* the position of our own pain.

course, this unpretentiousness of Wittgenstein's is based on his conviction that pretending more can only mislead us and that the construction of a *theory* will at most promote the building of Potemkin villages.[12] Wittgenstein had no illusions about the fact that this deliberate renunciation of a theory proper would render his investigations extremely complicated: 'The difficulty of renouncing all theory: One has to regard what appears so obviously incomplete, as something complete' (*RPP* i. § 723). The decision to make do without a theory does not mean that one must put up with something incomplete; what it means is that one grasps and does not forget that what seems to be incomplete is everything there is and that more is not to be had. However, in order to grasp that what seems incomplete is all you can get you will need criteria to help your decisions, and in order to discover the right criteria you will need a systematic grouping, perhaps even a classification, of the phenomena populating the terrain you wish to examine. Thus renouncing all theory does not amount to renouncing all analysis and systematic procedures; what it means is that one has resolved to get by without 'ornamental copings' and that instead one will, for example, quite deliberately draw 'auxiliary lines'.

A classification is nothing more than a means for getting clearer about the criteria needed, and in this sense it cannot accomplish more than to serve as a guiding principle for the further course of one's investigation. It is not an end in itself but is meant to contribute to the discovery of useful questions and to our decisions about the validity of possible answers.

Here a further preliminary note may be in place. Wittgenstein has a reputation for being a behaviourist, a verificationist or a kind of anti-realist. He certainly was not a behaviourist. And it will not be necessary in this context to go into the question of the extent to which the labels 'verificationist' or 'anti-realist' may fit him.[13] Often Wittgenstein avers that his remarks are 'grammatical' ones, that is, remarks that are based on conceptual considerations and not on introspection;[14] only what can be checked on intersubjectively is admitted to be of possible value. In spite of this one might get the

[12] In Wittgenstein's writings the term 'theory' is generally used to refer to a scientific theory or to an account which tries to emulate a scientific theory.

[13] Cf. my article 'Bedeutung und Verifikation', *Grazer philosophische Studien* (1982).

[14] Cf. below, Chapter 5, Appendix.

impression that the criteria mentioned in the classifications described above are irreducibly subjective. After all, how do we find out whether a psychological phenomenon has genuine duration, constant or variable intensity, a characteristic course, characteristic accompanying feelings, and whether it is subject to the will? Quite a few readers would find it natural to reply that this is to be found out by means of introspection. And if this were the complete answer to those questions, then Wittgenstein's efforts would from the very beginning be doomed to be in vain.

But there is something that can be regarded as mediating between the subjective and the objective, between the inner and the outer, namely our characteristic expressive behaviour. It is this highly important criterion for the application of psychological concepts which brings language to the fore, as the expression of our feeling and thinking is essentially linguistic but at the same time closely connected with 'immediate' responses. Immediate expression and linguistic expression—these are the elements which Wittgenstein tries to use in order to grasp how it is possible to get a conceptual hold on the subjective.

4

Expression

'EXPRESSION' is a central concept of the language of psychology as well as of some of its theories. In Wittgenstein's considerations it plays a decisive role, in particular in such phrases as 'immediate' or 'primary expression'.[1] There is, however, yet another context where Wittgenstein deals with the concept 'expression', namely the context of aesthetic appraisal, criticism, or description. The connection between this use and the employment of phrases like 'expression of a sensation', 'expression of an experience', or 'expression of pain' is not obvious but it will gradually become apparent.

An example which Wittgenstein mentions several times is that of an 'expressive musical phrase'. Here the question is how it is possible to communicate or describe the expression of a given musical phrase. In such cases it is not uncommon to object in a general way that music (or perhaps all forms of art) cannot be described at all. But this objection is, if not refuted, then at least weakened by pointing out the fact that we do find certain characterizations more *appropriate* than others. What is undeniable, however, is that words will often fail us and that we may try to reproduce the expression of a given piece of music by means of gestures which underline and are supposed to help to describe the characteristic or interesting element of the musical phrase in question. Thus it will happen that one of several players tells one of the others: 'You must not play it *this* way [*gesture*], the tune is to be played *that* way [*a different gesture*].' And when people listen to music it quite frequently occurs that one of the listeners tries to draw the attention of another to a certain phrase by *expressing* some particular feature by means of gestures. But if the other person is unfamiliar with the work in question, he will not get the point; and

[1] By a *primary* expression Wittgenstein means an utterance or a description of an experience (or an account of a dream, for instance) which is essentially based on conceptual connections that have not been learnt. If we are confronted with differences between primary kinds of expressive behaviour, then we are bound to assume that the relevant experiences themselves are different. Cf. MS 131, 13. 8. 46.

if he does not understand music at all, gestures will not help him to grasp it. The expression in question will remain inaccessible to him. This appears to correspond to those cases where a man is incapable of following a discussion among experts for the reason that he is unfamiliar with their terminology; it thus does not seem to be a peculiarity of our example.

Now imagine that a person who understands music is looking through a window into a recording studio and observes the gestures of the players discussing questions of musical interpretation and also the gestures of listeners inside the studio who draw each other's attention to certain characteristics of the music they are listening to. It may be that the observer, who does not hear a sound, will find what he sees ridiculous; but he will certainly not get much of an idea of what the music is like.

And one will be equally unsuccessful if one is confronted with a verbal description of music, even if experts regard this description as appropriate. Suppose someone hears the following words:

Beneath her flying fingers the music mounted to its unbelievable climax and was resolved in that ruthless, sudden *pianissimo* which is like having the ground glide from beneath one's feet, yet like a sinking too into the very deeps of desire. Followed the immeasurable plenitude of that vast redemption and fulfilment; it was repeated, swelled into a deafening, unquenchable tumult of immense appeasement that wove and welled and seemed about to die away, only to swell again and weave the *Sehnsuchts-motiv* into its harmony; at length to breathe an outward breath and die, faint on the air, and soar away.[2]

The hearer will have no idea of what the music described sounds like unless he knows that the words are about a certain passage from *Tristan und Isolde* and he is familiar with that passage.[3]

If it is a question of characterizing the expression of a piece of music, gestures and words are obviously dependent on a specific context. If there is no discernible connection with an object, they have virtually no function whatsoever. 'What I am really saying of it [a musical phrase] or my gesture is evidently quite insufficient. They

---

[2] Thomas Mann, *Tristan* (New York, 1979), 155–6.

[3] Of course, if a description is as characteristic as the one quoted above, then, even if someone does not know the music in question, he will not associate the words with a completely different kind of music, for instance with Bach or Webern. But it would none the less be an extraordinary coincidence if, unaware that the music in question is by Wagner, he managed to arrive on the basis of nothing but the words quoted at an idea of the sound roughly corresponding to the music itself.

may, if they are accompanied by this music, appear appropriate but they would not give anyone who was not familiar with the music an idea of its character' (MS 130, p. 57). It cannot, on the other hand, be denied that a listener who is really wrapped up in the music will find certain gestures, facial expressions, or movements appropriate while others will appear unsuitable. Certain elements of the expression of a musical phrase can, as Wittgenstein admits, be explained by means of an analysis of the harmonic structure but this will be impossible, for instance, if it is a question of 'the seriousness, the significance' of that gesture which is expressed by the last variation of the Allegretto of Beethoven's Seventh Symphony. Here my 'explanation will in the end consist in my *accompanying* the sounds with a gesture and my mien. And I am satisfied by this explanation' (MS 130, pp. 60–1).

What Wittgenstein wishes to emphasize is that an expression which we understand, for example the expression of a musical phrase, invites or stimulates us to react in a certain way. What this reaction is like will depend on the medium of expression, on our knowledge of this medium, and on our natural, perhaps even instinctive forms of behaviour. One of these 'instinctive' kinds of reaction is producing an accompaniment of the expression; another kind is looking for and quoting parallels taken from other areas: 'It might perhaps be possible to find a phrase in a poem which corresponds to this expression of the language of music. And that would give me great satisfaction.' (MS 130, p. 62, cf. *RPP* i. § 35) Wittgenstein's repeated mention of the satisfaction given by such reactions indicates that these reactions are particularly basic or immediate ones. By means of accompanying a phrase or finding a parallel to it we react in an immediate way to a direct stimulus, even if the particular case, such as an example from music, involves highly culture-specific information.

The example of our responses to music is of special significance for the reason that in this case there are, besides the possibility of complete failure to understand, various degrees of understanding and misunderstanding to be found. As far as these different degrees of understanding and misunderstanding are concerned, we as observers may reach agreement, even though this type of reaction is fairly remote from those practices where we are used to giving marks for more or less competence and understanding. In most cases where a person completely fails to understand a piece of music this failure will simply be expressed verbally by remarking: 'That does not mean anything to me', 'Baroque music leaves me cold', even 'I am deaf to music'. Another case is the entirely unsuitable reactions produced by members of remote cultures when confronted with our music (or of our own inappropriate responses to the music of a foreign culture). More interesting and more complex are the many forms of misunderstanding music. First of all, there are striking ways of misunderstanding an expression, as for example when someone hearing a ländler-like movement by Schubert breaks into exuberant clapping or loud whistling.[4] A less striking case of misunderstanding music is where a listener (or a player) makes gestures underlining a merely ornamental figure or an up-beat which should demonstrably bear no accent.

Such cases of misunderstanding are not always distinguishable from cases of understanding things in a different way. Thus there can be arguments about questions like whether certain notes should only accompany a tune and hence be played more softly or whether the 'correct' expression comes about only if these notes are accentuated. But mostly it is quite likely that we shall be able to decide if someone has misunderstood the expression of a certain phrase or if he has understood it in a way different from another possible interpretation. The usual criterion is that the person concerned either says 'I do not understand it' or says 'I understand this differently' or 'I understand it *this* way' and at the same time plays or sings the phrase in question or makes a characteristic gesture. What this brief consideration of understanding the expression of a musical phrase shows is that, first, understanding the expression of such a phrase cannot clearly be separated from understanding the phrase itself and that, secondly, understanding the phrase itself is in its turn connected with characteristic ways of expressing it.[5]

---

[4] Here it is of course assumed that these are reactions to the *music*. This is meant to exclude cases like those where someone behaves this way in order to annoy other people or where he *pretends* not to understand.

[5] Cf. MS 137, 15. 2. 48, in *C&V* 70: 'There is a certain *expression* proper to the appreciation of music, in listening, playing, and at other times too. Sometimes gestures form part of this expression, but sometimes it will just be a matter of how a man plays, or hums, the piece, now and again of the comparisons he draws and the images with which he as it were illustrates the music. Someone who understands music will listen differently (e.g. with a different expression on his face), he will talk differently, from someone who does not. But he will show that he understands a particular theme not just in manifestations that accompany his hearing or playing that theme but in his understanding for music in general.'

The fact that one has understood a piece of music or a musical phrase shows itself in certain responses and in an inclination to use certain verbal expressions or parallels which indicate that one ascribes a certain kind of organization or structure to the piece or phrase in question. The ways of getting these responses or inclinations across are not settled once and for all but, as a matter of fact, there is a high degree of agreement as regards that which we tend to count as 'suitable', 'appropriate', 'fitting', 'similar', 'adequate', and so forth.

Our understanding of the expression of a piece of music does not normally remain silent; it manifests itself in characteristic ways. And it is precisely the existence of such characteristic ways which allows us to speak of misunderstanding music or of understanding it in a different way and to argue about different interpretations. Often the expression of understanding, taking in, and responding to a piece of music is in the nature of an imitation: there are typical mimetic movements corresponding to rhythm, melody, and intensity.

However, the most immediate way of conveying how one has understood the expression of a musical phrase is rendering it by singing or playing it. Whether I have understood a piece of music and hence its expression will show itself in the way I play or sing it; it will become clear from the expression I bestow on it. The way the understanding of an expression is connected with the expression of the interpretation is peculiar: it may so happen that a performer with brilliant technical qualities completely fails in rendering a musical phrase while a stumbling amateur may hit its expression perfectly. And there are 'expressive' interpretations of a piece of music which fail to render its sense as well as inspired interpretations which miss the mark.

Such judgements will always be based on a comparison between the intended expression which is 'contained in' the work in question and the expression indicated by its listener or performer. As regards this situation we keep expressing ourselves in a way which suggests that the musical work is a kind of text which can be grasped, paraphrased, and translated correctly or incorrectly, this way or that way. And this analogy, it seems, is to a large extent appropriate: the degree to which the expression of our understanding agrees with the expression of the piece concerned will depend on our more or less perfect mastery of a certain technique and on the agreement of the expression given to his interpretation by one performer with that indicated by his colleagues or rivals.

There is, however, at least one respect in which there is an essential difference between understanding what is expressed by a verbally articulated text and the expression of this understanding, on the one hand, and the understanding of a piece of music and the expression of that understanding, on the other. The way I understand a text and whether I understand it correctly are, to put it in a simplified manner, to a large extent a matter of how and whether I understand its propositional content. (Of course, the degree of dependence on propositional content varies according to the use made of the linguistic expressions concerned. For this reason the kind of text meant here is one where contextual factors have little relevance.[6]) Understanding a musical work, on the other hand, involves a strong element of direct and unreflective response, while speaking of a propositional element in our understanding of music will always have a marked flavour of metaphor.

The extent to which the understanding of a work of music is connected with forms of immediate reaction is mirrored by typical phrases like 'His feet twitched to the rhythm of that "allegro rubato"', 'She could not help letting her hands follow the flow of the tune played by the strings', and so forth. But it is also to be found in the most sober characterizations of musical works in so far as these characterizations go beyond a mere list of harmonic and rhythmic details. Here language depends on figurative elements; it needs to hark back to emotions and experiences, it needs analogies with natural forces and eruptions, no matter how objectively you wish to formulate your observations. (Similar reflections apply to not purely conventional directions given by composers who want to indicate how their works are to be performed. Wittgenstein points out that it is doubtful if everyone can grasp Schumann's 'Wie aus weiter Ferne' (As if from afar).[7]) In short, to a certain extent,

---

[6] That does not mean that in the case of utterances whose intelligibility is highly situation-dependent the literal *meaning* of the words will play a less significant role than in the case of a written text. Even if you wish to *distract* from the content of your utterance, you are, as long as you are employing linguistic means at all, bound to exploit the meanings of the words used (cf. D. Davidson, 'Communication and Convention', in *Inquiries into Truth and Interpretation* (Oxford, 1984), 272). At this point I am only concerned with the fact that the intelligibility of a complete written or a recorded spoken text is relatively independent of the non-linguistic context.

[7] *RPP* i. § 250. Neither here nor in other passages of a similar character does Wittgenstein claim that understanding locutions of this kind is in any way dependent on a kind of meaning different from literal (or 'primary') meaning, e.g. figurative or metaphorical meaning. One might speak of 'secondary meaning', but according to Wittgenstein that merely amounts to using an expression with its primary meaning in

which may vary from person to person, our reactions to music are similar to our reactions to actions or events which are primarily directed at or responded to by our emotional feelings. For this reason the expression of our understanding may here (again only to a certain extent) resemble our reactions to actions or events to which we tend to respond in an emotional manner: harmonious gestures, dance steps, strong facial expressions, and so on. The immediate element in the expression of our understanding of music determines to a high degree the role of our reactions as criteria for our having understood the music, as well as the degree of their reliability. A person who does not understand a piece of music will react in a way which is wrong or inappropriate, while a person who understands it will make the right gestures und use appropriate words.

But how is one to judge whether a certain expression is correct or incorrect, appropriate or inappropriate? The question is whether we know any objective, explicable, and analysable rules which can be appealed to whenever one wishes to give reasons for such judgements. One tends to suppose that natural and immediate expression should be allowed to play a role only where there are no intersubjective criteria at our disposal. For one thinks that if it is a question of giving reasons and explaining one's judgements, citing evidence which permits of being analysed is preferable to appealing to examples which resist further analysis.

The problems concerning the notion of an expression of the understanding of a musical phrase, however, show that in cases of this kind we shall not get very far if we rely on our usual ideas about explanation and analysis. If a person simply does not understand music I cannot by means of verbal explanations plus a few examples make it clear to him why his reactions indicate lack of understanding, nor why certain other reactions would have indicated that he had understood. If I wish to point out to him what various forms of reacting to *music* mean, I shall have to teach him *music*, that is, he will at least have to learn to listen, he will have to be told about musical forms, he will have to be able to identify the characteristic sounds of various instruments and their typical roles in an orchestra,

an unusual context (*LW* §§ 797 ff.). For a criticism of the idea of metaphorical meaning, see D. Davidson, 'What Metaphors Mean' in *Inquiries into Truth and Interpretation* (Oxford, 1984). Cf. my 'Wittgenstein's Notion of Secondary Meaning and Davidson's Account of Metaphor'.

and so forth. Only when he is apprised of these and many other things, that is, only when he has been 'trained' (to use Wittgenstein's word), will he for his part be able to react to music with understanding and to judge the appropriateness of other people's expressions. Once he has mastered the 'language of music', he will as it were automatically or *spontaneously* respond to music. This shows that 'immediate' expressions of our understanding of the language of music are by no means natural in the way our expressions of pain for instance are. Those expressions of understanding music presuppose knowledge and skills without, however, entailing deliberate recourse to such knowledge and skills.

A person who is able to express his understanding of music succeeds in doing so by reproducing what he has understood with an appropriate expression, for instance by playing or singing it the right way; or he succeeds through accompanying his listening with suitable gestures or through discovering parallels from other areas, for instance a poem by Eichendorff which exactly 'corresponds to' or 'agrees with' a certain passage in Schumann. From discovering such parallels we get 'great satisfaction', as Wittgenstein observes. But are these possibilities always open to us?—Let us consider the following case:

But how is it if someone pronounces a sentence in a very expressive way? If, for example, someone pronounces a certain phrase in a tone and in a manner in which only an American can pronounce it? Should I *here* be able to reproduce the expression in any other way? (MS 130, pp. 57–8)

Here one might think for example of Philip Marlowe's words in the screen version of the final dialogue of Raymond Chandler's thriller *The Big Sleep*. The expression which the words bear in the film cannot be rendered in a different medium; no translation can do justice to it; and once you have heard them spoken by Humphrey Bogart you will feel that nothing can ever really take the place of that. But even if one has never heard that, one may still imagine what it would sound like, and then one will say: 'Yes, that is the way it *must* be, that is unmistakable.' Of course, if one speaks American English well, one may be able to imitate that expression. But the expression itself, that which we call unmistakable, is something to which nothing different will correspond. It can be separated neither from this context nor from this kind of performance:

But it is a quite specific expression, after all! It expresses something quite specific!—But note that what it expresses is not explained through our being able to replace it by this and that but through its *surroundings*. For it is in them that what he says appears *expressive*. For what appears expressive to us would not be called expressive by someone who is so to speak unfamiliar with its implications. (MS 130, p. 58)

We feel that the expression is something peculiar, something specific, something which we are able neither to explain in a satisfactory way nor to replace by anything corresponding to it. For this reason we are inclined to speak of a *specific experience* and to leave it at that. But if we follow this inclination, Wittgenstein says, we shall be misguided and make a double mistake. For, first of all, it is not the experience itself to which the expression owes its specificity; and, secondly, something can be said about why we feel that the expression is somehow specific. The above-quoted passage indicates that the specificity of an expression is a function of its surroundings, which is why the experience in question presupposes an understanding of the context of the expression. A person who is not familiar with the Chandler atmosphere will not get much out of those words or that special way of pronouncing them. Thus the experience of a specific expression is not an independent phenomenon which resists all further attempts at elucidation.

There are several later passages where Wittgenstein returns to this subject, namely the question of experiencing something specific, and there he discusses it in different connections. The printed text of the *Philosophical Investigations* contains allusions to this kind of problem, too, but these allusions are extremely hard to make anything of, as they are not placed in the right kind of context.[8] In order to get a better grasp of this type of problem, we shall now leave the examples we have been discussing so far and try to get clearer about what Wittgenstein means by the term 'specific'.

There is a relatively extensive though inconclusive and apparently rambling discussion of 'specific' phenomena in *Remarks on the Philosophy of Psychology* (*RPP* i. § § 600 ff., 1.11.1946 ff.; cf. *LPP* 133). Here it is colour impressions in particular (and, for purposes of

---

[8] The remarks I am thinking of are: 'The grammar of the expression "a quite particular" (atmosphere). / One says "This face has a quite *particular* expression", and maybe looks for words to characterize it' (*PI* 66). 'Something new (spontaneous, "specific") is always a language game' (*PI* II, xi, p. 224). I hope the meaning of this last remark will become clearer at the end of this chapter.

comparison, experiences of sound) which are called specific. Thus
we read, 'Red is something specific' (619–20), 'Colours are
something specific' (628), and in two out of three cases statements of
this type are enclosed by quotation marks indicating that they are
not statements by Wittgenstein himself but objects of his investigation.

What does a speaker who uses a sentence like that ('X is
something specific') want to say by that? Here Wittgenstein
distinguishes three closely connected ideas: (1) X is simple, not
composite; (2) X cannot be explained (by means of words), it is
unanalysable (undefinable, cf. *RPP* i. § 160); (3) X is an object that
can be grasped by means of a special kind of cognitive faculty; if one
does not have this kind of faculty, one is not in a position to come to
know what X is.

1. *Red is simple*. This means that red plays a special role in the
context of our colour concepts; it is a primary colour, not a mixed
colour. We should find it hard to imagine a community where red is
supposed to be a secondary colour between orange and bluish-red,
even though such a possibility is not to be excluded for either logical
or physical reasons. Similarly we should not know what it would
mean if someone said he saw the tricolour as something uniform in
the same way as he saw red (cf. MS 133, 3. 11. 46). Such a statement
would be in complete contrast with our normal use of colour
concepts.

2. *Red cannot be explained*. It is impossible to teach the use of
colour concepts without ostensive gestures, that is, by employing
only words.

3. *The experience of redness presupposes a special faculty*. A blind
man cannot see objects and hence no coloured surfaces. For this
reason he does not know what is meant by 'red'.

All three of these claims contain a sound core but at the same time
the seeds of various misunderstandings. The statement that red is
simple says something about the role this colour concept plays in
our language and it also says something about our techniques of
learning and teaching this language, where these techniques may to
some extent depend on our biological constitution. For us it is
evident that red is a *part* of the tricolour, and if we invented a story
in which people call the tricolour non-composite and uniform, we
should say: 'Here we describe a language game that we *cannot learn*'
(*RPP* i. § 606).

The thesis that red is simple is a statement about our concept of this colour and is in this sense a statement about the 'essence' of red.[9] But here we must not forget that the contrasting pair 'simple'——'composite' does not really come in here, for 'red is composite' is in virtue of our language game excluded from the very beginning. For this reason the word 'simple' has not been used in its proper sense but as it were as a kind of reminder emphasizing a certain feature of that language game, namely the fact that red is one of the primary colours. The statement, 'Red is something simple, something specific' does not refer to an empirical property, and hence we cannot say things like, 'Now I have *seen* that red is simple.' Thus our thesis cannot be justified or refuted by means of empirical statements. What it does is to indicate a characteristic feature of the grid by means of which we impose a certain structure on our experience. That is the point of Wittgenstein's remark: 'Red is something specific; but we don't see that when we look at something red. Rather we see the *phenomena* that we *limit* by means of the language game with the word "red" ' (*RPP* i. § 619).

The second thesis, according to which red cannot be explained, says at least three things: (*a*) that redness cannot be explained without the help of ostensive explanations; (*b*) that colour expressions cannot be explained by means of something of a different kind, that is, something which has nothing to do with colour; (*c*) that only someone who is able to perceive or experience red will be able to understand the meaning of 'red' (this claim shades into thesis (3) and will be discussed below).

It is an 'important fact', as Wittgenstein underlines, that we need ostensive gestures in order to explain colour words (cf. *RPP* i. § 609). It goes without saying that pointing also plays an important role as a criterion for determining whether a certain colour word has been learnt correctly. On the other hand, ostension is neither an infallible instrument of teaching nor a necessary or sufficient criterion of having learnt a colour word. As Wittgenstein points out in many places, ostensive gestures are by themselves insufficient, since it is not possible to isolate an intended feature by means of such gestures; after all, we are not in a position to point as it were to

---

[9] Cf. *RPP* i. § 622. It is not clear from Wittgenstein's observations at this point whether or not he approves of this way of speaking. However, he does not argue against it.

properties but only to objects.[10] There will always be the possibility
of a mix-up, an erroneous collection, or an unjustifiable separation
of the intended characteristics: 'And note this: one doesn't point to
red, but to something red. That is of course to say: the concept
"red" is not determined by pointing . . .' (*RPP* i. § 613).

Neither pointing by itself nor the use of words by itself will
suffice to give a satisfactory explanation of 'red'. But is it true that
colours cannot be explained through something which does not
itself belong to the realm of colour? It is true to this extent, that
without the criterion of pointing to a colour there is no checking
and thus no training for the mastery of colour words. On the other
hand, pointing to red objects is not the only necessary condition of
successfully learning 'red'. Words too are needed and what is
especially important is an introduction to activities where the use of
colour words plays a role, serves a purpose, and has a point.

The activities where colour words come in useful are immensely
varied. They include not only 'the naming of colours, the
comparison of colours', but also making statements about 'the
connection between colour and light and illumination, the connection of colour with the eye' (*RPP* i. § 628). At this stage of learning
and teaching colour words, it obviously may also help to mention
parallels from other areas, especially if one is dealing with such
characteristics of colours as the distances between different shades,
their degrees of saturation, or their intensities. It must be
remembered in this connection that it is not one single factor—neither pointing, nor words, nor indicating point or purpose—which suffices to explain colour concepts. Understanding
colour concepts presupposes mastery of a variety of activities and
techniques, and only after a number of such activities and
techniques has been mastered will whatever is specific about a
certain colour dawn upon the learner.

The third thesis amounts to saying that a person who is incapable
of having a sense impression of red will never know what 'red'
means and will hence not be in a position to understand the concept
'red'. The idea behind this thesis is that in order to make a blind or
colour-blind man understand what we mean by 'red' it will be
necessary to give him a new perceptual or cognitive faculty or to

---

[10] Which does not mean, however, that we succeed in identifying objects by means
of this kind of pointing.

find some other way of generating an impression of redness in his brain.

What is true is that a person who differs from us in not being able to identify colours by means of his sense of sight will not be in a position to participate in most of our language games involving colour concepts; and the few games he may by means of certain devices be able to join in will not be played by him the same way as by us. A man who is red–green blind, for example, will sometimes be able to identify red in virtue of the location of the colour, but if it occurs at an unfamiliar spot of his visual field he will no longer be able to state its location. Thus he will for instance be unable to make independent comparisons between colours. A blind man may be able to learn to mix and to produce colours (in the sense of painter's colours, coloured lights, etc.) and he may also be in a position to assert after having manipulated some mechanism: 'This is red.' He would not be able to verify such an assertion without relying on some more or less complicated apparatus.

Comparison of different shades of colour and unmediated verification of colour statements are evidently elements of the foundations of our use of colour concepts. A person who is not able to perform these operations will also be incapable of grasping that which is 'specific' about colours. This fact, however, should not mislead us into thinking that experiencing something red—the sense impression of something red—constitutes the specificity of the concept 'red'. What we explain in explaining this concept is not the experience had by us, nor do we in any way 'employ' this kind of colour experience for the purpose of explanation.[11] It is only mastery of language games involving the words 'red' or 'redness' which will allow us to point out the specificity of this concept and to speak of a specific content of experience. But that does not mean that we have specific *experiences* which are generated by certain language games. What is specific lies *in the language game*: it lies in the facts that these colours and not those other ones are primary colours, that we describe degrees of saturation in such-and-such ways, that colours are mixed by means of certain techniques, and so forth.

---

[11] Cf. MS 133, 4. 11. 46: 'Does he who is explaining "red" point to a content of experience?' Of course, the answer is no.

All this does not mean, however, that such experiences are not real or that there are only oblique ways of referring to them. What it means is that what we are inclined to call the specific element of these experiences owes its existence to our techniques of using certain concepts and to their being embedded in the relevant practices. For this reason Wittgenstein remarks: 'Quite right: one can't imagine any explanation of "red" or of "colour". Not, however, because what is experienced is something specific, but rather because the language game is so' (*RPP* i. § 602).

The temptation to locate the specificity of an experience in the experience itself is particularly great in the case of psychological verbs; and according to Wittgenstein this is due to the fact that here one cannot indicate parallels when one tries to explain the meaning of those verbs. While with certain experiences of taste and smell, for instance, it is possible to remind us of analogous tastes and smells and thus give whoever is asking questions about them at least an idea of what one is talking about, such a possibility does not exist in the case of concepts like 'memory', 'pain', and 'fear'.[12] If someone asked what it was really like to remember something, we should not know how to give him an answer of the type we could give had he asked what the taste of sweetbread was like. There we are tempted to reply that remembering is remembering—a completely specific process with which one is simply familiar. One might say: 'When I remember yesterday's toothache, for example, I remember neither my behaviour nor do I feel toothache again; I am entertaining a kind of picture, but it is not of the same sort as a painting or a photograph—rather, it is something specific.' (Cf. *RPP* i. § 159.) In such a case, it seems, we are bound to use the same words again and again—words like 'it occurs to me', 'I am entertaining this picture', and so on—but there is no satisfactory parallel of the kind we may be able to mention in the case of a musical phrase or when savouring a certain taste. And this inclination to return to the same, albeit unsatisfactory words is evidence of our inclination to assume a specific experience.[13]

----

[12] Cf. *RPP* i. § 200: 'What can be adduced against the expressions "specific psychological phenomenon" or "irreducible phenomenon"? They are misleading: but what is their source? One wants to say: "If someone is unacquainted with sweet, bitter, red, green, notes and colours, one cannot make the meaning of these words intelligible to him." On the other hand, if someone hasn't yet eaten a sour apple, what is meant can be explained to him.'

[13] In Jackson's account of Wittgenstein's lectures on the philosophy of psychology we read: 'We ask the man who says this "What happens in you?" and he replies "I did

But questions like 'What is going on in your mind when you are remembering?' or 'What is it like to be in pain?' are just as misguided as attempts at explaining these processes or states by means of descriptions of experiences. The man who asks the question does not learn anything this way, and the man who gives answers of this kind keeps being misled. A person who tries to get a kind of inner memory picture in order to answer a question about the nature of memory behaves like the man who tries to develop a private system of designation by paying special attention to an inner experience: 'The expression "specific psychological phenomenon" corresponds to that of the private ostensive definition' (*RPP* i. § 200). To attempt to point to a specific experience is just as useless and harmful as to attempt to create a private language. One can speak of rules and of language only where there are methods of checking, standards, in brief, the possibility of training and learning. A person who does not know what pain is can be informed about it only by being made to feel pain; but if, for example, I pinch him, then this is a public, intersubjectively perceivable act which will fulfil its purpose only in a situation offering the usual verbal and non-verbal surroundings.

The nature of an experience which we tend, for want of a better term, to call a 'specific' one can be elucidated only under appropriate circumstances. The situation is similar to that described in the Grimm brothers' fairy-tale about the man who wanted to find out what fear is or in Wagner's *Siegfried*. It is necessary to find or bring out a situation in which the person in question can learn to apply the word concerned. Only when Siegfried is confronted with what he has never seen before does he understand 'the anguish of longing' and 'the heart in its tumult' and is at last able to use the word 'fear'.

According to Wittgenstein, the lesson which we should learn from such considerations is that whatever appears specific in an experience will have its basis in the relevant language game, that is,

a sum in my head"; "I can't say anything more about it but I did do that", so this is a strong case of wanting to say "a specific experience", because it's the case where you naturally say that it's describable only by those words.' (See G. Hallett, *A Companion to Wittgenstein's 'Philosophical Investigations'* (Ithaca, NY, 1977), 732.) This is to some extent similar to certain attempts at reproducing the specific expression of a musical phrase; here too we are sometimes inclined to recur again and again to a certain gesture or word. One difference, however, consists in this: that here the gesture or the word may seem suitable or appropriate while the words we tend to go back to when trying to explain or describe 'memory', 'pain', etc. leave us unsatisfied.

in the techniques and institutions which determine what it is in such cases to be right or wrong. Therefore it will quite generally be useless to answer questions about the nature of a psychological phenomenon by saying that it is something peculiar, something specific. First of all, this will help neither the person asking the question nor the one giving such an answer and, secondly, it will create the mistaken impression that here there is nothing to be explained. But the explanation is bound to fail only if one presumes that the characterizing word 'specific' is intended to refer to a private experience. What we have to understand is that 'the word "specific" (or an analogous one), which one would very much like to use here, does not help. It is as little of a resource as the word "indefinable" when one says that the word "good" is indefinable. / What we want to know, to get a bird's-eye view of, is the use of the word . . .' (*RPP* i. § 160). A bird's-eye view or conspectus of the use of a word is possible once one has understood the functioning and the peculiarities of those language games in which the word plays a role. What is entailed by such a bird's-eye-view and how one has to go about it in order to get there, is yet another set of questions. It is important to see right from the start what is justified and what is misleading in our use of phrases like 'a specific experience' or 'a specific expression'. And what we have learnt through the questions considered so far is that specificity is not a property of the experience itself but the effect of a language game which enables us to talk about the experience and to get our meaning across.

These considerations may also help to understand the following extremely puzzling remark from the *Philosophical Investigations*: 'Something new (spontaneous, "specific") is always a language game' (p. 224). What Wittgenstein presumably means by this remark is that a new form of expression requires an adequate and suitable context. (And here 'context' is naturally meant to be a very comprehensive term.) Thus if you wish to speak about music, you must not be ignorant about music. And you may speak about pain only if you yourself have had certain experiences and have learnt to make a number of moves in certain language games. That which is 'new' is not a pure and unfamiliar sound experience or a pain experience which is completely dissimilar to anything one has ever felt before. Even though both experiences are to a greater or lesser extent connected with instinctive, immediate forms of reaction, the experiences as such are 'meaningless' for myself ('I have no idea of what I am having') and they are uncommunicable unless there has been a minimum of instruction in the language games concerned. Even our so-called 'spontaneous' forms of reaction—certain types of gesture or dance steps when listening to music, exclamations like 'Ouch!' or 'Help!' or more complicated forms of behaviour in the case of pain—will acquire sense only within a language game and hence through their connections with certain kinds of conduct and through being embedded in relevant practices. And the 'specific', finally, is equally a function of a language game. What is specific in a colour experience is not, as far as we can make it intelligible, a matter of private experiences; it is dependent on the roles played by our colour concepts, which in their turn are not given to us by nature but have to be learnt. The specific character of a musical phrase simply does not exist unless there is some understanding of music.

A *new* experience is not even an experience if the relevant concepts are lacking, that is, if one has not learnt to make a number of moves in the language game in question. And if we do not know the techniques to be used in the language, there will be no *spontaneous* reactions to our experiences, let alone any possibility of identifying and articulating what is *specific* in them.

5

Experience

In the course of his early attempt at a classification of psychological phenomena Wittgenstein wonders if he ought to call the whole field of the psychological the field of experience (see p. 28, above; cf. *RPP* i. § 836). But even independently of a discussion of the problem of whether or not this terminology can be justified, it is necessary to see how the concept 'experience', which is central to Wittgenstein's entire philosophy of psychology, is to be understood.

The chief motive and focus of Wittgenstein's considerations regarding the concept of experience is the question of what it means to say that one can see a certain object or figure at one time as this and at another time as that, e.g. the figure ꟻ as an F and then as the mirror-image of an F (Wittgenstein calls this a mirror-F). That which distinguishes this kind of 'seeing-as' from ordinary seeing seems to be a certain element of interpretation. Whenever there is nothing peculiar about the circumstances under which I am looking at a table, it will be misleading or even wrong to say that I am seeing it *as* a table; for if this locution is appropriate, it must be legitimate to ask what other things it could possibly be seen as, and in ordinary perceptual situations there would be no answer to this question. For this reason neither the question nor an assertion supposedly answering it would make any sense. But if the context is different and we are, for instance, dealing with a children's game where a table serves as the wicked sorcerer's castle, the table being stood on its top while the legs are seen as towers or battlements, then it may happen that all of a sudden one pauses and says that now one has seen the table as a table.

One of the peculiarities of this situation is this: that asked what it is that one has seen, one is inclined to answer both by showing only one picture and by showing *two*, namely a picture of a table embellished to look like a castle *and* a picture of the plain table. We are aware that the seen object itself has not undergone any changes, but we wish to indicate that there has been some sort of change affecting our visual image. We feel that there has been some inner occurrence, and when we notice this feeling we are stimulated to theorize.

The first and most obvious step towards a deliberate analysis of this occurrence consists in trying to separate sensuous elements from intellectual ones. Thus one may say that of course the 'pure' sense impression has not changed in the least. Both before and after that occurrence one has seen the very same table and, as it were, received the same picture; it has only been *interpreted* in different ways. But a mere separation of a pure sense impression from the possible interpretations of this impression is evidently unsatisfactory in this case, for the thought one really wishes to express is precisely this: that the object has been *seen* differently. It is not the possibility of different interpretations which worries us and makes us reflect upon the details of that situation but rather the peculiar experience of the sense impression itself appearing to change, so that the recourse to interpretation looks like an explanation one tends to give *afterwards*.

How is this experience to be characterized? It is, on the one hand, clear that we are seeing the same thing both times; on the other hand, we do not want to say that what changes is merely our *conception* of what is seen. For there is after all a difference between a case where one and the same figure is used in two different contexts and then interpreted accordingly and a case where that figure is once seen as this and later as that and the change itself is, as we want to say, *experienced* by us.

If one looks at the well-known figure,

which can be seen either as a rabbit or as a duck, and says: 'Now I am seeing it as a rabbit', it is easy to be confused into conceiving this expression as a description of a state of affairs which by different means might be grasped in a more direct way. One is aware that the figure can be seen in two different ways, and now one is seeing it *this* way and thinks that one is having an immediate impression which is only *indirectly* described by those words 'Now I am seeing it as . . .'. This feeling is based on a natural but by no means harmless illusion which involves the suggestion that it might be possible to regard sense impressions in such a way that pure elements can be clearly separated from interpretative ones. This illusion is, among other things, due to the fact that we are not clear about the role of sentences with 'seeing as'; we take certain sentences to be essentially descriptive ones while in reality they do not have the function of descriptions at all. Wittgenstein emphasizes that the statement 'I am now seeing this as a rabbit' is not an indirect description of an experience but a typical *utterance* of such an experience (cf. *RPP* i. § 13). In Wittgenstein's view the idea that an utterance of the sentence 'Now I am seeing it as a rabbit' is a description of an experience is due to an illusion similar to the one which can make us believe that the complaint 'I am in pain' is the description of an experience and not its utterance.

A sentence like 'Now I am seeing it as a rabbit' does involve an interpretation; this, however, is not an interpretation of an experience but an interpretation of what has been seen. But as we are confused about the nature of that experience, we are inclined to claim that the experience itself involves an act of interpreting, and then we wonder exactly what part is played by that act: 'The question whether what is involved is a seeing or an act of interpreting arises because an interpretation becomes an expression of experience. And the interpretation is not an indirect description; no, it is the primary expression of the experience' (*RPP* i. § 20).

The confusion about the real character of an experience of seeing something as something arises through our inclination to regard it as composite or as the result of two processes which, although their theoretical distinction seems easy enough, are then extremely hard to fit together. Seeing is a state, interpreting is an activity—how can they come together in an act of seeing-as? (Cf. *RPP* i. § 1.) Seeing-as is not a state in the sense in which seeing can be said to be one. Whenever I look around the room I am in, I shall simply see things; I do not normally see them as this or that. I see things on my desk, I recognize them, I notice details about them, but that is far from being a peculiar experience.

Let us suppose that the duck-rabbit picture has been standing on my desk for quite some time. All of a sudden I notice for the first time that this picture, which for me has always been a picture of a duck, can be seen as a picture of a rabbit. What is it that is happening at that moment? In a flash a certain aspect becomes visible, I shall try to produce the change at will by directing my eyes in such a way that the picture is 'phrased' (*RPP* i. § 22) differently in order to get clear about the process going on in my mind. Now I know that the picture can be seen this way or that way; and experiencing the change seems to depend on my being aware of the different possibilities. This awareness, however, is not a kind of seeing; it is an intellectual element which only through the process of seeing something as something becomes an experience of such a peculiar type.

This account makes it appear as if seeing-as were the result of two different processes: seeing, plus awareness of a certain change, lead to seeing-as. This would be similar to a case where I see a man, remember a certain face, and then notice a similarity between these two. Here the seen face plus a memory image result in noticing a similarity. And this kind of noticing of a similarity may really be regarded as a new and separate process apart from seeing and remembering.

But if we examine the notion of seeing something as something, we shall soon notice that here things are different. Whenever I see the duck-rabbit picture as a picture of a rabbit, there is not a separate process of normal seeing taking place simultaneously. Nor will it do to say that normal seeing is suspended while I am seeing that picture as a picture of a rabbit. Thus seeing-as is not a process which takes place in addition to, and possibly accompanying, a process of normal seeing. On the other hand, attentive normal seeing is not said to be a peculiar experience whereas seeing-as is. Does the answer to the question arising here amount to saying that the awareness of a change will 'colour' our normal seeing and thus lend it the character of a peculiar experience?

This is the form in which the problems surrounding the notion of seeing-as are presented in the very first remarks on the philosophy of psychology and in which they reappear in a number of later reflections. But Wittgenstein nowhere reaches clear conclusions that might serve to settle his questions. He asks certain questions again and again. To what extent is seeing-as a matter of having an experience? To what extent does it depend on an act of interpreting? Which elements of the process could be called 'seeing', which 'understanding'? It repeatedly happens that Wittgenstein is side-tracked by subordinate questions and moves away from these problems, as if he wanted to explore lateral paths, leaving the main complex to one side, in order to reach it, not through the main entrance, as it were, but by way of some side-gate. Only towards the end of December 1948 does he get down to an extended discussion of those questions, and then he discovers, as so often happens in his writings, that the questions have to be asked differently. This does not mean, however, that he simply changes the subject. His technique of dealing with these problems mirrors the problems themselves in a striking manner: Wittgenstein changes his question in such a way that we get the impression of constantly looking at one and the same problem while his mode of discussing it makes us see new aspects of it. These aspects, while they may not grant us a final solution, will at least give us a more comprehensive picture of the subject.

The following example is Wittgenstein's starting-point. Suppose I am taking a walk with a friend; suddenly a rabbit is crossing our path and I notice that my friend looks surprised, makes a certain gesture, and utters a sound indicating that the sight has struck him. Never before in his life has he seen a rabbit; he does not know what kind of animal ran past us. He is not familiar with this phenomenon. I for my part may not even have seen the rabbit very clearly, but I shall none the less need only a brief glance to identify the animal: 'Oh, I see, a rabbit!' And now I wonder if my friend's seeing was a process of a different kind from my seeing. More generally, does someone who sees something without recognizing it have 'a different visual experience from someone who knew the object at once'? (*LW* § 540) Here the answer obtrudes itself upon us that there must be a difference in the visual experience, even though, for instance, we may both of us react in the same way to a request to draw a picture of what we have seen. That is, his picture may look the same as mine, and perhaps it is even more exact and more detailed than the one I have drawn.

However, a question about what has been seen is not the same as a question about the experience of seeing something. We must try to find out about the way the other person has seen the rabbit and about how he will describe his experience. The first difference between his account and mine will of course consist in the fact that he will not use the word 'rabbit', whereas I employ it quite naturally. His description of the animal and its appearance or movements will be rather awkward and cumbersome and he may even have to resort to gestures and drawings. It is the difference in our ways of reproducing the experience which will incline us to assume a difference in the experience itself.

Here one might object that the whole difference is due to the fact that the other person simply lacks the relevant concept. He does not know what a rabbit is; so it is not surprising that he is obliged to give a more complicated account. This objection can be met by modifying the example. Suppose my friend knows just as well as I do what a rabbit is and what it looks like. He merely did not recognize it straight away; for this reason he looked at it in surprise and than exclaimed in a surprised tone of voice: 'Oh, a rabbit!' In this case too his description will be different from mine. Again he will make use of gestures and pictures or vivid expressions, though to a lesser degree than in the former example. Thus he will for instance say something like this: 'All of a sudden I saw something on my right side. It had long ears and was running in a zigzag, quickly trying to get away from us. Only then did I notice that it was a rabbit.' This account too is clearly different from my laconic statement: 'I saw a rabbit crossing our path.' And again the difference between these descriptions suggests a difference between the experiences.

Remember the original way of putting the problem: there we started from our own case and our noticing a peculiar experience. Our further investigation amounted to a painstaking analysis of our memory of that experience. There was an act of paying attention (which according to Wittgenstein is a criterion of genuine duration, and hence of a state of consciousness in contrast with a disposition, *RPP* ii. § 50), and this act was our reason for looking back on the experience and considering it. Both paying attention to something and considering something involve *thought*, and in this way we arrived at the confusing question of to what extent the experience is constituted by an intellectual and to what extent by a purely visual element.

Our new way of posing the problem looks different. First of all, it does not start from my own case but from another person's experience. Secondly, we compare this person's verbal description of his experience with a description given by someone else (in our example, by myself) who in the same perceptual situation did *not* have that experience. Thirdly, we avoid the imposition of preconceived psychological notions, for 'we must be careful not to think in traditional psychological categories. Such as simply dividing experience into seeing and thinking . . . ' (*LW* § 542).

This change of perspective away from myself and towards other people and the new focus on utterances in the third person—this 'objectivization' of the relevant state of affairs, as one may call it—is of course not intended to deny the reality of the experience in question. It never occurs to Wittgenstein to negate the factuality of inner experiences. He rather tries to grasp the peculiar and problematic features of experiences by looking at them 'from the other side', as it were, for the reason they appeared problematic was that starting from one's own experience did not lead to a convincing way of dividing up the different elements and more or less characteristic properties constitutive of such experiences. For this reason Wittgenstein warns us: 'Do not try to analyse your experience internally!' (*LW* § 548).

But the objectivized account leads to a situation which is quite similar to the one reached starting from the subjective point of view. As regards the object of the description, there appears no difference between a person with and a person without a peculiar experience. Whatever difference there is results from the fact that the visual experience is expressed differently in each case. One person makes a simple statement while the other one expresses his surprise, his attention, and his concentrated consideration of the object in question, his attempts at interpreting and understanding what he sees. So the objectivized account too leads to a division into those two elements of seeing and interpreting, and again it seems as if the peculiar character of experiences of the kind we are interested in is due to the addition or admixture of an interpretative element. Thus we shall now have to ask whether an objectivized account will make an essential difference and whether it may turn out to be more adequate than a subjective one, which is based on introspection and memory.

There is one obvious difference between a subjective and an objective or objectivized approach which is frequently stressed by Wittgenstein, and it consists in this, that the subjective account, by contrast with the objective one, does not offer an intersubjectively helpful criterion for testing the relevant statements. This is a disadvantage, not only because other people will not know how to deal with my statements, but also because I myself, if I keep insisting on the purely subjective approach, will have no means of testing my own statements.

Of course, the difference between a subjective and an objective way of looking at things does not reside in the number of people who are present. Even in silent soliloquy can I objectivize my investigation by formulating it in such a way that another person could join in the discussion. This is the reason why a necessarily private way of indicating sense data, feelings, experiences, etc. must not play any role in an objectivized account. A mere statement like 'I see it *this* way' remains useless unless something is added to it. However intensely I may feel about it, it will leave myself just as much in the dark as my audience. This consideration gives the following remark its point: 'Always eliminate the private object for yourself, by supposing that it keeps on altering: you don't notice this, however, because your memory keeps on deceiving you' (*RPP* i.§ 985). This implies no claim about the existence or non-existence of entities that might rightly or wrongly be called private objects; the problem of the reality of such entities is not in question here. What Wittgenstein wants to bring out is his methodological maxim to leave allegedly private objects out of account, as it will help neither myself nor others to arrive at a better understanding of what I am saying.

Now we may for example want to ask which criterion of a visual experience is at the disposal of an objectivized account. Wittgenstein's answer is that it is 'the reproduction of "what is seen"' (*LW* § 563). As we have noticed, however, the rendering or reproduction of what is seen may in the case of our peculiar visual experience agree with a reproduction of what is seen in a normal case of seeing something. But this agreement is present only on the surface; it is an agreement of the pictures drawn or of the words used by the two speakers. Here Wittgenstein mentions the following example: 'I look at an animal in a cage. I am asked: "What do you see?" I answer: "A rabbit."—I gaze into the countryside; suddenly a rabbit runs past. I exclaim: "A rabbit!"' (*LW* § 549). If only the verbal form of expression is taken into account, there is virtually no difference between those two cases. But if one considers the utterances in their wider context, then one will no longer wish to claim that the words used express the same thing. Even though 'both things, both the report and the exclamation, can be called expressions of perception and of visual experience', it is none the less true that 'the exclamation is so in a different sense from the report; it wrests itself from us. It is related to the experience as a cry is to pain' (ibid.).

The relation between cry and pain which is here alluded to by Wittgenstein is not some identifiable definite causal relation. What is meant is rather the characteristic way cry and pain are embedded in situations of human life. The fact that a cry wrests itself from a person who is utterly surprised is not something which no one except for this person would be able to notice; it is a fact which we as 'outsiders' may well be in a position to grasp and recognize from his movements, the tone of his voice, his facial expression, just as we are in a position to recognize a cry of pain from its typical features. When a person utters a certain kind of cry, we do not normally need to ask him if this was a cheerful cry, a cry of anger, or a cry of pain. The situation, and his behaviour within it, will normally leave no doubt about the nature of his cry. And in the same way, purely verbal agreement notwithstanding, the reproduction of what is seen may make it clear whether we are confronted with a 'report' or an 'exclamation', that is, with a simple description of what has been perceived or with an expression of a peculiar experience.

The difference between a report about what has been seen and an expression of a visual experience lies both in one's *reactions* to what one sees and in the *consequences* of seeing it for the rendering or reproduction of what has been seen, that is, in the way this rendering or reproduction enters into various language games. In the first case (that of a report) the rendering of what has been seen is a simple description of things and events. In the second case (that of an exclamation) there are, according to the kind of experience concerned, different characteristic forms of reaction which are mirrored, if not by the chosen words themselves, then by the way they are pronounced, by the tone of voice, and other circumstances. Typically, it is not only the voice or the phrases used which express all this but also gestures and movements of the face; for example, you imitate what you are observing, you narrow your eyes, you speak in a tone of surprise or disbelief, you make certain comparisons. Here there are of course considerable differences between various kinds of perceptual experience. If you know what a rabbit is but are surprised by one crossing your path, your reaction will hardly be more than a mere 'Can I really trust my eyes?' As regards the consequences, however, the rendering or reproduction of what one has seen may be very different from those in the case of a simple report. Thus it will often be the case that a person who is surprised by what he has seen will continue with an *explanation* which specifies why he is surprised and why he has had a special experience when seeing that rabbit.

In cases of seeing-as things are more complicated yet. The reaction of a person who has had a peculiar perceptual experience or is just having one will express itself in his gestures, in his face, and in a typical phrase like 'I have seen this as that', perhaps even in a certain perplexity and in his looking for appropriate analogies which could render his experience more vivid. But while in normal cases of surprise the relevant consequences will consist in explanatory remarks such as 'I should never have thought that there are rabbits in the centre of Oxford', etc., in cases of seeing-as reference will be made to the experience itself, and one will try to give an idea of the peculiarity of that experience.

As has already been stressed, in these cases reference to the experience cannot be a straightforward kind of pointing to it. And it is useless to place your interlocutor in the same situation as you were when you had the peculiar experience of seeing something as such-and-such, and then to tell him that now he is having the same experience as you had earlier on. Such an arrangement, unless it is part of a psychological experiment, will at best serve to teach the other person what the expression 'change of aspect' means or to make him familiar with a certain kind of aspect. But it does not help us to get a better understanding either of the phenomenon of seeing-as or of the corresponding concept. The kind of reference which is intended by Wittgenstein and which in his opinion might help us to get clearer about the peculiar experience takes its start from the *expression* of the experience. And the expression may be helpful because it will suggest natural ways of continuing a description. Of course, Wittgenstein does underline that here there are 'hugely many interrelated phenomena and possible concepts' (*LW* § 581) but at the same time he hints at a few more closely circumscribed types of cases which may help to explain his meaning. Among the possibilities he hints at there is, first, the use of a conceptual explanation and, secondly, the reproduction of experiencing an aesthetic aspect by means of giving an account of what one has experienced.

Now one cannot be absolutely certain what Wittgenstein here intends by a conceptual explanation. He writes: 'Sometimes the conceptual is dominant in an aspect. That is to say: Sometimes the experience of an aspect can be expressed only through a conceptual explanation. And this explanation can take many different forms' (*LW* § 582). But the examples which are scattered over several manuscripts suggest that what he has in mind are explanations containing characteristic formulations such as 'There was an abrupt change, and then I saw *y*', or 'At first I saw nothing but confusion but gradually the picture became organized and suddenly I saw a face', and so forth. These are explanations which are most easily formulated by means of formulas like 'sudden change', 'organization of the visual image', etc., and these formulas cannot really be replaced by examples, which here could at most serve to specify the general notion. These are cases where the use of such formulas and general concepts is a natural expression of, or an immediate reaction to, the experience in question. A typical consequence of such a reaction would be to continue by mentioning analogies, for instance 'It was as if I had suddenly seen the picture in a different light', or by using typical phrases like 'All of a sudden I saw . . .', or 'The scales were removed from my eyes and I realized . . .'.

The second possibility mentioned was that of experiencing an aesthetic aspect, for example hearing a tune in a certain way. Here Wittgenstein alludes to several characteristic forms of expressing such an experience: gestures or movements with one's hands, involuntary dance steps, and in particular playing or singing the tune in a way which underlines the experience, for instance by stressing the felt rhythm or by accentuating an unexpected part of a transition: 'I hear it differently, and now I can play it differently. Thus I can render it differently' (*LW* § 587). Expressing the experience is here essentially connected with an activity: a way of accompanying the tune which comes to the fore in certain movements or an unusual way of playing, singing, or whistling the tune suggesting the peculiarity of one's experience. Parallels to this can be found in the realm of visual experiences; thus one may underline the experienced visual aspect by tracing a certain line in a drawing with a bold pencil stroke or simply with one's finger.

In these last cases experience and activity appear particularly closely connected (cf. *LW* § 586). Here our response to a certain experience is a natural reaction. It comes automatically, just as certain concepts force themselves on us in the case of conceptual explanations (*LW* § 591). Of course, the immediacy of such reactions and the suggestiveness of those concepts are by no means purely natural phenomena. Even though they may be based on primitive or instinctive forms of behaviour (in the way this is true of our natural pain expressions), they tend to be shaped by certain activities, conventions, and types of explanation which are typical of the relevant language game.

This shows that the sequence experience——reaction——consequences is not to be read in only one direction. Such consequences (that is, follow-up explanations, the specific continuation of an expression of a peculiar experience in various kinds of language game) do not remain without influence on the type of reaction concerned and even on the way the experience is felt. This is one reason for thinking that the phenomenon we are interested in cannot easily be divided into separate parts corresponding to either seeing or interpreting, experience or activity, and this is so both in the case of a subjective and in that of an objectivized approach. Naturally an objectivized approach has this advantage: that it allows us to place an experience in a wider context which a subjective approach, if consistent, cannot take into account. And only if an experience is seen in the context of its expression and its consequences will it become possible to draw helpful conceptual distinctions and to make explanatory comparisons.

These distinctions and explanations will always be restricted to individual cases and their relevance will remain limited. There simply is no common denominator making for uniformity, and that is a fact which we shall have to put up with:

There are many ways of experiencing aspects. What they have in common is the expression: 'Now I see it as *that*'; or 'Now I see it *this* way'; or 'Now it's *this*—now *that*'; or 'Now I hear it as . . .; a while ago I heard it as . . .'. But the explanation of these '*that*'s and '*this way*'s is radically different in the different cases. (*LW* § 588)

Appendix: Meaning Blindness and Introspection

In his book on Wittgenstein's notions of rule and private language Saul Kripke makes some points which are closely connected with the considerations of the present chapter. Kripke is right in emphasizing that Wittgenstein's remarks are not compatible with a behaviourist theory; but at the same time he makes the surprising claim that Wittgenstein's method of investigation and his way of employing thought experiments are to be regarded as largely introspective procedures.[1] While Kripke approves of Wittgenstein's thesis that the psychological processes which may accompany meaning and understanding are not constitutive of what we mean by 'meaning' and 'understanding', he declares that in his opinion Wittgenstein runs the risk of promoting too mechanistic a conception, even though his own investigations are essentially introspective ones. In Part II of the *Philosophical Investigations*—that is while working on his manuscripts on the philosophy of psychology—Wittgenstein, according to Kripke's reading, became aware that he had run that risk, and this is said to be particularly evident in his remarks on meaning blindness. Summarizing, Kripke writes:

Could there be a 'meaning blind' person who operated with words just as we do? If so, would we say he is as much in command of the language as us? The 'official' answer to the second question . . . is 'yes'; but perhaps the answer should be, 'Say what you want, as long as you know the facts.' It is not clear that the problem is entirely resolved. Note that here, too, the discussion is introspective, based on an investigation of our own phenomenal experience. It is not the kind of investigation that would be undertaken by a behaviourist.[2]

What is obviously correct is Kripke's statement that Wittgenstein does not proceed in a behaviourist fashion, although he does, as Kripke also notes, sympathize with certain aspects of a behaviourist attitude. Kripke's further claim, however, according to which Wittgenstein proceeds introspectively, cannot be correct, if my remarks about an 'objectivized' approach (pp. 60 ff., above) are true. It must also be remembered that there is no reason to suppose that behaviourism and introspection are the only alternatives to be considered here, so that from a rejection of behaviourism one could infer the soundness of an introspective method. But quite apart from this point, I shall try to show that Kripke's claim is misguided,

---

[1] S. Kripke, *Wittgenstein on Rules and Private Language* (Oxford, 1982), 48.
[2] Ibid. n. 29.

that his reconstruction of Wittgenstein's way of asking his questions is wide of the mark and his answer correspondingly inadequate.

As a first step, we shall have to find out what the point of Wittgenstein's remarks about meaning blindness is.[3] In order to support his claim Kripke not only refers to a few remarks from the second part of *Philosophical Investigations* but also to the highly instructive Preface by Rush Rhees to his edition of the *Blue and Brown Books*. In this preface Rhees writes that to the question of why language does not appear to be a mere mechanism but something alive Wittgenstein tends to answer by pointing out that signs gain their life through intercourse with other speakers, through being used in linguistic exchanges, and that this answer will often be sufficient. In some cases, however, it may be possible to raise the objection

that someone might do all that, make the signs correctly in the 'game' with other people and get along all right, even if he were 'meaning-blind'. Wittgenstein used that expression in analogy with 'colour-blind' and 'tone-deaf'. If I say an ambiguous word to you, like 'board', for instance, I may ask you what meaning you think of when you hear it, and you may say that you think of a committee like the Coal Board, or perhaps you do not but think of a plank. Well, could we not imagine someone who could make no sense of such a question? If you just said a word to him like that, it gave him no meaning. And yet he could 'react with words' to the sentences and other utterances he encountered, and to situations too, and react correctly. Or can we *not* imagine that? Wittgenstein was not sure, I think. If a man were 'meaning-blind', would that make any difference to his use of language? Or does the perception of meaning fall outside the use of language?[4]

Now it is possible that Kripke has been misled by Rhees's account, for that which is here described as 'meaning blindness' is not at all

[3] The curious expression 'meaning blindness' (*Bedeutungsblindheit*) occurs in Fritz Mauthner's *Beiträge zu einer Kritik der Sprache* (Frankfurt etc., 1982) i. 309, where it is, however, used with a completely different meaning from that intended by Wittgenstein. (I owe the reference to Mauthner to Hannes Marek.) But I regard as unlikely that Wittgenstein in any way deliberately took this notion from Mauthner. What cannot be excluded, however, is that there is some relation between the much-discussed concept 'soul blindness' (which is also mentioned by Mauthner) and Wittgenstein's use of the word 'meaning blindness'. Two possible sources are Ernst Mach, who mentions soul blindness in his book *Erkenntnis und Irrtum* (Darmstadt, 1976, 45–6, where he also speaks of 'word blindness'), and William James, who discusses various phenomena of soul blindness in ch. 2 of his *Principles of Psychology*.

[4] R. Rhees, Preface to Wittgenstein, *The Blue and Brown Books* (Oxford, 1972), pp. xiii–xiv.

the same phenomenon as that intended by Wittgenstein in his
remarks written in the late forties. To put it briefly, Rhees gives an
exaggerated account of what is meant by a meaning blind person.

Even if the intended notion of meaning blindness is not clearly
definable, Wittgenstein does mention sufficiently many examples to
indicate which kinds of cases are *obviously* excluded. Thus it
becomes clear that a meaning blind person is not blind in the sense
in which someone may be born without eyesight. What a meaning
blind person is lacking is not a certain kind of sensation or sense
impression (cf. *RPP* i. § 189). It would not even be correct to claim
that a meaning blind man is incapable of making anything of
questions about the meanings of words in general or of ambiguous
words in particular. Wittgenstein explicitly states that a meaning
blind man can now say that a certain meaning has occurred to him
and later that a different meaning has occurred to him, just as he is
able to think of different bearers of one and the same proper name
used on different occasions (cf. *RPP* i. § 242).

The absence of the capacity which a meaning blind person lacks
does not, as Rhees rightly emphasizes, prevent him from being just
as able as the rest of us to take part in most language games. On the
other hand, what he is lacking is not something which only very few
people have like 'the eye of a painter' or 'the ear of a musician'. No,
what he is lacking is something like a 'musical ear'. He is similar to
someone who is able to distinguish 'piano' and 'forte', 'allegro' and
'andante' but incapable of making anything of Schumann's direction
to play something 'as from afar' or of the indication 'Play this [or
hear this] as if it were the answer' (*RPP* i. §§ 250, 247).

Among the examples Wittgenstein keeps mentioning in his
manuscripts of the late forties is our understanding of jokes like the
oft-quoted 'Weiche, Wotan, weiche!' On the one hand, the words
can be read as an instruction for Wotan to retreat and, on the
other, as an answer to Wotan's question about whether one has a
preference for hard- or soft-boiled eggs. Another example is the
capacity to hear the end 'a' in the name 'Maria' differently according
as to whether one speaks of Carl Maria von Weber or of Maria
Callas. Wittgenstein also hints that a meaning blind person will not
be able to make much sense of Goethe's well-known remark about
proper names.[5] That which a meaning blind person is lacking is like

---

[5] Cf. Wittgenstein, *Zettel* § 184; Goethe, *Dichtung und Wahrheit*, II. 10: 'A man's
proper name is not like a cloak, which hangs but loosely around him and at which
one may tug or pull if need be, but rather like a perfectly fitting dress, even like his

the feeling absent in a person who is completely indifferent to nuances of the spelling of words and who would thus be unable to make anything of the following remark by Grillparzer:

I cannot describe the dreadful impression which the *h* in the English word *ghost* makes on me. When the word is spoken it does not sound particularly solemn, but whenever I see it written it does not fail to have its effect on me; I believe I am seeing a spectre before me.[6]

All the capacities or abilities mentioned so far are of fairly 'refined' kinds. The cases taken from music presuppose certain skills and knowledge, and the linguistic examples go far beyond the mere rudiments of language mastery. And the following example, which Wittgenstein mentions several times, is subtle indeed:

But remember how the names of famous poets and composers seem to have absorbed a peculiar meaning. So that one can say: the names 'Beethoven' and 'Mozart' don't merely sound different; no, they are also accompanied by a different *character*. But if you had to describe this character more closely—would you point to their portraits, or to their music? And now the meaning-blind man again: He would not feel that the names, when heard or seen, were distinguished by an imponderable Something. And what would he have lost by this? (*RPP* i. § 243)

Here it is a feeling for an imponderable Something which the meaning blind person is lacking, and this feeling will surely not be acquired without some instruction. If we look at all the examples concerning meaning blindness mentioned so far, it will soon become manifest that at least a number of these cases are not at all far-fetched but, on the contrary, really to be met with. Musicians who cannot properly interpret Schumann's directions, people who are not able to understand puns, and those for whom 'spelling is just a practical question' (*RPP* ii. § 572)—they all are figures who are not taken from Wittgenstein's imagination but types of people we are familiar with. Rhees's question of whether we are incapable of imagining a case of meaning blindness will thus be just as mistaken as his claim that Wittgenstein was not sure of the answer to be given to that question. A phenomenon which we can characterize by means of so many analogies is not difficult to imagine; indeed, we

skin, which has grown fast all over him and which one may not scrape or flay without hurting him.'

[6] F. Grillparzer, diary entry of 1811, *Sämtliche Werke* (Munich, 1964), iii. 271. Wittgenstein refers to this passage in his MS 135, 28. 7. 47. Cf. *RPP* ii. § 572.

shall hardly need any imagination at all, since we can largely rely on experience.

To put it more generally, what a meaning blind person is lacking is neither a kind of sense experience nor mastery of a certain skill but an experience of a meaning or of a specific kind of meaning. (Cf. *LPP* 105–6.) It is in the nature of what we call a feeling, a sensibility, or perhaps a 'nose for something'. A meaning blind person is like a musician who plays mechanically whatever is put before him or like a person who drinks different kinds of wine without tasting any differences. In some cases it is possible to help these people to acquire what they have been lacking. Some musicians can be taught to play more expressively, whereas others will never learn it; some wine drinkers can be enlightened on the differences between certain aromas, whereas others will remain insensitive. If I succeed in making another person feel such experiences, then this will not be due to my having exercised some inexplicable, undiscoverable influence on his soul. What has happened is that I have taught him a technique, a way of reacting, and perhaps a certain vocabulary, which of course does not mean that the technique or the reactions or the words are the same thing as the experience in question.

What is the interest of an enquiry into the abilities of a meaning blind person? According to Rhees and Kripke the interest lies in this, that here we are dealing with a problem concerning our mastery of our language. They think that it is a question of whether or to what extent a meaning blind person would use our language the same way as us. Wittgenstein begins by putting his question in a similar way:

When I supposed the case of a 'meaning-blind' man, this was because the experience of meaning seems to have no importance in the *use* of language, because it looks as if the meaning-blind could not miss much. But it conflicts with this, that we sometimes say that some word in a communication meant one thing to us until we saw that it meant something else. (*RPP* i. § 202)

In the use of language, that is, in our everyday intercourse, experiencing the meaning of a word appears to play no role. We give information and orders, we put questions and formulate answers without ever feeling that an alleged special atmosphere surrounding our words comes in or that an 'imponderable Something' or the 'savouring' of an ambiguity is of particular relevance. Thus our first impression is that a meaning blind person will miss little or nothing. Then, however, we remember that even in normal linguistic intercourse it can happen that a word is first understood in one meaning and later in another. If someone says: 'I'll just go to the bank', I can take this as referring either to a building on the other side of the street or to the land next to the river. Suppose I take it in the latter sense. But now the speaker continues: 'I have to take out a lot of money.' Now I notice that he has meant the establishment on the other side of the street and shall, if required, react accordingly. But how about the meaning blind man? At first one might think that he will miss a fair amount, for *ex hypothesi* he has no sensitivity for the ambiguity of the word 'bank'. Whenever he moves from one meaning to another, he does it mechanically, as it were, without ever remarking either to himself or to another person something like, 'Now I see the word "bank" in a completely different light.' Thus there really is a difference, but how important is it? Let us have another look at the case of ourselves, who are not meaning blind:

First, however, we don't feel in this case that the experience of the meaning took place while we *were hearing the word*. Secondly, here one might speak of an experience rather of the sense of the sentence, than of the meaning of a word.

The picture that one perhaps connects with the utterance of the sentence 'The bank is far away', is an illustration of *it* and not of one of its words. (*RPP* i. §§ 202–3)

The experience which we are interested in does not take place while one is hearing or pronouncing the ambiguous word or words. Only after the sense of the entire sentence or of a larger unit of speech has become clear can I become aware of the fact that a certain word in that sentence was to be understood differently from the way I took it. It is through this dawning of the proper or intended meaning that the experience of a 'switch' of meaning is generated which Wittgenstein likes to compare to the switch of a seen aspect. It is this experience which a meaning blind person lacks.

This case does not really concern an experience of *word* meaning; the switch concerns the meaning of an entire sentence. This difference is important for the reason that here the situation is different from one in which the meaning blind man is really at a loss. A paradigmatic case of meaning blindness may for example arise if one is first asked to read the sentence 'I HAD A RUSK FOR

BREAKFAST' in what one might call its natural sense, meaning that I ate a kind of zwieback, and then asked to see the word 'RUSK' in isolation and read it as a proper name. Here a person who is *not* meaning blind is free to react in more than one way. Perhaps he will 'blink with the effort' as he tries 'to parade the right meanings before [his] mind in saying the words' (*PI* II. ii, p. 176), and he will be able to report certain associations that have come to his mind. A meaning blind person, on the other hand, is completely at a loss in this case. He does not know what he is supposed to do, while in the case of the ambiguous word 'bank' in ordinary linguistic intercourse he acts and reacts in the same way as us, except for what we shall say when on *later* occasions we describe our experiences of meaning.

From this account it will have become clear that Wittgenstein is not really concerned about the question asked by Kripke of whether a meaning blind person can use words the same way as we do; for Wittgenstein's presentation of the situation leaves no doubt about it that the linguistic behaviour of a meaning blind person is indistinguishable from that of a normal person only up to a certain point. One difference lies in this, that a meaning blind person will not be able to cope with certain questions regarding isolated ambiguous words and will in this respect be incapable of taking part in the language game. The same consideration yields an answer to Kripke's second question of whether a meaning blind person 'is as much in command of the language as us'. This answer—in contrast with the 'official' view as depicted by Kripke—cannot be an unconditional 'yes', for the answer will depend on whether or not the capacities which the meaning blind person is lacking are regarded as essential. In other words, is the meaning blind person like someone who is incapable of using negation or is he like someone who is incapable of speaking competently about Schumann's piano music? If the former, then the meaning blind person does not have the same kind of command of our language as us, but if the latter, then there will be no real reason to doubt his mastery of our language.[7]

But what has all this got to do with an *experience* of meaning? The connection lies in this, that anything we say about experiences, be it to ourselves or to others, will be intelligible only to the extent

[7] A corresponding answer will have to be given to Rhees's question of whether the perception of meaning falls outside the use of language.

that our sentences involve characteristic forms of expression, comparisons, gestures, etc. As Wittgenstein remarks at one point (*LW* §§ 712–13), some words simply *are* gestures or bearers of a certain tone, and because of that, for example, we are in certain situations unwilling to replace them by so-called synonyms. If a man reacts to a certain passage in Schumann by quoting a line from a poem by Eichendorff, we may say that he has an experience of a certain kind, an experience which we too may be able to feel. The consequences of his expression of his experience will also fit a recognizable pattern; he will mention certain parallels and analogies to which we may for our part react in a suitable fashion. But someone who is not able to respond in any way or at most by a mechanical repetition of what he has heard and who is also unable 'to continue correctly' is similar to a meaning blind man. And just as we may succeed in teaching a 'Schumann blind' person how certain sequences, transitions, and pauses are to be understood and to be interpreted, so we *may* in the case of a meaning blind person succeed in teaching him a certain technique for 'savouring' the meanings of words. We know sufficiently many criteria for judging whether he is doing so purely mechanically and hence merely pretending to have a certain experience, for only if he is for example able to respond spontaneously and by using expressions he has not heard from others shall we admit that he really has the experience in question.

These considerations suffice to show that Wittgenstein's remarks about meaning blindness are not, as Kripke claims, based on introspection; Wittgenstein does not try to establish his view by means of 'an investigation of our own phenomenal experience'. Of course, most of us do have experiences of meaning, and these experiences will be accessible to introspection. What we say about these experiences will be intelligible only to the extent that our utterances correspond to certain patterns, be they ever so vague. If someone lacks certain kinds of experience altogether, we shall be at a loss to know what to make of claims about his having or not having such experiences; we may just as well assume that he is blind to those processes which are normally connected with experiences of this kind. We may speak of experiences only if the surroundings (the situation, our utterances, and other reactions, as well as our ensuing actions) are of the right kind. It is an alleged sort of experience *simpliciter* that Wittgenstein's interlocutor intends with his question: ' "If you didn't *experience* the meaning of the words, then how could you laugh at puns?" [What is the difference between a hairdresser and a sculptor?—A hairdresser curls up and dyes, and a sculptor makes faces and busts.]' To which Wittgenstein replies *in propria persona*: 'We do laugh at such puns: and to that extent we could say (for instance) that we experience their meaning' (*LW* § 711). Laughing is not the same thing as having the experience; but only of someone who does laugh at puns may we make the fairly safe assumption that he has a feeling for the ambiguity of words. A person's laughing at the right point is *one* criterion of his experiencing the meaning. If such reactions and many other ones besides remain absent, we may really be confronted with a meaning blind person.

6

Objects of Vision

WHENEVER Wittgenstein speaks of problems of perception or sense impressions he—like most philosophers—concentrates on the sense of sight: vision takes pride of place. What distinguishes his way of dealing with these problems from more traditional approaches is the fact that he tends to discuss vision or our normal seeing of something in connection and confrontation with the doubtlessly puzzling problems arising from phenomena of aspect seeing. One likely reason for this procedure is Wittgenstein's intention of depriving ordinary vision of its character of un-problematic normality by comparing it with a set of problems which obviously raises innumerable questions. Thus he writes: '"Seeing the figure *as* . . ." has something occult, something ungraspable about it. One would like to say: "Something has altered and nothing has altered."—But don't try to explain it. Better look at the rest of seeing as something occult too' (*RPP* i. § 966). A comparison of ordinary seeing with seeing-as, however, may easily lead to misunderstandings of the latter notion, as we tend to overrate the similarities between them. For this reason Wittgenstein observes in a suppressed remark: 'Comparison with *seeing* is risky. And *that* is what I should learn from it. Of course, there really are analogies, but there are conceptual differences too' (MS 135, 20. 7. 47).

Both of the remarks which are quoted in the preceding paragraph were written in summer 1947, a few months after Wittgenstein had discussed Köhler's presentation of gestalt psychology extensively in his lectures. After a fairly long interruption, he had again taken up work on his manuscript. From 12 July until 3 August he wrote daily in his ledger, and the content of his entries suggests that he kept a copy of Köhler's *Gestalt Psychology* at hand, as the allusions to this book are numerous and detailed. It may well have been that this discussion of Köhler's views among other things stimulated Wittgenstein to make constant comparisons of seeing and seeing-as.[1] Similarly, the fact that Köhler's treatment of the problems of

[1] Of course, Wittgenstein discussed the subject in much earlier writings too. Cf. e.g.

perception suggests such a comparison may have increased Wittgenstein's interest in the gestalt theoretic approach.

The fact that the material published as Part II of the *Philosophical
Investigations* contains only one mention of Köhler and no mention
of gestalt theory at all must not mislead us into overlooking the fact
that Köhler's book was the most important single influence on
Wittgenstein during those years.[2] But even the material which is
contained in the second part of the *Philosophical Investigations*
makes it difficult to overlook the impact of Köhler on Wittgenstein's thinking. Of course, the most striking examples of this
are the illustrations; but there are also a number of allusions to
certain thoughts and concepts which are characteristic of Köhler's
theory. On the last page of the *Philosophical Investigations*, for
instance, there is an implicit reference to Köhler which is of general
and fundamental significance:

The confusion and barrenness of psychology is not to be explained by
calling it a 'young science'; its state is not comparable with that of physics,
for instance, in its beginnings. (Rather with that of certain branches of
mathematics. Set theory.) For in psychology there are experimental
methods and *conceptual confusion*. (As in the other case conceptual
confusion and methods of proof.)
The existence of the experimental method makes us think we have the
means of solving the problems which trouble us; though problem and
method pass one another by.[3]

The quoted expression 'young science' is taken from Köhler's book
Gestalt Psychology whose second chapter bears the title 'Psychol-

the following passage from the early thirties: 'The different experiences I have when I
see a picture first one way and then another are comparable to the experience I have
when I read a sentence with understanding and without understanding. / (Recall
what it is like when someone reads a sentence with a mistaken intonation which
prevents him from understanding it—and then realizes how it is to be read.) / (To see
a watch as a watch, i.e. as a dial with hands, is like seeing Orion as a man striding
across the sky.)' *PG* 42.

[2] The other authors mentioned by Wittgenstein during the late forties did not
really exercise any *influence* on his thinking. William James's *Principles of Psychology*
provided him with stimulating opinions and examples. G. E. Moore's frequently
mentioned paradox was a fresh stimulus to resume thinking about a subject which
Wittgenstein had been interested in from the very beginning of his philosophical
career and thus to look at the Fregean theme 'assertion—supposition—belief' from a
new point of view. Cf. Ch. 9, below.
[3] *PI* II. xiv, p. 232. The manuscript draft of this remark mentions Köhler's name
while it is absent from the typescript version (= *RPP* i. § 1039).

ogy as a Young Science'. Köhler there defends the view that many difficulties arising in psychological investigations are due to the fact that, compared to physics for example, psychology as a discipline is a young science. While physics has, according to Köhler, already reached a stage of maturity, psychology is still in its leading-strings. And implicitly this amounts to saying that the present problems which psychology is dealing with are somehow analogous to those problems that physics had to wrestle with before overcoming its teething troubles and that psychology will have to take a similar path to that of physics in order to emulate it and become a mature science. This is precisely the claim which is denied by Wittgenstein in the above-quoted remark from the *Philosophical Investigations*. In his view the confusion and barrenness of psychology are not to be overcome by emulating physics and striving to follow in its footsteps.

But how, according to Köhler, can psychology emulate physics? This question appears especially urgent if one remembers Köhler's claim that psychology must not proceed purely quantitatively but should take its start from 'qualitative' phenomena. Thus he writes, for example, that 'the various qualitative types of behaviour are no less important than are the quantitative differences within a given type'. The qualitative aspect, however, is regarded as more significant inasmuch as 'the discrimination of qualitative types must be accomplished in the first place'.[4] But this priority of the qualitative aspect is to be understood in purely temporal terms; the qualitative phenomena are a mere starting-point and are thus to be regarded as a stage of the research programme that should soon be overcome. The aim remains that of a scientific discipline striving to follow the model of physics. For the time being, however, the psychological problems which could be dealt with in a really scientific spirit are few because psychology is only at the beginning of its development. Köhler writes: 'If we wish to imitate the physical sciences, we must not imitate them in their highly developed contemporary form. Rather, we must imitate them in their historical youth, when their state of development was comparable to our own at the present time.' In brief: 'Physics is an old science, and psychology is in its infancy.'[5]

---

[4] W. Köhler, *Gestalt Psychology* (New York, 1975), 26.
[5] Ibid. 28, 27.

In Wittgenstein's view this diagnosis is misguided: psychology is not a science comparable to physics. Physical problems are such that they can be solved satisfactorily by means of the consolidated methods and techniques developed by the scientific discipline of physics. If they cannot be solved that way, they are pseudo-problems or questions remaining external to physics itself. Psychology, on the other hand, is confronted with a number of problems which can neither be solved by established scientific means nor rejected as mere pseudo-problems, which of course does not mean that it never encounters any problems that can be solved in a scientifically acceptable fashion. But problems which can be solved in a scientific way are in Wittgenstein's opinion of no philosophical relevance. The questions he is interested in are those which cannot be attacked by scientific means or solved by techniques imitating scientific procedures; that is, he wants to deal with questions which are due to 'conceptual confusion'.

Here it is natural to wonder why it should not be possible to solve or get rid of these problems by means of more exact definitions and the operationalization of the concepts in question and thus to apply a method which has evidently been successful in other areas. Wittgenstein's answer is that there are concepts which are simply not accessible to such a kind of treatment, and among those concepts there are some psychologically relevant ones. He writes:

Psychological concepts are just everyday concepts. They are not concepts newly fashioned by science for its own purpose, as are the concepts of physics and chemistry. Psychological concepts are related to those of the exact sciences as the concepts of the science of medicine are to those of old women who spend their time nursing the sick. (*RPP* ii. § 62)

The problem touched on by this remark is among the most delicate and most difficult ones to be found in Wittgenstein's philosophy; it can in this context only be indicated but not developed with all its ramifications. For again one gets the impression that Wittgenstein is simply ignoring the possibility of defining and operationalizing concepts in order to reach a more exact understanding of what we can grasp only vaguely and incompletely if we insist on proceeding without strict scientific means.

This, however, is not the salient point. Wittgenstein does not defend a point of view according to which any progress within a scientific discipline is mere appearance. Rather, he wishes to stress that psychological concepts are similar to other everyday concepts in so far as they have a *sufficiently* determinate sense and a very large field of application where they may behave rather waveringly and unpredictably, thus leading to confusion, especially if one tries to use them in new contexts or with a restricted meaning. Our everyday concepts owe their senses to the way they are used. Their senses cannot be changed without simultaneously changing their uses, and it is impossible to do that by mere stipulation.

Wittgenstein does not deny that in psychology there are experimental techniques which may lead to sound results, but in his view they will not help us to reach satisfactory insights into the relation between different psychological concepts (as, for example, 'sensation', 'impression', 'experience', 'perception', 'pain', 'imagination', etc.) or their mutual relevance. This is the reason why Wittgenstein thinks that the problems which worry us and the experimental method 'pass each other by'. The hope of clarifying our psychological concepts by means of scientific and experimental techniques has no tenable basis, as we know too little about the relations between the relevant concepts and techniques and are in no position to learn anything about those relations by applying these techniques.

In order to solve conceptual problems, we do not need experimental methods; what we need is a completely different procedure, namely a philosophical clarification of our concepts. And this is where Köhler's mistake resides: physics has been able to advance towards increasingly helpful explanations and other achievements by using stricter and more purely quantitative methods; psychology, on the other hand, is not in a position to solve any of its conceptual problems or to answer any question arising from conceptual confusion by relying on experimental techniques. For in psychology, as in mathematics, there are *foundational* problems.[6] Psychology, like mathematics, can continue to apply its unproblematic techniques and methods without getting any nearer to a solution of its foundational problems, as a solution of these

---

[6] Cf. *LW* § 792 (also *PI*, II. xiv, p. 232): 'An investigation is possible in connection with mathematics which is entirely analogous to the philosophical investigation of psychology. It is just as little a *mathematical* investigation as the other is a psychological one. It will *not* contain calculations, so it is not, for example, logistic. It might deserve the name of an investigation of the "foundations of mathematics".'

problems requires 'treatment' from a philosopher or a psychologist who has learnt his Wittgensteinian lesson.

In order to see what a psychologist who is knowingly or unknowingly involved in foundational problems can learn from Wittgenstein, it will be helpful to take one of these problems as an example and thus to discuss the first of the categories mentioned in Wittgenstein's attempt at a classification, namely the category of sensation.

One of the basic starting-points of Köhler's gestalt theory is his fundamental rejection of the traditional explanation of perception by reference to atomic, punctiform stimulations of our sense organs. This traditional explanation holds that through our senses we receive a mosaic of stimuli and that the fact that we perceive *objects*—and not merely dots and coloured surfaces—is to be explained indirectly, by means of a theory of learning. The mosaic theory, which claims that those atoms are the only things which are perceived immediately, makes it enormously difficult to explain certain facts, for instance the fact that we recognize a tune and are able to re-identify it even if it is played in a different key or by different instruments.[7]

If we are to simplify our theory of perception and to avoid the absurdities of many indirect explanations, we shall, according to the gestalt theoretic view, have to assume that what has been perceived

---

[7] It was by means of this and similar examples that Christian von Ehrenfels developed his concept of *Gestaltqualität*, which forms the basis of all subsequent gestalt theories, and hence also of Köhler's theory. Cf. e.g. the following passage: 'if . . . someone remembers a melody in a key different from that in which it was originally heard, then he does not reproduce at all the sum of his earlier individual presentations, but a quite different complex which possesses only the property that its members stand to each other in a relation analogous to that of the earlier complex. This relation is, according to our present conception, founded in a new positive element of presentation, the tone-Gestalt. This new element is such that one and the same tone-Gestalt always determines an identical relation among the elements of its tonal substrate (the presentations of the individual tones).' Ehrenfels, 'On "Gestalt Qualities" ', in B. Smith (ed.), *Foundations of Gestalt Theory* (Munich, 1988), 92. In this paper Ehrenfels takes up certain ideas and observations noted by Mach, cf. the following passage: 'If two sequences of tones start from two different tones and proceed according to the same ratios of vibration, we shall, through our sensations, recognize in both sequences the same melody just as directly as we recognize the same shape [*Gestalt*] in two geometrically similar figures with similar positions. The same melody played at different pitch may be called a tone structure of the *same tone gestalt* or . . .'. E. Mach, *Die Analyse der Empfindungen und das Verhältnis des Physischen zum Psychischen* (Darmstadt, 1985), 232.

is more than the sum of the individual stimulus atoms and forms from the very beginning an integral, circumscribed object with the property of transposability and thus offers the possibility of being recognized in new or unusual or modified contexts. To put it in a very simplified fashion, we directly perceive not stimulus atoms but objects or groups of separate objects.

At least as far as the rejection of the mosaic theory and of the empiricist theory of learning is concerned, Wittgenstein is probably in agreement with this view. But according to Wittgenstein the gestalt theoretic view has its own problems, which are particularly likely to come to the fore in those cases where one talks about seeing different aspects of an object. An example of this would be the well-known duck-rabbit picture. Another example, which is especially instructive, is described by Köhler:

The contour of the land is the same on a maritime chart as it is on a map of the usual type; i.e. the geometrical line which separates land and water is normally projected on the retina. None the less, when looking at such a map, say, of the Mediterranean, we may completely fail to see Italy. Instead we may see a strange figure, corresponding to the area of the Adriatic, and so forth, which is new to us, but which happens to have shape under the circumstances.[8]

Wittgenstein thinks that this does not show at all that here there are really two different visual objects, as one might infer from Köhler's formulation when he writes that, 'instead' of Italy, we may see a different figure. In Wittgenstein's opinion we may at most claim that in this situation there is a plausible reason for choosing a certain way of expressing oneself; for there is, as he emphasizes, an essential difference between the statement 'That shows that two different things are seen here' and the statement 'Under these circumstances it would be better to speak of "two different objects of sight" ' (*RPP* i. § 1035). According to Wittgenstein only the second formulation is justifiable.

What is the point of this brief criticism? Wittgenstein thinks that when Köhler claims that seeing two different aspects of something is literally a case of seeing two different *objects*, he goes beyond the meaning of the concepts 'visual object' and 'see'. Wittgenstein holds that it is useless and thus theoretically harmful to say that when we

---

[8] Köhler, *Gestalt Psychology*, 107.

see two different aspects of one and the same object two different
visual objects are given to us. Even though it may be justified to
introduce the term 'visual object' to facilitate a description of this
situation, one must not forget that this is merely a *façon de parler*
which implies neither the existence of two different objects nor the
existence of mental correlates of those alleged objects.

Wittgenstein's criticism is directed against the idea that whenever
there are two different visual impressions there will also have to be
two different visual objects corresponding to them. Köhler is right
in thinking that what is seen is simply to be accepted and not to be
regarded as something different according to a preconceived theory.
But that does not justify the claim that in the case of two different
visual impressions we *see* two different objects (where 'see' is used
in the same sense in which it occurs in the statement 'I see a tree', for
instance). One may put it in a slightly simplified manner and say
that we must not confuse the sense of the word 'object' as it occurs
in the statement 'I see two different objects' (that is, two different
trees, two different chairs, etc.) with the sense it has in those cases
where we are speaking of the same tree twice, once seen as what it is,
that is, a tree, and another time as something else, for example as a
human being or a motor car, etc. In this latter case the speaker sees
the same tree both times, albeit different aspects of it, and in
speaking of *two* visual objects he refers neither to the tree nor to
two alleged trees but to those different aspects.

Thus the gestalt theoretic conception runs the risk of ascribing
too much ontological independence to its visual objects. But what
we have not understood so far is how much of a risk that is—after
all, this criticism seems to affect a purely theoretical, even
speculative element of that conception. To get clearer about it, we
shall have to find a more clearly defined context where real errors
may be discovered that are due to the idea that an object of
perception is a unified, circumscribed object which can be directly
grasped as such an object.

One of Köhler's main theses amounts to the claim that the
perception of pure gestalts is a precondition of the possibility of
lending sense to an object. In other words, it is said that one first
recognizes objects or groups of objects as gestalts (and thus sees
them as visual objects, for example) and then, in a second step, gives
them a meaning. Of course, the notion of 'sense' or 'meaning'

employed in this context is extremely vague. But before continuing this discussion let us look at Köhler's own formulation of his thesis:

Sensory units have acquired names, have become richly symbolic, and are now to have certain practical uses, while nevertheless they have existed as units before any of these further facts were added. Gestalt psychology claims that it is precisely the original segregation of circumscribed wholes which makes it possible for the sensory world to appear so utterly imbued with meaning to the adult; for, in its gradual entrance into the sensory field, meaning follows the lines drawn by natural organization; it usually enters into segregated wholes.[9]

It is this thesis of the priority of gestalt over meaning which Wittgenstein wishes to reject when he remarks that noticing a gestalt switch is perceiving a *meaning*,[10] for example hearing a tone either as the beginning of a new musical phrase or as the end of the preceding phrase. By saying this Wittgenstein does not want to claim that our biological constitution makes us incapable of recognizing certain gestalts without knowing their meanings, that is, without knowing their possible uses, their symbolic value, their names, and so on. Rather, the point is that the hypothesis that we can perceive gestalts without giving them a meaning is vague and useless if we are trying to clarify and understand basic concepts like 'perceive', 'see', 'feel', and so forth.

Wittgenstein does not deny, for instance, that a man who lived a thousand years ago could have grasped the idea that a drawing of a railway engine was the representation of an object. But this man would not have been able to introduce this drawing into a language game. He would merely have been able to say things like 'This figure here . . .'. Unaided he would not even have been in a position to say 'The thing which has been drawn here . . .', since without additional information he could not have known whether or not this figure was a representation of something. (In particular, the question whether it was a drawing of one or more things would have been absolutely unanswerable for him.) We, on the other hand, are not only able to see this drawing as a representation of something but as a representation of various things: of a railway engine, a sculpture of a railway engine, a toy railway engine, and so on. And here it would be obviously mistaken to claim that every

---

[9] Köhler, *Gestalt Psychology*, 82.
[10] 'It is—contrary to Köhler—precisely a *meaning* that I see' (*RPP* i. § 869; cf. *LPP* 102, 333).

time we see the figure as this or that we are perceiving a different gestalt to which we are in addition ascribing a meaning.

Of course, it cannot be denied that we can see something as an independent, separate object without being able to specify what kind of object it is. And if the claim that without this capacity we should never have been able to invest any objects with meaning is regarded as a scientific hypothesis, it may well be justifiable. But if the thesis of the priority of gestalt over meaning amounted to no more than such a hypothesis, it would be fairly irrelevant regarding foundational problems about our psychological concepts. As soon as it is taken as a thesis about our concepts, however, Wittgenstein's criticism appears convincing for the following reason. When the word 'see' is used in its normal way, we speak of seeing trees, houses, motor cars, children, and so on. To say merely that I see 'an object' or 'a thing' is legitimate and intelligible only in a context which is well defined in most other respects. Thus I may say that to the left of that tree over there, behind that house, I can see an object. What we do not and cannot say are things like 'To the left of that thing over there, behind that thing, I can see an object', etc. That this sort of utterance is excluded does not merely amount to saying that the language of perception could not work that way but that here we cannot even speak of perception at all, for perception does not mean seeing or hearing pure gestalts without further characteristics; no, it involves perceiving that things are this or that, and it is precisely this fact which makes it possible that on certain occasions one and the same thing can be seen *as* either this or that.

Objects fulfil certain functions in our lives, and these functions are connected with the meanings we ascribe to them. But Wittgenstein does not want to establish a counter-thesis to the one held by Köhler; he does not want to claim that perception *presupposes* meaning or something of that kind. He merely wishes to point out that an act of direct perception refers not merely to a pure gestalt or to a circumscribed Something but includes its meaning or part of its meaning.

If we are, for example, looking at a maritime chart we may suddenly notice that at one time we see Italy as figure and the Mediterranean as ground while at another time we see the Mediterranean as figure and Italy as ground. But that does not mean that at one time we grasp this and at another time that object and in addition certain meanings. What it means is that we perceive a thing together with its meaning and notice that it is possible to see it as having a different meaning. That is the point of Wittgenstein's statement that we see not only gestalts, but also meanings. The thesis of the priority of gestalt over meaning does not agree with the content of our normal concept of seeing something; and that is why Köhler's attempt to give pride of place to pure gestalts runs the risk of causing conceptual confusions.

Excursus: Sense Data

Moore's Theory

It is striking that Moore, in his discussions of the problems of sense perception, seems to deal with one sense only, the sense of sight. This fact has been noticed by several commentators, and in spite of Moore's protests against some of their remarks, it is quite obviously true that virtually all his examples concern *visual* perception. In a reply to his critics Moore claims:

I have always both used, and intended to use, 'sense-datum' in such a sense that the mere fact that an object is *directly apprehended* is a *sufficient* condition for saying that it is a sense-datum; so that, according both to my usage and my intentions, directly apprehended smells and tastes and sounds are just as much sense-data as *directly seen* objects.[11]

It remains a fact, however, that the *seeing* of objects constitutes Moore's paradigm of sense-perception.

In this context Moore asks various types of question, for example 'What is it that I am judging, when I judge, as I now do, that that is an ink-stand?'[12] or 'What is it that happens, when . . . we see a material object?'[13] And in general he proceeds to answer these questions by giving an outline of the elements he believes to be involved, not only in every standard case of actually seeing a physical object or material thing, but also in every case of dreaming or having hallucinations or images or after-images. According to

[11] G. E. Moore, 'A Reply to My Critics', in P. A. Schlipp (ed.), *The Philosophy of G. E. Moore* (Chicago, 1942), 639.
[12] G. E. Moore, 'Some Judgements of Perception', in *Philosophical Studies* (London, 1922), 224.
[13] G. E. Moore, *Some Main Problems of Philosophy* (London, 1953), 29.

Moore experiences of this latter kind can, at least up to a point, be quite indistinguishable from perceiving material things; the entities experienced in both kinds of experience, he says, can stand in the same relation to the subject of these experiences.

Obviously the entities experienced both in cases of sensations proper and in cases of dreaming, hallucinating, etc. cannot be physical objects. These entities are what Moore calls 'sense-data' or, as he sometimes prefers to say, 'sensibles'. These sense data, or sensibles, are to be distinguished, not only from the physical objects which they may, in cases of genuine sense perception, be said to present, but also from a number of mental occurrences that may be connected with my having, or perceiving, or experiencing, certain sense data.

The distinction intended by Moore can perhaps be brought out in *this* way. When, for example, I am looking at a certain physical object—a teacup (say)—then what I am directly perceiving or, as Moore prefers to say, *directly apprehending* is not the material teacup, but a sense datum of this teacup; my apprehending it, however, is not the same thing as the sense datum I am apprehending; it is a mental process which, in turn, can be the object of my attention.

This is the reason why Moore keeps insisting on his distinction between sensations and sense data. Even if sense data cannot, as a matter of fact, exist unperceived, they are not mental occurrences of the same kind as our perceiving them; even if they are in some sense dependent on my mind, they are not dependent on it in the same way my seeing, hearing, smelling, etc. are dependent on my mind. As Moore puts it:

I look at [an envelope], and I . . . see a *sense-datum*, a patch of whitish colour. But now I immediately turn away my eyes, and I no longer see that sense-datum: my seeing of it has ceased to exist. But I am by no means sure that the sense-datum—that very same patch of whitish colour which I saw—is not still existing and still there . . . it seems to me at least *conceivable* that it should be still existing, whereas my *seeing* of it certainly has ceased to exist. This is one reason for distinguishing between the sense-data which I see, and my seeing of them.[14]

But what are Moore's reasons for introducing sense data at all? It is remarkable that Moore does not seem very worried by this

---

[14] G. E. Moore, *Some Main Problems of Philosophy* (London, 1953), 31.

question. And this indicates a fundamental change of the philosophical climate between his day and ours. Moore was far more anxious to persuade his contemporaries to accept the common-sense belief in physical objects, the real existence of the world, etc. than to justify his assumption of the existence of sense data. And it may very well be the case that he himself saw fewer problems regarding *their* existence than regarding the past existence of the material world, for example. Accordingly he does not make much of the usual argument from illusion and similar attempts to justify the assumption of sense data but simply proceeds to analyse the role which sense data are supposed to play in certain types of judgement, especially in judgements of perception.

Let us take what Moore considers a typical judgement of perception, such as 'This is a teacup' (uttered in the conspicuous presence of a teacup). Now, according to Moore, it is evident that this judgement is not a judgement about the material teacup standing on the sideboard, or at least not exclusively about that material teacup. What I am talking about in uttering this judgement is what Moore calls a 'presented object', something which is neither the material object itself nor something in my mind, but something of which I could believe or presume that it is part of the surface of the material object concerned. But if in judging that this is a teacup I am really making a judgement about a sense datum, or a presented object, then I cannot possibly wish to say of this sense datum that *it* is a teacup. I may be unclear about the nature of sense data, but surely I do not believe that I can pour tea into them.

What follows from this is that judgements of perception are to be analysed in a way which is far more complicated than is suggested by their surface structure. The word 'this' in 'This is a teacup' is, according to Moore, to be taken to refer to a sense datum, while the predicate 'teacup' says something about a material object standing in a certain relation to this sense datum.

The simple reason why *this* (the object I am referring to in my judgement of perception) cannot be a material object is that I cannot normally see—*directly* see—a *whole* object. When I am looking at a teacup I only see part of the surface of a teacup, never a whole teacup. It could be different in the case of *transparent* objects, like soap-bubbles or whisky-glasses, and for this reason Moore seriously considers the question of whether objects of this kind need to be treated in a different way from opaque objects.

But why does Moore think that judgements of perception are judgements *about* sense data which at the same time, however, predicate something of material objects? After all, one might object, even if, as a matter of fact, my perceiving of physical objects always involves the direct apprehension of sense data, this does not obviously mean that what I am talking about are those sense data.

Moore, although he does take this objection into consideration, does not seem to take it very seriously. He simply replies that in a certain sense it is correct to say that my judgement is about the material teacup, but the sense in which this *is* correct is not independent of my talking about the *presented* teacup, that is, the sense datum. Accordingly, Moore claims, we must distinguish between a sense in which we can be said to see the object of which we predicate that it is a teacup (even though this object is never *directly* seen) and a sense in which we see the sense datum 'corresponding to' that material teacup.

There may, however, be yet a third sense of 'see', depending on whether the sense datum is identical with the seen surface of the material object concerned or not. That is, if what I directly apprehend in the process of seeing an object is part of the material object's surface, then this part of the surface and my sense datum are identical; and in this case no third sense of 'see' is needed. But if my sense-datum is to be regarded as distinct from the relevant part of the surface of that object, then we need a third sense of 'see' for seeing that surface, and that will differ both from the sense in which I can be said to see a material object and the sense in which I can be said to see the corresponding sense datum.

Whether we really need three senses of 'see' or can make do with two senses of the word is a question to which Moore did not find a definite answer. Sometimes he inclined one way and sometimes the other. In some sense the final answer seemed to him to depend on whether sense data could be said to continue to exist when they were not perceived any longer. Surfaces of material things can be said to exist even if they are not perceived; thus, if sense data are identical with parts of the surfaces of physical objects, then it must make sense to claim that they can exist unperceived. On the other hand, it seems natural to suppose that sense data do not continue to exist when they cease to be given to a perceiving subject; and hence it seems unlikely that sense data can be understood to be identical with parts of the surfaces of material objects. Thus, in a reply to one of his critics, Moore confesses: 'I am strongly inclined to take both of these incompatible views. I am completely puzzled about the matter, and only wish I could see any way of settling it.'[15]

Wittgenstein's Criticism

In Wittgenstein's writings after his return to Cambridge in 1929 problems of sense perception are discussed fairly frequently. It would, however, be misleading to say that Wittgenstein had a *theory* of perception. The concepts of seeing, immediate experience, visual image, etc. crop up in all kinds of context, sometimes in order to be given detailed treatment, at other times merely to illustrate a given point.

Wittgenstein's way of discussing these concepts is a very far cry from Moore's patient and somewhat repetitive way of dealing with his problems. Indeed, it is a very far cry from *all* earlier ways of doing philosophy. One of the main differences is Wittgenstein's unprecedented insistence on what one may call the 'natural habitat' of our concepts, that is, the linguistic and non-linguistic contexts in which our expressions are normally used.

It is this insistence on the natural habitat of our concepts which plays an important role in Wittgenstein's best-known discussion of concepts of perception, his treatment of the distinction between seeing something and seeing something as such-and-such. This distinction is dealt with in Part II of the *Philosophical Investigations* and at greater length in his *Remarks on the Philosophy of Psychology*. By pointing out certain peculiarities of the actual use of the relevant expressions and the possible consequences of conceivable uses of these expressions Wittgenstein shows the extent to which seemingly private experiences *can* be communicated and how little the solution of philosophical problems and puzzles depends on what cannot be communicated.

Wittgenstein's remarks on the distinction between seeing and seeing-as and his discussion of the experience of seeing a certain aspect or a change of aspect are not *directly* related to the things that Moore has got to say about perception. In the first half of the 1930s, however, both in his writings and in his lectures, Wittgenstein talks

---

[15] 'A Reply to My Critics', 659.

about sense data in a way which is directly relevant to the theses maintained by Moore. In a lecture in 1935 Wittgenstein addresses himself to one of the questions which Moore had found so poignantly puzzling. He says:

The philosopher does not tell us how to decide the question . . . whether or not a sense datum is identical with, or part of, the surface of an object, and . . . the question whether the chair or its surface is brown. If these were questions of natural science we should need to be told how to decide them, what the method of verification is. . . . But how to decide whether whiteness or a surface or a sense datum is circular? The philosopher does not tell us how to decide between these, and what is more confusing is that often a question such as these *has* an application, which makes a philosopher think it has when he asks it.[16]

Here Wittgenstein claims that Moore's question regarding the identity of a sense datum with the surface of a physical object is pointless, even illegitimate, for the reason that Moore could not specify a method for verifying the statement that a given sense datum is identical with a certain surface. By implication he says that there are, or can be, questions concerning sense data and surfaces which are not only intelligible but answerable; *these* questions, however, will not be philosophers' questions but questions of science: questions, for example, regarding optical illusions or other strange phenomena of perception, which can be decided if a verification procedure is available.

But why (we may ask ourselves) is it impossible to verify the philosopher's question? The most obvious and perhaps most satisfactory answer Wittgenstein gives to this question is that there is no criterion of the identity of sense data in the philosopher's sense. To be sure, if in ordinary conversation my interlocutor answers the question as to *what he has seen* by drawing a picture or producing a photograph, the questions of whether he has seen the same thing I have seen or whether he has seen today the same thing he saw yesterday *can* be answered. Here we have evidence, we have criteria, and we know how to use them.

Moore's question, on the other hand, about what is seen when I see a sense datum does not admit of this type of answer. Sense data

---

[16] A. Ambrose (ed.), *Wittgenstein's Lectures: Cambridge 1932–1935* (Oxford, 1979), 128–9.

in Moore's sense are necessarily private; if I produce a photograph or a drawing, then what I or another person will 'directly' see will again be a sense datum, and we do not have the foggiest idea of how to find out whether this sense datum is the same as the former one.

But even in this formulation the problem still sounds far too reasonable, for according to Wittgenstein there is no real problem here but only confusion. For it is not that a criterion of identity has not yet been discovered, in which case we could still hope to find one. It is that there is no *possible* criterion of identity for the philosopher's notion of a sense datum, both in the sense that such a sense datum is not accessible to *other* people and in the sense that a past sense datum is not accessible to *myself*.

Wittgenstein elucidates this point by means of an example about auditory and physical sounds:

Can you in a continuous sound distinguish the part you are hearing at the moment and the part you remember hearing? You can hear a click, and there is no part of it which you can remember as coming before or after another part; whereas with a sustained violin note you can remember the part which has gone before. The problem then is to find an intermediate stage at which you can say you both hear and remember.
The confusion lies in thinking that the physical sound and the sense-datum are both continuous. The physical sound is continuous, but the sense-datum is not.[17]

This, of course, applies not only to auditory sense data but also to visual ones. But even Wittgenstein's remark (which comes from lecture notes and may be incomplete) is not entirely felicitous. What he means is that of a sense datum I cannot *say* that it has duration; and it would be equally nonsensical to assert that it has duration. Sense data simply are not objects of the type to which talk of duration applies.

Now one may wish to object that this is going too far—'Either a sense datum has duration or it has not; if it has not, then of course I cannot apply a criterion of identity, but that is because there simply is not enough time to apply it.' But this is not Wittgenstein's view of the matter. He thinks that the language of everyday life—and this is the language whose concepts we normally discuss when doing philosophy—does not function like a well-constructed calculus in that it does not always permit a yes/no answer to the question of

---

[17] D. Lee (ed.), *Wittgenstein's Lectures: Cambridge 1930–1932* (Oxford, 1980), 71.

whether a given predicate is true of a certain object. According to Wittgenstein a statement makes sense only if the relevant expressions occurring in it are associated with certain criteria in such a way that procedures can be specified for deciding whether a predicate applies to this or that object and under which circumstances an alleged object can be counted as one and the same.

One result of this conception is that if in a given case there are no criteria to be applied, then the sentence in question does not make sense. But this does not mean that all senseless sentences are nonsense of the same type. There is on the one hand what we may wish to call 'simple' nonsense, for example 'This teacup is in B minor'. Here there simply is no procedure for deciding whether teacups are in B minor (or, for that matter, in any other key); and even if this sentence occurred as a line of a poem or a song and thus acquired some emotional significance, it would still remain nonsense of the simple sort.

On the other hand, there are sentences which lack sense in a different way. These are what Wittgenstein tends to call 'grammatical sentences', that is, sentences expressing rules—or specifying conditions for the application of rules—for the employment of linguistic expressions. Such sentences do have a use in our language games, Wittgenstein says, but this use is a very specific and limited one. They can play a role in the context of teaching a language or, for example, when reminding someone that he has misused a certain expression. Thus if somebody tells a story in which two people are described as playing a game of patience I may remind him that one plays patience by oneself. And this reminder is a grammatical sentence, which does not supply any factual information but indicates the correct way of using a given expression. For this reason we may say of sentences of this type what Wittgenstein remarks apropos certain tautologies, namely that they are 'degenerate propositions on the side of truth' (*RFM*, iii. § 33).

Even though grammatical sentences lack sense, they are not useless. However, they easily mislead us into thinking that they supply information about something. Thus we may be led to believe that the statement that sense data are private expresses a discovery about sense data, whereas really it is no more than a grammatical reminder to the effect that when I speak of seeing what another person sees I may be talking of the object he is *looking at* but not of his sense datum. Wittgenstein stresses this point in a remark of 1934 or 1935 from his 'Notes for Lectures on "Private Experience" and "Sense Data"':

'Surely', I want to say, 'if I'm to be quite frank I must say that I have something which nobody [else] has.'—But who's I?—Hell! I don't express myself properly, but there's *something*! You can't deny that there is my personal experience and that this in a most important sense *has no neighbour*.—But you don't mean that it *happens* to be alone but that its grammatical position is that of having no neighbour. (p. 283)

None of this excludes the possibility of talking about sense data. But if I decide to do so, Wittgenstein says, I not only have to take care not to confuse normal sensible sentences and grammatical sentences but I shall also have to take my decision seriously, that is, I must not speak of sense data as if they were merely another kind of object—different from ordinary physical objects, but none the less objects about which we can speak in similar terms. For this notion is quite mistaken, as Wittgenstein points out in the *Blue Book*:

those who say that a sense datum is a different kind of object from a physical object misunderstand the grammar of the word 'kind' . . . They think they are making such a statement as 'A railway train, a railway station, and a railway car are different kinds of objects', whereas their statement is analogous to 'A railway train, a railway accident, and a railway law are different kinds of objects'. (p. 64)

If I seriously want to speak of my sense data, Wittgenstein says, I must put up with the consequences. One such consequence is that I shall have to use a notion of identity different from the one appropriate to physical objects. Thus whereas we normally use the word 'same' in a transitive way, sense data may be such that we cannot help saying that A = B and B = C, but A ≠ C. After all, in the realm of sense data we have to take things as they are given to us; we cannot change our point of view without losing sight of those data.

A second consequence of taking sense data seriously is that I shall have to put up with the incommunicability of what I think I am 'really' seeing. This means that I shall have to get myself into a solipsistic mood, as Wittgenstein says at one point. But then much of what I am tempted to say becomes pointless, misleading, utterly wrong. If I try to point to my sense data, for example, I cannot do it with my finger; it must be a kind of *visual* pointing and hence incommunicable. In the *Blue Book* Wittgenstein says:

When in the solipsistic way I say '*This* is what's really seen', I point before
me and it is essential that I point *visually*. If I pointed sideways or behind
me . . . the pointing would in this case be meaningless to me; it would not be
pointing in the sense in which I wish to point. But this means that when I
point before me saying 'this is what's really seen', although I make the
gesture of pointing, I don't point to one thing as opposed to another. This is
as when travelling in a car and feeling in a hurry, I instinctively press against
something in front of me as though I could push the car from inside.
. . . When I made my solipsistic statement, I pointed, but I robbed the
pointing of its sense by inseparably connecting that which points and that
to which it points. I constructed a clock with all its wheels, etc., and in the
end fastened the dial to the pointer and made it go round with it. (p. 71)

Thus if Wittgenstein is right, then Moore's analysis of judgements
of perception according to which such judgements are both about
sense data and material objects is misguided for at least two reasons.
First, Moore does not keep separate what needs to be separated,
namely normal empirical sentences from grammatical sentences and
sentences about physical objects from sentences about sense data.
Secondly, Moore believes that sense data can be named and pointed
to in a manner analogous to that in which we name and point to
physical objects. This, however, is a mistake. The language games
we can play when using expressions for sense data are entirely
different from those we can play with words for physical objects;
they are as different from each other as our language games with
words for railway stations are different from language games with
words for railway shares.

7

Memory

MANY of our everyday or scientific considerations regarding psychological processes are based on a simple model, which even at second glance may still appear convincing. This is the model of a magic lantern, of an incessantly and inexorably running film, of a constant succession of representations. There is no difficulty in reconciling this model with any of the traditional conceptions of sense perception; but problems arise as soon as our knowledge of the past is in question. For, on the one hand, it is inconceivable to have real knowledge without having memories while, on the other hand, it appears extremely difficult for a view agreeing with the model of a magic lantern to accommodate memories without at the same time depriving them of their essential function of informing us about something which is not present—that is, about the past—and of possibly constituting the past for us. The reason why questions about the place of memory may become problematic is that in the magic lantern there only appears to be space for that which is going on now: here there is never more than one image at a time, and even though this image may be immensely complex and involved, it will never by itself indicate whether or not it is an image of something past. How am I, the owner of the magic lantern, to know if a representation concerns something present, or something future, or something past? Does the stream of consciousness contain any indicator assigning the right position in the sequence of time to the objects of the passing flow of images, or do we have to reckon with the possibility that our division of represented events into past, present, and future ones is without a foundation and perhaps a mere illusion?

The basic question about the locus of memories according to the magic-lantern model is this: 'What makes a representation a *copy* of an earlier representation?' It is this question which is asked with particular vigour by William James. He begins by defining the concept of memory in terms of 'the knowledge of an event, or fact,

with the additional consciousness that we have thought or
experienced it before'.[1] From this definition it immediately follows
that a mere representation of an event is not in itself sufficient to
mark it as a memory, for what it still lacks is the consciousness of a
former experience. James thinks that the image must be richer than
that if it is to form an 'object' of memory: it will in addition have to
comprise (1) 'a general feeling of the past direction in time'; (2)
orientation about our whereabouts on the memory path through a
relative date, which in many cases involves symbolic means; (3) a
context of adjoining events or facts which helps to specify the
relevant event or fact; and (4) the thought that it is part of the
experience of myself, the subject of the relevant representation.[2] But
even this complex 'object' is not sufficiently determinate to count as
one of memory. What is missing is the crucial 'characteristic quality
of reality', without which there would be no way of distinguishing
between a fantasy of something supposedly past and a real memory
image. To be sure, within the scope of a purely subjective approach
it will not do merely to add the condition that the event in question
has really taken place and has really been perceived by me; the
reality of that event is not a property of my present representation
and cannot be read off from it. According to James, the missing
characteristic, which turns the relevant 'object' into an object of
memory, is an emotion, and hence a subjective mark, forming an
essential constituent of memory: 'the object of memory is only an
object imagined in the past to which the emotion of belief adheres.'[3]

Some of Russell's remarks on memory are in a similarly
subjective vein. Russell emphasizes that there is no *logical* relation
between what we call our knowledge of the past and the past itself;
not even the existence of a past will logically follow from our
assertions of knowledge about past events.[4] In order to illustrate
this view Russell develops his well-known hypothesis according to
which it is logically possible that the world has sprung into being
five minutes ago and together with it a population with 'memories'
to which no reality corresponds. Once this logical possibility is
recognized, it becomes particularly urgent to discover some
characteristic which distinguishes memories from other kinds of

[1] W. James, *The Principles of Psychology* (New York, 1950), i. 648.
[2] Ibid. 650.
[3] Ibid. 652.
[4] B. Russell, *The Analysis of Mind* (London, 1971), 159–60.

contents of consciousness. In this context Russell appeals to two feelings or kinds of feeling, namely feelings of pastness, on the one hand, and feelings of familiarity, on the other. Feelings of pastness may for instance be connected with the decreasing intensity of a representation, with the increasing faintness of a memory image; and these phenomena will often be accompanied by relative dates, which may be inferred ones. These feelings contribute to assigning our memories to their proper positions in the time-order. Feelings of familiarity will help us to decide how far we can rely on something that appears to be a memory, if there is no further reason for doubting it. Whenever the degree of familiarity dwindles, we tend to call the memory claim in question or we reject it altogether.[5]

Wittgenstein's remarks on the concept of memory can be read in part as replies to a conception which includes elements of the theories held by Russell and James. In particular, there are three characteristics of that conception which are criticized by Wittgenstein, namely the idea of a *memory image*, the notion of the *experiential content* of a memory, and the thesis that a memory is embedded in certain *feelings*. These three topics, which are mentioned time and again in Wittgenstein's remarks on the philosophy of psychology, are not always strictly separated by him, for it may happen that an image is regarded as part of an alleged content, and the experiential content may be interpreted as a specific feeling or as something which depends on a feeling. Here Wittgenstein's objections are not chiefly directed against those concepts as such or against possible existential claims involved in their use; they are directed against certain theoretical applications of these concepts and against certain aims that go along with some existential claims.

These qualifications regarding Wittgenstein's critical statements are in place. If for instance we said in a general way that Wittgenstein criticizes the concept of a memory image, it would be completely unclear what this criticism might be supposed to achieve. After all, memory images are something which we all of us know from our own experience; we can see them 'before our inner eyes', we can articulate and describe them in such a way that other people too will be able to imagine what they are like. No, it is not the real occurrence of such pictures which is disputed by Wittgenstein; he asks where the concept of an inner image is *needed*

[5] B. Russell, *The Analysis of Mind* (London, 1971), 161–3, esp. 163.

(*RPP* i. § 109). The legitimacy of this question becomes manifest as soon as we think of everyday situations where the concept of memory is used, for in such situations allusions to memory images appear to play no considerable role. When we make a memory statement, we do not normally appeal to anything inner; without further ado we simply volunteer information about the past: 'If someone asks me what I have been doing in the last two hours, I answer him straight off and I don't read the answer off from an experience I am having. And yet one says that I *remembered*, and that this is a mental process' (*RPP* i. § 105).

So far, however, this amounts to no more than saying that we, as a matter of fact, need not always appeal to memory images to answer a question about the past 'from memory'. But it seems that Wittgenstein means to be able to make a more radical claim, namely that it is possible to give a description of something past from memory *without* an accompanying inner picture or, in other words, that such a description makes sense. This is the reason why he wonders whether there could be people who are able to give exact descriptions of certain details from memory while denying that they are seeing the described object before them, that is, 'People who would find the expression "I see him before me" *totally inappropriate*' (*RPP* ii. § 144). Although Wittgenstein does not answer this question with an unequivocal yes, it is rendered clear by the context that such a possibility is not to be excluded. But the conceivability of such a state of affairs does not imply that we cannot answer the question of whether visual representations do occur;[6] all that follows is that reliable memory statements do not themselves yield a sufficient reason for maintaining that memory images really must exist. Memory images are not a generally necessary condition of memories.

This hint at the conceivability of reliable memory statements in spite of the complete absence of accompanying memory images springs neither from a mere whim nor from a theoretical urge to explore all possibilities. It is likely that the fact that the later

---

[6] As so often happens in philosophical discussions, in treatments of the concept of memory too the visual aspect is generally given pride of place in comparison with the other faculties of sense perception. An exception is Schopenhauer, who calls the sense of smell our 'sense of memory' (*Paralipomena*, 'Psychologische Bemerkungen', § 353). Wittgenstein, in a suppressed remark, wonders if there is a criterion for deciding whether or not a remembered smell is the right one (MS 136, 23. 12. 47; here Wittgenstein uses the English word 'whiff').

Wittgenstein displays little confidence in notions like 'picture' or 'image' is due to his critical attitude towards some of the central ideas of the *Tractatus*; thus he regards it as misguided to think 'that one has already done everything by speaking of a "picture" ' (*RPP* i. § 726). The concept of a picture or image may mislead us because it suggests certain possibilities of application which are not really open to us in the given case. Thus it is plausible to think of the possibility of a comparison when something of a pictorial nature is mentioned: we place a portrait beside the original, a photograph beside another photograph, a drawing beside a photograph, and so forth. What kind of comparison may we think of, however, if the picture concerned is a memory image? Take the case of someone who recognizes a person and at the same time notices in which ways this person has changed since their last encounter. If here you make an uncritical attempt at applying the notion of a picture, you will be apt to explain this perception by claiming that it is due to a confrontation of a visual image and a memory image, *'as if* two pictures were getting compared here' (*RPP* i. § 1041). But this idea is erroneous because a memory image cannot be placed beside either a different inner picture or beside the object of memory. Even though it may be possible to scrutinize my memory images, to analyse them, and to produce various descriptions of them, I cannot while I am seeing a certain memory image look at any other kind of picture.

The misleading character of the idea of comparing a memory image with the original or with a different picture becomes important when we are dealing with questions like the following: What is it that we can learn from memory? To what extent may we rely on memory? To what degree is memory constitutive of knowledge? Suppose I am really having memory images in my mind. When I come to think about the question of whether the pictures which I am 'seeing' are really in agreement with former visual experiences and as it were copies of past sense impressions, I shall find that there is no method of confirming or refuting such an assumption. It may even be the case that in reminiscing I see things from a perspective which I am sure was not accessible to me at the time, yet the memory itself appears none the less reliable. As it is not possible to compare my memory images with different pictures, the idea of assigning these memory images the status of objective evidence must be generally excluded. That, however, does not mean that one should always distrust one's memory images; what it means is that they belong to a different category from generally accessible clues: 'My memory image is not evidence of that past situation; as a photograph would be, which, having been taken then, now bears witness to me that this is how it was then. The memory image and the memory words are on the *same* level' (*RPP* i. § 1131). Whether or not I am entertaining memory images is irrelevant to the degree of certainty of my memory statement. And even for myself a memory does not become more reliable if I have clear and vividly colourful pictures in my mind; the non-visual thought 'At the time such-and-such was the case' may accomplish much the same.

It cannot be denied that there is a categorial difference between memory images and evidence of the kind provided by photographs or dated drawings; but we may none the less wonder why it appears so plausible to compare memory with a kind of seeing into the past if the relation between memory images and the concept of memory is, as Wittgenstein seems to suggest, a purely contingent one. According to Wittgenstein it is, however, exactly this comparison of remembering and seeing into the past which is misleading: '*Dreaming* might be called that, when it presents the past to us. But not remembering; for, even if it showed scenes with hallucinatory clarity, still it takes remembering to tell us that this is past' (*RPP* ii. § 592). This move of Wittgenstein's may seem to come as a surprise. He claims that the comparison between remembering and seeing or looking into the past is completely ill-conceived for *this* reason, that only memory can teach us what is past. But here two problems arise immediately. First, what does it mean to say that only memory teaches us what is past? And, secondly, provided the first question has been answered satisfactorily, what is therefore wrong about the comparison between remembering and seeing into the past?

The objective intended by Wittgenstein's claim becomes clearer if one takes the remarks following the last quotation into account (*RPP* ii. §§ 593–4). There it is said that memory shows us the past just as little as our senses show us the present; and even if memory talked to us with an inner voice mentioning the date of the relevant memory, we should still have to find out what the specification of the time means and whether we may rely on it. The point hinted at by these remarks is apparently that it cannot always make sense to doubt our memories, for that would lead to a kind of regress. If it were always the case that such doubts made sense, there would never be any point in asserting that one recognizes something, that one knows the meaning of certain words, that one knows the sense of a certain gesture, and so on. In short, just as I cannot help accepting *these* memory-dependent states of affairs, so I shall have to accept without the slightest doubt the remembered temporal succession of innumerable events if I am ever to ask a meaningful question about any fact in time. And it is precisely this remembered temporal succession which gives content to our concept of the past and to this extent 'teaches' us what is past. Of course, this reasoning does not amount to saying that certain specific memories are certainly or even necessarily true; the point is merely that statements about the past have sense only if we need not be in doubt about the great majority of memory claims.[7] This idea is foreshadowed in a conversation Wittgenstein had in 1929 with Schlick and Waismann. There he distinguished between memory as 'a source' and 'memories that can be verified in a different way' (*WVC* 53). It is only memory as a source, as the origin of our consciousness of the past, which enables us to confirm memory statements independently of our own memory, for example through photographs or other kinds of evidence.

Memory as a source teaches us what is past. But does that entail that a comparison between remembering and seeing into the past is bound to be mistaken? At first one might think that Wittgenstein rejects this comparison for the reason that seeing is not subject to the will whereas remembering is. But this cannot be the reason because Wittgenstein explicitly holds the view that memory is in at least one important sense involuntary (*RPP* i. § 848, cf. p. 109, below). It is more likely that his rejection of that comparison is also connected with the idea of memory as a source; and the intended contrast with dreaming is presumably meant to point that out. To the extent that a dream presents something past it is receptive in character. We may have the feeling of being onlookers, and our dream reports describe what has been seen as if it were a film. Now

[7] The dependence of the *sense* of memory statements on the reliability of a large number of further memories becomes clear if one reflects upon examples of radical memory loss. An impressive example is discussed by S. Stich, namely the case of Mrs T. (*From Folk Psychology to Cognitive Science* (Cambridge, Mass., 1983), 54 ff.). This old lady is able to make virtually only one statement about the past, namely that President McKinley was assassinated (an event from her youth, which she has recounted time and again). But now she is not even capable of explaining the meaning of the words 'assassinate' and 'president', that is, she has *forgotten* what these words mean. Is it, then, really permissible to claim that she *remembers* that McKinley was assassinated?

it is true that in remembering we are apt to slide into a similar way
of speaking—and this may, among other things, be one of the
factors responsible for the comparison between remembering and
seeing into the past—but there are conceptually important differences which are only too easily overlooked. First, for a dream
representation of past events it is necessary that I really have images
in my mind, whereas memory is, as we have seen, possible without
images and does, as a matter of fact, get by without such images.
Secondly, and this is the decisive point, memory is creative in a
sense in which seeing is not. In many respects the past is literally
constituted by our memory, and this is often expressed by saying
that memory is the last court of appeal for certain assertions.
Primarily this is obviously true of one's own psychological
processes, in particular if these have remained tacit. To be sure, it is
sometimes possible for another person, who has been observing me
closely, to correct my own memory of an emotion, for instance; but
this kind of possibility must always be in the nature of an exception
and it must also be reconcilable with my other memories. Thus for
example I may not remember having felt jealous on a certain
occasion. A friend of mine who has kept a careful eye on me points
out that I am wrong, and by indicating a number of gestures,
utterances, and omissions *which I really do remember* he convinces
me that out of vanity or for some other reason I have been trying to
persuade myself that I was not jealous. Once I see this, my jealousy
may even 'come back' to me. But such a correction is bound to
remain an exception; under normal conditions my memory of my
own emotions and sensations, impressions, and views is unassail-
able. In addition, memory is creative also in this respect, that it has
the function of integrating all reminiscences—purely subjective
ones as well as intersubjectively accessible ones—into connected
and mutually consistent episodes, picture stories, or narratives. In
this sense I am not a passive beholder of my own memories, and this
is why memories are not just copies of an independently given past.
These are Wittgenstein's chief reasons for holding that the
comparison between memory and seeing into the past is misguided.

In the *Philosophical Investigations* we read that 'Remembering has
no experiential content' (*PI* II. xiii, p. 231), and Wittgenstein
wonders if this claim can be confirmed through introspection. After
all, it seems plausible to suppose that the absence of a content can be

detected by looking at whether the container in question is empty. This idea, however, is not as helpful as it may appear at first blush. For, first, 'looking' by means of introspection will at most permit individual, and hence no general, statements about the absence of a certain content; and, secondly, it will give no information about the meaning of the word 'remember'. There is no systematic relation between the meaning of that word and introspection; consequently such a relation will always be an accidental one. Nor is it by any means clear *where* one might look for a possible content and what might be the possible 'container' whose emptiness could confirm the thesis of the absence of a content. But it is not only the whereabouts of a possible content which puzzles us, but also the nature of the content itself. (Is a bowl 'empty' if it shows my mirror image? Is a bucket 'empty' if the wind produces whistling noises in it?)

Thus our first question will have to be what it is that Wittgenstein here means by 'content'; and we must not forget that 'content' and 'experiential content' are expressions which he normally uses to characterize the views of others or which he puts into the mouth of his *alter ego*. For this reason it is not surprising that the notions used for explanatory purposes tend to be of a kind which Wittgenstein regards with a critical eye. He writes: 'Well, the content of an experience is the private object, the sense-datum, the "object" that I grasp immediately with the mental eye, ear, etc. The inner picture' (*RPP* i. § 109). With this we seem to have returned to those memory images which are really dispensable, although their factual occurrence is not denied. But the expression 'content' is intended to allude to an aspect which we have so far left out of account, namely the privacy of the object, the interiority of the picture, in brief, the inaccessibility of the relevant Something to others. This emphasis on its private, inner, and inaccessible character is, according to Wittgenstein, useless and misleading. The fact that sense data, representations, or pain are 'private' is a 'grammatical' one; the assertion of their privacy will, outside a context of linguistic training, appear banal to such an extent that one tends not to take it literally and to proceed in the same way as in the case of 'War is war' and similar trivialities by looking for another meaning (cf. *LW* § 890).

If we want to speak of the content of an experience, we mean something which, while it has pictorial character, can be seen only by myself, and is hence 'a picture in its subjective meaning, when its purport is: "*This* I see—whatever the object may be that produces the impression." For the experience-content is the private *object*' (*RPP* i. § 694). The typical gesture which we wish to make in reflecting on this is a kind of pointing, if only an inner one, and we stress our demonstrative pronouns:

> The *content* of experience. One would like to say 'I see red *thus*', 'I hear the note that you strike *thus*', 'I feel pleasure *thus*', 'I feel sorrow *thus*', or even '*This* is what one feels when one is sad, *this*, when one is glad', etc. One would like to people a world, analogous to the physical one, with these *thus*es and *this*es. But this makes sense only where there is a picture of *what is experienced*, to which one can point as one makes these statements. (*RPP* i. § 896)

Wittgenstein does not claim that it is senseless or false to speak of an inner world. But he insists that this way of talking makes sense only to the extent that statements about inner facts or events can be explained by reference to outer ones, which are accessible to others too. This claim is connected with the extremely complicated chain of reasoning summarized in the formula 'An "inner process" stands in need of outward criteria' (*PI* § 580), but even if one wishes to do without the involved argument epitomized by this quotation, it is possible to support Wittgenstein's claim by pointing out that as regards some of the above-mentioned expressions the outer has conceptual priority. The sense we attach to expressions like 'inner object' or 'inner picture' is always a derived one; if our use of these expressions is not to remain unintelligible or purely metaphorical, we must be prepared to explain them by means of demonstrative or linguistic reference to intersubjectively accessible facts (which does not, however, amount to giving definitions or scientifically accurate explanations). But here we need to be careful and must not believe that a concept for something inner which has been derived from the outer paradigm is bound to have the same or a similar sense as the concept for that which is outer. It often happens that their uses come apart, and it is precisely the attendant tendency to overlook this which makes concepts for inner phenomena dangerous: 'The concept of the "inner picture" is misleading, for this concept uses the *outer* picture as a model, and yet their uses are no more closely related than the uses of "numeral" and "number"' (*LW* § 442).

   In order to relate these considerations specifically to the concept of memory, we shall think of a typical situation involving memories.

I am sitting in my easy chair, let my glance roam, and see 'before my mental eye' scenes from my last trip to England. These scenes become blurred and are replaced by new impressions: ' "Memories of those days rose up in me" . . . Here I am inclined to speak of a content of the experience, and I imagine something like words and pictures which rise up before my mind' (*RPP* i. § 111). Here we need not deny that what I am seeing is a kind of inner film; and the fact that I utter a sentence of the type of 'Memories of those days rose up in me' is a *criterion* of there being images of such scenes in my mind. When I am asked what it is that I am seeing before me, I shall by no means try to make gestures in the direction of my inside and to point to those inner pictures;[8] no, I shall describe what I have seen by means of words or by making a drawing. It may also be that I shall put photographs taken during my trip on the table, or that I shall reach for an illustrated book and use pictures of St Paul's, the Tower of London, and Winchester Cathedral to show what I had in mind. Now the alleged content of my memories—the pictures in my mind, the private object—plays no role any more; *everything* relevant has been spread out before the eyes and ears of my audience. It is even possible that in remembering my last trip to England I see pictures of Oxford before my mental eye, although I did not visit Oxford on that occasion. This *may* lead to a mistake in my memories, but it need not. It is not inconceivable, indeed, it may really happen, that one points to pictures of Oxford while saying, 'This is what I saw before my mental eye'; and that one will then point to pictures of Winchester and continue, 'And this is what I remembered.' This shows very clearly that *this* kind of content of a memory need not be that which is remembered and that it may be a mere accompaniment.

In so far as we have succeeded in clarifying the idea of an experiential content of memory, we have not found any close conceptual connection between 'content' and 'remembering'; a content which we have in mind *may* coincide with what we remember, but that is by no means *necessary*. However, the notion of experiential content is not to be restricted to scenes of a pictorial nature; as has already been indicated, it shades into something which it will be more suitable to call the 'characteristic content of a

---

[8] Even though it may be that I tap on my forehead or make a similar gesture—but that is not an attempt at 'pointing at something inside me': here this gesture has a different import from the one it has when we are philosophizing (cf. p. 104, above).

feeling' or simply a 'characteristic feeling'. It is not clear if Wittgenstein always manages to keep those notions apart. As regards both phenomena, he emphasizes that they are essentially accompaniments. If it is the pictorial character of such an accompaniment which comes to the fore, the expression 'experiential content' is in order; if we are, on the other hand, dealing with an example like that of comparing 'remembering' and 'tingling' (*PI* II. xiii), it is a question of a characteristic feeling.

Which feelings are characteristic of remembering? According to Russell, there are basically two types of feeling which are connected with remembering, namely a kind of feeling of familiarity, on the one hand, and a kind of feeling of pastness, on the other.[9] Now, Wittgenstein does not deny that there really are such feelings. But he notes that, first, they do not constitute easily recognizable qualities which can be given sharp intuitive or definitional boundaries; and that, secondly, their connection with remembering—as far as it exists at all—is not an essential one.

Of course, the feeling of pastness is not a characteristic of the images that may accompany an act of remembering. A memory image of an event which took place ten years ago need not be fainter than an image of something that happened yesterday. This is different from the case of a photograph which was printed ten years ago and is now visibly fainter than yesterday's snapshot. By a feeling of pastness Wittgenstein means something like a feeling of 'long, long ago',[10] which may accompany our reminiscences but which may also occur outside a context of remembering. Thus in his *Brown Book* Wittgenstein says that, as far as he is concerned, the feeling of pastness is well expressed by one of Schumann's *Davidsbündler Tänze*, that is, independently of any memories. This kind of feeling of pastness is not essentially connected with remembering, for just as it may occur without there being any remembering, so there will be many memory statements which are not accompanied by such a feeling. Indeed, it would be quite absurd to think of a statement like 'Today I shaved before breakfast' as associated with the feeling 'long, long ago' or a similar sensation. The point which is decisive for Wittgenstein is that this feeling is embedded in a context of gestures and linguistic phrases which makes it possible to talk about the feeling in a way that others can

---

[9] Cf. n. 5, above.
[10] *RPP* i. § 114, *LW* § 840, *BrBk* 184–5, *PI* II. xiii.

understand. Naturally, here the connection between feeling, tone, and word cannot be a 'logical' one: for while one person may grasp the hint regarding Schumann, another may not understand it at all. This latter person may however figure out what is meant if the speaker intones 'Rule Britannia' or if he wears a yearning look while producing an expressive sigh. All these forms of expression have the character of gestures—Wittgenstein calls the words 'long, long ago' together with the appropriate tone a 'gesture'—and hence they are communicable and can, like all gestures, be misunderstood. But the sense in which we understand them is neither entirely nor partially the same as that of words like 'I remember X', 'Now X comes back to me', or similar ones.

The case of familiarity is different. Whereas the feeling 'long, long ago' is clearly connected with a characterizable number of contexts, gestures, and kinds of tone, familiarity is not easily associated with certain forms of expression. In particular it is difficult to describe a typical case for applying the expression '*feeling* of familiarity'. Wittgenstein here imagines a situation in which someone returns after a long absence to his old room, 'enjoying his familiar acquaintance with all the old things' (*RPP* i. § 123). In this case there is a certain way of walking around the room, of looking at and touching the old things, and we may regard this as a characteristic expression of the feeling of familiarity, just as we regard a cat's purr as a characteristic expression of well-being (*RPP* i. § 122). With remembering, however, this feeling is only indirectly and by no means essentially connected. In particular, if we remember someone or something especially well, it is in no way appropriate to speak of a feeling of familiarity. If I were for example asked whether the face of my milkman seems familiar to me, I should reply, 'No, I see him every day' (cf. *RPP* i. § 120). It may at first glance appear paradoxical that whereas in the case of an encounter with people or things which I have not seen for a long time or of recognizing a barely known face I may indeed speak of having a feeling of familiarity, mentioning such a feeling is quite out of place when referring to people or things which I see every day. But this air of paradox is due to the assumption that such a feeling of familiarity is closely connected with acquaintance and must decrease or increase according to the degree of acquaintance. This assumption, however, is unfounded, unless you wish to regard the complete absence of any expression, or perhaps total indifference, as a typical indication of the highest degree of the feeling of familiarity. Only in very special or particular situations may we speak of a *feeling* of familiarity, for example in a situation where I grasp a violin which I have not played since my boyhood days and feel that my fingers are as it were finding their places automatically. Not only is such a feeling, as a matter of fact, rare but it is, in addition, not essentially connected with remembering. We have already seen that many memories are not associated with such a feeling. But it may also happen that I have this feeling about something I certainly do not remember, for instance when looking around my room in the Holiday Inn at Heathrow, even though I have never been there before and thus cannot have any memories of that room (but have for example stayed in other hotels belonging to that chain).[11]

It appears generally misguided to assume a systematic connection between remembering and a certain kind of feeling or a certain sequence of feelings. At any rate, this is the impression one gets if one regards the existence of characteristic forms of expression as a necessary criterion of the assertability of the presence of certain feelings. After all, what is the typical expression which is supposed to be connected with remembering? Many memory statements are made without any characteristic expression; some are made with an expression of the feeling 'long, long ago'; other ones with an expression of anger, bliss, or yearning. None of these feelings is constitutive of remembering, and each of them may occur without memories. There is no such thing as a characteristic expression of an alleged feeling of memory, and hence there is no basis for speaking of an identifiable, isolable feeling of memory.

At the time of working on the *Blue Book* (1933–4) Wittgenstein proposes to distinguish various forms of remembering.[12] He begins by pointing out that looking into one's memory is different from straightforward remembering. He calls looking into one's memory a 'very peculiar' activity, but he does not specify what the peculiarity

[11] Cf. D. C. Dennett's example of the 'Ballad of Shakey's Pizza Parlour' ('Beyond Belief', in A. Woodfield (ed.), *Thought and Object* (Oxford, 1982), 53 ff.). Here a man is drugged in pizzeria X and in a state of unconsciousness transported to an absolutely identical pizzeria Y, where he wakes up. This example might be construed in such a way that the man's feeling of familiarity is responsible for memory *mistakes* on his part.

[12] A. Ambrose (ed.), *Wittgenstein's Lectures: Cambridge 1932–1935* (Oxford, 1979), 56.

consists in. The kinds of remembering which he then tries to distinguish are (1) that which 'passes in time, cinematographically', (2) remembering something all at once, and (3) the capacity to reproduce or repeat something (a poem, a tune, etc.). Looking into one's memory would presumably fall under category (1), straightforward remembering under (2). Category (3) seems to be more clearly separated from the other two than those are from each other. If one puts (1) and (2) together and confronts them with (3), then the resulting distinction amounts more or less to Ryle's distinction between remembering as an 'occurrence' and remembering as 'having learned something and not forgotten it'.[13]

In Wittgenstein's remarks on the philosophy of psychology from the late 1940s we do not find any such distinction, at least not an explicit one (which does not mean that he would now regard remembering as a uniform phenomenon). The earlier contrast between categories (1) and (2) would probably not be appropriate any more, especially as category (1) is too exclusively explained in terms of a subjective process; a temporal succession of memory images and similar phenomena are merely regarded as accompaniments of remembering. And the characteristics of remembering now discussed by Wittgenstein do not mark a contrast between remembering as a process or event, on the one hand, and remembering as a capacity to reproduce something (to learn something without forgetting it), on the other. The only distinction which Wittgenstein draws, rather in passing, is that between 'remembering' and 'calling something to mind', where the criterion used for distinguishing these two is their respective voluntariness or involuntariness: 'memory [is] involuntary, but calling something to mind is voluntary' (*RPP* i. § 848). As far as the terminology is concerned, this distinction is perhaps not entirely fortunate. At any rate, it does not rest on striking observable characteristics but primarily on differences of our descriptions, which often mirror differences in the context of what is being described. If I call a certain movement for instance a voluntary one, this is not due to feeling (in my own case) or seeing or otherwise perceiving (in the case of another person) that the movement has not been brought about in the same way as when it is made involuntarily. In order to be able to use the contrast between 'voluntary' and 'involuntary',

---

[13] G. Ryle, *The Concept of Mind* (Harmondsworth, 1970), ch. 8. 7, pp. 257–8.

there must be a context in which one may speak of 'trying', 'striving', and so forth. If the circumstances under which I am lifting my glass are entirely normal ones, then there is simply no question of whether or not my movement is voluntary. It *may* happen, however, that I raise it to my lips in a deliberate and careful manner, for instance because I have recently upset a glass—possibly through an 'involuntary' movement of my hand—and here one may speak of a voluntary movement. In a similar way one may say of certain memories that one has *tried* to call them to mind and that this attempt has been successful. This sort of thing often involves preparations or accompanying activities, such as trying to get in a certain mood, closing one's eyes, looking at pictures of a given kind, whistling a tune, and so on. If one cannot speak of 'trying' it and if there is no hint of preparatory or accompanying activities, the memories concerned tend to be of the involuntary kind; otherwise they will be voluntary ones.[14]

Even though the distinction between voluntary and involuntary memories marks a point of difference between various uses of the expressions 'memory' or 'remember', it does not clearly separate different concepts of memory. And it is likely that such a separation is not intended by Wittgenstein. Instead, he mentions three characteristics of memories which apply to them, if not in all, then in many cases, namely their occurring in a flash, their being immediate, and the impossibility of their suffering from a failure of reference.

It often happens that one has to reflect for a long while before a certain fact or event will come to one's mind; but as soon as it occurs to one, it happens all at once: 'One can remember a situation or

[14] Terminologically Wittgenstein's distinction between remembering and calling to mind is not a very fortunate one because in the case of a voluntary memory the word 'remember' is just as much in place as in the case of an involuntary one. In addition, the entire complex of problems concerning the contrast between 'voluntary' and 'involuntary' is much more complicated than has here been indicated. One must not forget that because of the obscurity of many situations we are often incapable of deciding whether and why a certain act of remembering something is to count as voluntary or not—we do not, after all, notice everything. In cases of remembering we tend to classify indifferent and obscure cases among the involuntary ones; in cases of bodily movements it tends to be the other way around; and yet another type of case is that where one *defines certain bodily functions*, as for example the motoricity of the skeletal muscles, as involuntary ones. Furthermore, there are numerous actions (such as speaking or writing) of which it is generally not possible to say that they are performed 'involuntarily' but which we are at the same time extremely reluctant to call 'voluntary'.

occurrence *at a moment*. To that extent, then, the concept of memory is like that of instantaneous understanding or decision' (*RPP* i. § 837). This remark refers us to Wittgenstein's discussions of someone's understanding something in a flash (cf. *PI* §§ 191, 197; *RFM* i. § 123). To understand something in a flash does not mean that an infinitely complicated process is reeled off before one's mental eye in a fraction of a second, as if one were seeing an entire motion picture in the shape of a single slide. This and similar ideas are very peculiar indeed and they do not help to get a better understanding of the expression 'grasp something in a flash'. All one means when one uses this locution is that one feels capable of employing a certain expression, playing a certain game, or operating a certain mechanism correctly without mentally having to go through all the details of all the individual moves involved in these processes—the employment of the word, the rules of the game, the instructions for using the machine. In the same way, there is nothing mysterious in remembering a certain event, a tune, or a poem in a flash. All it means is that one feels able to describe that event, to whistle the tune, or to repeat the poem without lengthy considerations or efforts of imagination. And there is a further similarity between the cases of understanding and remembering something in a flash: one may get it wrong. Perhaps I believe I understand something, and then it turns out that I have not grasped it correctly; I may believe I remember something, but then the supposed memory proves not to correspond to reality.

The immediacy of remembering shows itself in the fact that a memory description need not be 'read off' from anything. As we have seen, memory images or other kinds of representation do sometimes agree with our memory statements, but such images tend to be accompanying phenomena or memory aids (and such an aid may consist in deliberately imagining *something different* from that which one is trying to remember). This immediacy applies to memories of external events just as much as to memories of thoughts and psychological states: I can describe yesterday's walk straight away, without having to reflect or to call anything to mind; and I can give an account of an idea I had last year or of the melancholy I felt in the spring without retracing the steps which led to that idea or imagining myself in a melancholy mood.

The characteristic of the impossibility of reference failure indicates a certain similarity between remembering, on the one hand, and intending or meaning, on the other. Of course, this does not mean that in remembering we cannot make mistakes; what it means is that, as far as the *reference* of a person's memories is concerned, that person himself is the last court of appeal. Let us, for purposes of illustration, think of the following example. Someone says: 'When I mentioned a consummate ass, I meant X.' If I point out to the speaker that X—that is, the man who is really called 'X'—*cannot* for one reason or another be the person intended (for example, because the speaker does not know X), he may reply: 'You are quite right, I did not mean X, I meant Y', or 'You may be right, the man I mean is someone who has done such-and-such'. There are many respects in which I can correct the speaker's utterance—for instance, if he has confused certain names, or if his description is incoherent, etc.—but whether or not he meant this or that person is a question which only he himself can decide, even if we shall never find out who the intended person is. In a similar way we may be able to recognize the speaker's memory statement as mistaken and to correct it; but who or what the memory is about is again a question which only he himself can decide. Of course, both in the cases of intending and meaning as well as in that of remembering there exists the possibility of radical failure, but a definitive conclusion to that effect can only be drawn by the speaker himself. And in such a case he may say: 'I believed I remembered X, but now I see that I got it wrong—there is no such person as X' (or, 'I have never met X', etc.).' This form of expression—'I believed I remembered such-and-such'—by means of which the speaker admits his mistake (just as he shows his uncertainty by using a phrase like 'I believe I remember that'), serves to bring out the subjective element of remembering (cf. *RPP* i. § 107). But the word 'subjective' hardly amounts to more than saying that the speaker himself is the last court of appeal which decides whether he is uncertain or in error.

These three characteristics—happening in a flash, immediacy, and impossibility of reference failure—place remembering in the vicinity of intending and meaning, of which similar things can be said. Thus remembering is completely different from sensations or feelings, for genuine duration (which is essential to the latter) is not a necessary condition of remembering; and there is also no characteristic expression of remembering, just as there is no characteristic expression of intending or meaning. In at least one respect, however, there is a general difference between remembering, on the one hand, and intending or meaning, on the other. Whereas in the case of memory I can speak of voluntary or involuntary acts of remembering, this distinction applies neither to intending nor to meaning.

There is no doubt that memory, the faculty to remember things, is at the basis of all knowledge and of numerous intellectual as well as practical skills. We have no idea of how talking or playing the piano, science or ballroom dancing might be possible if we lacked the faculty of memory. It is obvious that memory is extremely important, and this is why we feel that we should get to the bottom of this phenomenon. And there is a widely held conception which suggests itself as useful in the attempt to understand this phenomenon, namely the conception of memory as a kind of store, where certain impressions leave traces which will remain recognizable or become faint and which we may call up, scrutinize, forget. This basic idea has been accepted by many philosophers, who have in some cases contributed further images to supplement this conception. A particularly vivid account is given by Plato in his *Theaetetus*, where Socrates asks his interlocutor to imagine

that our minds contain a block of wax, which in this or that individual may be larger or smaller, and composed of wax that is comparatively pure or muddy, and harder in some, softer in others, and sometimes of just the right consistency. . . . Let us call it the gift of the Muses' mother, Memory, and say that whenever we wish to remember something we see or hear or conceive in our own minds, we hold this wax under the perceptions or ideas and imprint them on it as we might stamp the impression of a seal-ring. Whatever is so imprinted we remember and know so long as the image remains; whatever is rubbed out or has not succeeded in leaving an impression we have forgotten and do not know.[15]

In a similar way Locke, in a well-known passage of his *Essay*,[16] speaks of memory as a storehouse in which our ideas are laid up. This device is regarded as necessary by Locke because man's mind is

[15] Plato, *Theaetetus*, 191c, d. Translation F. M. Cornford, *Plato's Theory of Knowledge* (London, 1935), 121. Cf. the image of knowledge as an aviary in the mind (197c ff.). This latter image is quoted by J. A. Fodor as a paradigmatic example of a 'horizontal' faculty psychology (*The Modularity of Mind* (Cambridge, Mass., 1981), 12).

[16] Locke, *An Essay Concerning Human Understanding* (London, 1961), II. x. 2.

too restricted to keep a large number of ideas under review simultaneously; so a storage depot is needed where ideas are kept and from which they may be taken out whenever the situation requires it. In this storehouse, however, our ideas 'quickly fade and often vanish quite out of the understanding, leaving no more footsteps or remaining characters of themselves than shadows do flying over fields of corn; and the mind is as void of them as if they never had been there.'[17] So here again we encounter the basic conception of a store where impressions are kept provided they have imprinted themselves on the mind and as long as these traces do not fade away completely.

But it is not only philosophers, let alone only philosophers of the past, who appeal to this notion of memory as a storehouse of such traces. There are psychologists of a scientific orientation who regard this conception as basic and formulate their theories accordingly. Wolfgang Köhler, for example, writes that 'all sound theories of memory . . . must contain hypotheses about memory traces as physiological facts' and they 'must also assume that the characteristics of traces are more or less akin to those of the processes by which they have been established'. For 'otherwise, how could the accuracy of recall be explained, which in a great many cases is quite high?'[18] Whereas most philosophers vaguely locate the storehouse of memory in the mind, Köhler assigns it a physiological place. In this way his hypothesis of a kinship or correspondence between triggering impression and stored trace gains a kind of definiteness which the more metaphysical accounts given by Plato and Locke are lacking.

This more definite conception of memory, in terms of stored traces which can be described and perhaps even explained in a physiological way, is criticized by Wittgenstein in two respects:

An event leaves a trace in the memory: one sometimes imagines this as if it consisted in the event's having left a trace, an impression, a consequence, in the nervous system. As if one could say: even the nerves have a memory. But then when someone remembered an event, he would have to *infer* it from this impression, this trace. Whatever the event does leave behind in the organism, *it* isn't the memory.

[17] Locke, *An Essay Concerning Human Understanding* (London, 1961), II. x. 4.
[18] W. Köhler, *Gestalt Psychology* (New York, 1975), 149. Cf. N. Malcolm, *Memory and Mind* (Ithaca, N Y, 1977), 192.

The organism compared with a dictaphone spool; the impression, the trace, is the alteration in the spool that the voice leaves behind. Can one say that the dictaphone (or the spool) is remembering what was spoken all over again, when it reproduces what it took? (*RPP* i. § 220)

Before we go into some of the details of this criticism a preliminary remark will be in order. Here Wittgenstein criticizes neither the idea that some events leave in our nervous system certain traces which are somehow connected with our memories nor the comparison between an organism and a dictaphone spool. He turns against these ideas only in so far as they become incompatible with our actual notion of memory, that is, in so far as they postulate states of affairs or forms of expression whose assumption is implausible or incoherent.

What this conception of memory as a trace in the nervous system implicitly asserts is the existence of a mediating link between impression and memory (however this latter may be articulated). And here the alleged mediating link is not only supposed to be a real and possibly inevitable physiological substrate of memories, it is supposed to be the essence of memory. This would mean that we have to read off or infer our uttered or thought memory statements from those traces in our nervous system. Roughly speaking, the kind of model here envisaged involves the following idea. Impressions and thoughts are in some form coded and stored; they are recorded. And these records represent those impressions or thoughts. By re-reading these records I become aware of the original impressions or thoughts, that is, I infer them from the representations in my nervous system. Now, part of this account may for reasons of convenience simply be accepted, even though it is surely justifiable to wonder whether the assumption of the existence of certain parts of this model is more plausible than the assumption of their non-existence. Wittgenstein merely says that the traces in the organism—our 'records' or 'representations'—may be all kinds of things but are certainly not *memories*; the concept 'memory' must not be applied to them. To be sure, this is by itself not an argument against the model we have characterized; but it seems to me that it is possible to infer a number of reasons for Wittgenstein's criticism from the passage quoted and from some further remarks.

All these reasons amount to saying that we need more than mere traces in a memory store if we are to decide whether or not something is to count as a memory. Let us first think of the case of a false memory statement. I believe I remember having been in Marienbad last year, but I am wrong—I have been in Karlsbad. Where does my mistake reside? Did I make an error in recording the fact? Has the storing caused a certain defect? Or did I make a mistake in reading the record? We shall never find out. And to this extent the envisaged model is nothing but superfluous ballast. But let us suppose further that I correct this mistake without external assistance, for instance by thinking of the route by which I reached the destination of my trip and calling various images to mind. In which way will our model allow such a correction? It is, on this model, conceivable that through various considerations we hit on incompatible records, and it may also be acceptable that there is an inner decision procedure which leads to cancelling the less plausible record. But what appears hardly intelligible according to the model is the common phenomenon of the right thing popping into one's mind after the false memory has been discarded. For where should the true record come from, if it has not been there from the very beginning? And if it has been there from the very beginning, the supposed existence of the mistaken record becomes impossible to explain. The only way out of this difficulty would be the assumption that all memory mistakes are a kind of reading error. But that would in its turn be incompatible with the equally common phenomenon that we let documents and considerations persuade us of the falsity of a certain memory claim while experiencing not the slightest change in the subjectively certain memory record which has turned out to be false. Had my mistake been a mere reading error, I should have been able to read this memory record correctly, without getting any assistance from outside.

A second reason for rejecting the envisaged model is that it does not indicate any way of explaining the reference of our memories. Of course, it may be that quite a few of the alleged traces in the memory store are somehow associated with definite descriptions which can, in the process of looking in that store, somehow be decoded and thus permit clear reference to what is remembered, but the overwhelming majority of our memories cannot possibly be based on definite descriptions. It is quite obvious that—even for myself—many of my memories acquire shape and definiteness only through pointing to objects, people, pictures, etc., or through reproducing or repeating sounds and smells. I may claim that I remember Mr X. without being able to mention any feature which is characteristic of him. But as soon as I see Mr X., or a picture of Mr X., I say, 'That is Mr X.', and this shows that I really remember him. If, however, I do not recognize him, I shall have to admit that I do not remember him. But where does the difference lie, according to our envisaged model? Whether or not my memory statement has a reference cannot, on this model, depend on whether or not I am able to point to Mr X.; for according to it memories are read off or inferred from traces in my nervous system. As actual recognition is not a criterion of correct reading off, the question of whether or not I remember correctly must remain undecided—and this consequence is absurd.

How do I succeed in keeping memories apart from other types of contents of consciousness? According to the simple model of 'reading off' traces the answer to this question must assume differences between various psychological faculties which are part of the very structure of the nervous system and potentially detectable. That is, the mind is regarded as somehow able to distinguish various contents according to their origins. To illustrate this by means of a simplified example: sense impressions arrive on track I, feelings on track II, memories on track III, etc. The mind recognizes that it is dealing with memories from the fact that it must first read their traces, whereas impressions, images, and other contents of consciousness do not require that. This conception, however, involves two difficulties which deprive it of its possible plausibility.

First, it remains completely obscure how the mind could succeed in keeping different kinds of memories apart. We all know the experience of feeling unable to decide whether or not certain images which we have in our minds reproduce something which we have really seen or something which we have merely imagined or 'seen' in a dream. In order to decide such a question, we need more context, and even that does not always suffice. In that event the question must remain open. The case of the traces would be analogous: that which has been recorded may correspond to a picture, but whether it is a picture of a real occurrence or of a dream or of hallucination cannot be read off from the picture itself; the trace by itself does not suffice to determine the kind of memory. (We cannot gather from a written record which lacks all further information whether it is about something real or about something

invented. A conventional drawing[19] of an everyday occurrence does
not show whether it reproduces a real event or a dream.) But as a
matter of fact, we are rarely in doubt about whether what we
remember is a real occurrence or a dream. Shall we thus need a
second kind of 'track' which would divide memories into different
categories? Or shall we have to assume that the different kinds of
memory are recorded on different tracks? It seems that this sort of
speculation leads to absurd results; for the more differences we
notice, the more devices in the nervous system we shall have to
postulate. And these merely postulated devices will surely lack any
explanatory power.

Secondly, the defender of the envisaged model of memory traces
overlooks the fact that present impressions, feelings, etc. themselves
tend to involve memories. To see a house involves knowing what a
house is; and knowing what a house is implies that one remembers
the concept 'house', that one is able to describe houses which one
has seen on previous occasions, and many other things. It simply is
not possible to draw a clear dividing line between 'purely present'
contents of consciousness and those which include memories of
things past. To be sure, one might imagine that in all cases of
psychological processes quite a number of traces are simultaneously
activated and contribute to our performances; but under that
assumption the hypothesis of memory traces and the envisaged
model lose all their presumed explanatory value. Just as a number of
traces may be activated without my regarding the result (for
example a judgement about what I am seeing before me) as a
memory, so there is no reason to suppose that in a different case I
call a certain content of consciousness a memory for the reason that
I have read it off a certain trace.

In the last analysis the envisaged model of memory traces is
misleading because it ignores the creative element in remembering:
what Wittgenstein used to call 'memory as a source'. If I remember
a certain passage from the Fourth Symphony by Brahms and hear
the sequence of tones before my mental ear, do I listen to a
reproduction of a certain performance? If yesterday I heard the
Fourth conducted by Kleiber and the day before yesterday I heard
it conducted by Karajan, then my memory is likely to be influenced

---

[19] This condition, that the drawing be a 'conventional' one, serves to exclude those
cases where the peculiar style of the drawing enables us to see whether that which is
represented is a dream, a hallucination, or something else.

by both, and it may even be that I am able to reproduce—that I am
able to call into mind—differences between those two performances. But no matter which kinds of traces may be there in my
nervous system, *I* am the one *now* 'playing' Brahms's Fourth
Symphony. It is my present performance—what I am doing
now—which makes memory such a puzzling thing and at the same
time such an important agency. But it is precisely because the
present performance of remembering is the crucial aspect that the
various metaphors of traces in a store can at best articulate part of
the puzzle of memory.

8

Emotion

IN a remarkable passage of his *Principles of Psychology* William James writes:

My theory . . . is that *bodily changes follow directly the perception of the exciting fact, and that our feeling of the same changes as they occur* IS *the emotion*. Common-sense says, we lose our fortune, are sorry and weep; we meet a bear, are frightened and run; we are insulted by a rival, are angry and strike. The hypothesis here to be defended says that this order of sequence is incorrect, that the one mental state is not immediately induced by the other, that the bodily manifestations must first be interposed between, and that the more rational statement is that we feel sorry because we cry, angry because we strike, afraid because we tremble, and not that we cry, strike, or tremble because we are sorry, angry, or fearful, as the case may be.[1]

Then James comes to what he calls 'the vital point' of his whole theory and mentions what has since come to be called a thought experiment:

If we fancy some strong emotion, and then try to abstract from our consciousness of it all the feelings of its bodily symptoms, we find we have nothing left behind, no 'mind-stuff' out of which the emotion can be constituted and that a cold and neutral state of intellectual perception is all that remains. It is true that, although most people when asked say that their introspection verifies this statement, some persist in saying theirs does not. Many cannot be made to understand the question. When you beg them to imagine away every feeling of laughter and of tendency to laugh from their consciousness of the ludicrousness of an object, and then to tell you what the feeling of its ludicrousness would be like, whether it be anything more than the perception that the object belongs to the class 'funny', they persist in replying that the thing proposed is a physical impossibility, and that they always *must* laugh if they see a funny object. Of course the task proposed is not the practical one of seeing a ludicrous object and annihilating one's tendency to laugh. It is the purely speculative one of subtracting certain elements of feeling from an emotional state supposed to exist in its fulness,

---

[1] W. James, *The Principles of Psychology* (New York, 1950), ii. 449–50.

and saying what the residual elements are. . . . What kind of an emotion of fear would be left if the feeling neither of quickened heart-beats nor of shallow breathing, neither of trembling lips nor of weakened limbs, neither of goose-flesh nor of visceral stirrings, were present, it is quite impossible for me to think. Can one fancy the state of rage and picture no ebullition in the chest, no flushing of the face, no dilatation of the nostrils, no clenching of the teeth, no impulse to vigorous action, but in their stead limp muscles, calm breathing, and a placid face? The present writer, for one, certainly cannot. . . . Every passion in turn tells the same story. A purely disembodied human emotion is a nonentity. I do not say that it is a contradiction in the nature of things, or that pure spirits are necessarily condemned to cold intellectual lives; but I say that for *us*, emotion dissociated from all bodily feeling is inconceivable.[2]

Wittgenstein mentions this theory and this thought experiment from William James more than once in his later writings on the philosophy of psychology. Of particular interest, however, is an earlier passage from the *Brown Book*, which was dictated in the academic year 1934/5. There, in the context of discussing the question of the correctness of our translations of foreign, or radically foreign, words, Wittgenstein writes:

You will find that the justifications for calling something an expression of doubt, conviction, etc., largely, though of course not wholly, consist in descriptions of gestures, the play of facial expressions, and even the tone of voice. Remember at this point that the personal experiences of an emotion must in part be strictly localized experiences; for if I frown in anger I feel the muscular tension of the frown in my forehead, and if I weep, the sensations around my eyes are obviously part, and an important part, of what I feel. This is, I think, what William James meant when he said that a man doesn't cry because he is sad but that he is sad because he cries. The reason why this point is often not understood, is that we think of the utterance of an emotion as though it were some artificial device to let others know that we have it. Now there is no sharp line between such 'artificial devices' and what one might call the natural expressions of emotion. Cf. in this respect: a) weeping, b) raising one's voice when one is angry, c) writing an angry letter, d) ringing the bell for a servant you wish to scold. (p. 103)

This passage contains several themes which keep cropping up in Wittgenstein's later philosophy of psychology and, interestingly enough, even the combination of themes is typical of his later thought. The first point concerns the fact that we justify our

---

[2] Ibid. 451–2.

ascriptions of psychological states to people by referring to facial expressions, gestures, and the tone of voice. This is important, not merely because these expressions often are our *only* grounds for attributing certain states to others, but also because they are often more *reliable* than what people say. After all, many of these expressions are what we call involuntary ones: they are difficult or impossible to suppress or imitate, and frequently our attempts at suppressing or imitating them are not successful, so that others can perfectly easily and with confidence tell how we feel.

The second point is a very involved one. Here Wittgenstein talks about our experiences of emotions, and the questions arising in this context are largely coloured by the problems already alluded to under the heading of observing one's own state of mind. But Wittgenstein seems to intend something narrower than what is suggested by the word 'observe'. When he speaks of experiencing a certain emotion he seems to mean that the occurrence of some emotions tends to go with certain typical feelings, and that this way of experiencing our emotions is possible only if these feelings concern a well-circumscribed part of our bodies. Wittgenstein mentions the frown which is felt in my forehead and the weeping felt in the area around my eyes. But this does not seem to apply to all kinds of emotions. Grief, for example, is not felt in a particular spot in one's body. Certain more specific manifestations, on the other hand, are felt in this way. Thus it may be the case that, being very sad, I weep; and this of course *is* closely related to my sadness and at the same time something that I do feel. Tears, however, can also be shed from joy, so the mere fact of crying is not very indicative of the emotion in question. But in the case of joy, at any rate, there normally are other typical feelings in certain parts of our face which tend to correspond to natural and thus reliable outer expressions of this emotion.

The third point mentioned by Wittgenstein again concerns the question of expressing an emotion. He says that the relation between feeling or experiencing an emotion and a certain place at which it, or part of it, is felt is often overlooked because 'we think of the utterance of an emotion as though it were some artificial device to let others know that we have it'. Now this connection may not appear altogether obvious. It consists, I suppose, in this: that the typical localized feeling going with a certain emotion is at the same time and through the good offices of our gestures, weepings, groans, and stammerings related to that which other people perceive as expressions or utterances of that emotion. And Wittgenstein wants to stress that these expressions or utterances are often very natural, not artificial, ones. What appears as a way of communicating a certain emotion is not normally primarily intended as such. When I sit at the breakfast-table and notice that my father's nose is twitching, his fingers jerking, his brows knit, and his face purple I literally see that he is angry. These unmistakable signs of his anger are not artificial devices he uses to tell me that he is angry; they are his natural, even instinctive, expressions of anger which, however, do tell me more clearly than words could that he is angry. Of course, he may, on another occasion, try to use these signs or symptoms as devices for trying to give me the impression that he is angry. This may work, especially if he manages to 'feel' part of what he is attempting to convey. But it is nevertheless a very different situation.

However, the roles of these expressions of our emotions are not always clearly separable; they tend to shade into each other. This is why Wittgenstein asks us to consider four different cases where our expressions are more or less natural or, as the case may be, more or less artificial. The first case is that of weeping which, I take it, is a paradigmatic natural expression. The second case is that of raising one's voice when one is angry. Normally this would also be a fairly natural expression which, however, can be relatively easily used, that is, artificially employed, to give the impression that one is angry. The third case is that of writing an angry letter. In this case the medium of writing by itself takes away much of the naturalness of the expression. Writing may come fairly naturally to some people, but even they have to look for the *mot juste* and to adjust their grammar, and these activities tend to take one's mind off the emotion that originally inspired the letter. The fourth case, in which you are ringing the bell for a servant you wish to scold, is a curious one. Here the means used, namely to press a buzzer or to pull a string, is decidedly an artificial one but it may still be a natural way of expressing your anger. The servant, however, will not normally be able to tell from the way the bell sounds whether you are angry or not.

As we have seen, one can use what are normally natural expressions of emotions as more or less artificial means of giving the impression that one feels a certain emotion. But our capacity to feign such expressions can also be relied on to cause oneself really to feel that emotion. This possibility is clearly suggested by James's words, and Wittgenstein mentions it in his later remarks on the philosophy of psychology. He writes:

And how does it come about that—as James says—I have a feeling of joy if I merely make a joyful face; a feeling of sadness, if I make a sad one? That, therefore, I can produce these feelings by imitating their expression? Does that show that muscular sensations are sadness, or part of sadness? (*RPP* i. § 451)

Wittgenstein's last question concerns the problem of whether there is a conceptual or merely an empirical connection between statements about emotions and statements about the expressions of emotions. If there is such a conceptual connection, then it will be admissible to say that having certain feelings in your facial muscles is part of sadness. If, on the other hand, there is no such connection, that is, if statements about the expressions of emotions only say something about empirical relations between those expressions and the emotions themselves, then it will be incorrect to claim that those muscular sensations are part of sadness. Thus Wittgenstein writes:

Suppose someone were to say: 'Raise your arm, and you will feel that you are raising your arm.' Is that an empirical proposition? And is it one if it is said: 'Make a sad face, and you will feel sad'?
Or was that meant to say: 'Feel that you are making a sorrowful face, and you will feel sorrow'? and is that a pleonasm? (*RPP* i. § 452)

Now what about the first question: is 'Raise your arm, and you will feel that you are raising your arm' an empirical statement? One thing we must remember is that this statement can be false. This is the case, for instance, when the person we are talking to has taken a drug which renders his limbs numb, so that he will feel nothing. Another possibility is that he is bombarded with so many exceptionally strong stimuli that the feeling of raising his arm will not register at all. The possible falsity of the statement seems to speak in favour of thinking that it is an empirical one. On the other hand, it will be false only under very special circumstances, whereas in normal situations it will be true. And we do feel sure that somehow it cannot normally help but be true that the feeling that one is raising one's arm is simply part of raising one's arm. Yet it surely is not a purely conceptual truth, that is, it is not what we may

wish to call an analytic statement. Is the same true of the statement
'Make a sad face, and you will feel sad'? Now of course, when we
really are sad we do not normally bother to find out about how it
feels to be sad. But in many cases of, as it were, minor sadness we do
observe ourselves, trace our feelings, and even compare them with
our feelings on other occasions. In such situations you may realize
that you are making a sad face and literally feel that you are sad. But
if you are not sad but attempt to make a sad face and succeed in
making a face which looks like the face of a sad person, does that
really *mean* that you feel sad? Wittgenstein reformulates the
question to make it sound even more pleonastic and says, 'Feel that
you are making a sad face, and you will feel sad.' But even this
formulation, I think, is not fully pleonastic; it is not, if true, a mere
conceptual truth. After all, it seems quite possible to make a sad
face, so to speak savouring the various aspects of the sensation, and
still be quite aware that you are not really sad. In that case the
statement in question would be false and *a fortiori* not a
conceptually true one. This impression is reinforced by Wittgenstein's remark:

Does one say: 'Now I feel much better: the feeling in my facial muscles and
round about the corners of my mouth is good'? And why does that sound
laughable, except, say, when one had felt pain in these parts before? (*RPP* i.
§ 454)

Of course one does not normally say things like that. And it is also
clear that such a statement sounds silly because when talking about
myself feeling well or better I do not intend to talk about what it
looks like to feel well or better. That would be treating myself as if I
were a different person, which of course is a possible attitude to take
but not in talking to others.

Wittgenstein does not really come to a conclusion at this point,
but he does throw doubt on the claim that certain sensations or
feelings are to count as constituents of our emotions. He writes:

Now granted—although it is extremely doubtful—that the muscular
feeling of a smile is a constituent part of feeling glad;—where are the other
components? Well, in the breast and belly etc.!—But do you really feel
them, or do you merely conclude that they *must* be there? Are you really
conscious of these localized feelings?—And if not—why are they supposed
to be there at all? Why are you supposed to mean *them*, when you say you
feel happy?

Something that could only be established through an act of *looking*—that's at any rate not what you meant.
For 'sorrow', 'joy' etc. just are not used like that. (*RPP* i. §§ 456–7)

Our words for emotions like sorrow, joy, etc. are used for states which we need not find out about. And whatever is part of these emotions is something we are immediately aware of, not through making an introspective effort or an inference.

In considering the problems concerning our concepts for the various emotions as well as their relations to sensations, muscular feelings, etc. special attention must be paid to the possibilities of arousing emotions artificially and of pretending to be in a certain emotional state. Looking at these non-natural situations, as we may call them, might help us to see what is really essential to such states.

An example which springs to mind in this connection is that of the actor who tries to play his dramatic part as convincingly as possible. William James quotes a number of actors who have given accounts of their experiences. Thus one actress says: 'I often turn pale in scenes of terror or great excitement. I have been told this many times, and I can feel myself getting very cold and shivering and pale in thrilling situations.' And another actress gives the following answer: 'Playing with the brain is far less fatiguing than playing with the heart. An adventuress taxes the physique far less than a sympathetic heroine. Muscular exertion has comparatively little to do with it.'[3]

The example of the actor is used by Wittgenstein too in his attempt to get clearer about what an emotion consists of and whether it is legitimate to describe it in terms of various components. He writes in his *Remarks on the Philosophy of Psychology*:

But wouldn't I say that the actor does experience something like real longing? For isn't there something in what James says: that the emotion consists in the bodily feelings, and hence can be at least partially reproduced by voluntary movements?
Is it so disagreeable, so sad, to draw down the corners of one's mouth, and so pleasant to pull them up? What is it that is so frightful about fear? The trembling, the quick breathing, the feeling in the facial muscles?—When you say: 'This fear, this uncertainty, is frightful!'—might you go on 'If only I didn't have this feeling in my stomach!'? (*RPP* i. §§ 727–8)

[3] James, *Principles of Psychology*, ii. 464.

I take it that it is unproblematic to say of an actor who is acting his emotional part convincingly that he really experiences something like the relevant emotion. I suppose it is very much a question of degree. On the other hand, there is something very puzzling in saying that a man who has *no reason* to yearn for anything feels something like yearning; or that a person who has absolutely no reason to be angry feels something like anger. But still, this kind of experience does exist, and actors are not the only people who know it; we all know it from occasions like reading thrilling books, watching romantic films, or hearing ghastly stories which arouse emotional feelings in us, even though there may be nothing in our real lives to cause them. In such situations of what one may call vicarious emotional feelings we can easily observe the palpitations of our hearts, the trembling of our hands, the biting of our lips, etc. But the relations between these occurrences and our emotions are still far from clear. We have seen that it is difficult or impossible to imagine certain emotions without their typical physical accompaniments. Thus it seems for example quite meaningless to imagine fear without fear-feelings in your heart and your stomach. When one is in the grip of a strong emotion one does say things like 'I'm so afraid; I cannot stand this feeling in my stomach any more', or 'If this state of uncertainty will continue much longer, I shall die of heart failure', etc. And yet, when Wittgenstein asks whether it is this kind of feeling which is so frightful when one fears something, we tend to answer, 'Of course not. The frightful thing is that which arouses the feeling.' A similar point is made by Wittgenstein:

The expression 'This anxiety is frightful!' is like a groan, a cry. Asked 'Why do you cry out?', however—we wouldn't point to the stomach or the chest etc. as in the case of pain; rather, perhaps, at what gives us our fear.

When anxiety is frightful, and when in anxiety I am conscious of my breathing and of a tension in the muscles of my face—does that mean that I find *these feelings* frightful? Might they not even signify an alleviation? (*RPP* i. §§ 729–30)

There can be little doubt that it is not the feelings accompanying one's state of anxiety which are frightful. Or, to change our example, think of the case of exhilaration. It is not the tension caused by the upward-moving corners of your mouth which you find exhilarating, nor the extraordinary lightness you feel in your chest. Rather, it may be the good weather, or the good news, or the fact that you slept marvellously which fills you with high spirits. In such cases we are dealing with the causes of our emotion, and they are easy to indicate. Other states have no straightforward causes in this sense. If I am worried about the future in general, it would be foolish to suggest that the uncertain state of the future is the cause of my worrying. It may be possible that the future is in a certain sense the object of my emotion in a similar way to which the cook who has spoiled my dinner is the object of my wrath. But that does not get us very far because there are obviously many emotional states of excitement, nervousness, languor, etc. which have neither a clear cause nor anything one might wish to call an object. But in these cases too we should not find it natural to say that the feelings of nervousness are what we find enervating, or that the palpitating heart is what we find exciting.

The distinction between emotions with and without a clear cause or object is, I think, what Wittgenstein has in mind when he asks us to compare fear and anxiety with care. The original German word translated as care is 'Sorge'. And Wittgenstein continues by asking himself what sort of description is given by words like 'Ewiges Düstre steigt herunter', translated as 'Perpetual cloud descends'. These words are spoken by the figure of Sorge in the last act of Goethe's *Faust*. Sorge, or care, represents an emotion which is typically causeless and objectless. It is a state you can be in in spite of material and physical well-being; it is directed at nothing. It does not typically go with very strong accompanying muscular or other physical feelings. And still you can describe it. That is the point of Wittgenstein's quotation from Goethe. He wants to bring out that you can describe an emotion or, if you like, the *content* of an emotion by using words in a certain way, even though you cannot refer to any causes or objects or accompaniments of that emotion. Now it would of course be interesting to use this idea in looking at the other emotions, that is, those which do have causes, objects, and accompanying feelings. And this is what I propose to do after I have gone a bit more thoroughly into a few more questions arising from the theory suggested by William James.

In his most extended discussion of James's theory Wittgenstein writes:

James says it is impossible to imagine an emotion or a mood without the corresponding bodily sensations (of which it is composed). If you imagine the latter absent then you can see that you are thereby abolishing the very existence of the emotion. This might happen in the following way: I imagine myself sorrowing, and now in the imagination I try to picture and to feel myself rejoicing at the same time. To do that I might take a deep breath and imitate a beaming face. And now indeed I have trouble forming an image of sorrow; for forming an image of it would mean play-acting it. But it does not follow from this that our bodily feeling at that point is sorrow, or even something like it. To be sure, a person who is sorrowful cannot laugh and rejoice convincingly, and if he could, what we call the expression of sorrow would not really be that, and rejoicing would not be the expression of a different emotion.—If the death of a friend and the recovery of a friend equally caused us to rejoice or—judging by our behaviour—both caused us sorrow, then these forms of behaviour would not be what we call the expressions of joy or sorrow. Is it clear a priori that whoever imitates joy will feel it? Couldn't the mere attempt to laugh while one was feeling grief bring about an enormous sharpening of the grief? (*RPP* ii. § 321)

The passage in James to which Wittgenstein here alludes is evidently the quoted one in which James claims that it is impossible to abstract from our consciousness of an imagined emotion the feelings of its bodily symptoms. But while James argues his case simply by pointing out that if we subtract those physical feelings from our image of a given emotion nothing will remain of the original emotion, Wittgenstein introduces a new element into the discussion. He describes a case in which a person tries to imagine being in a certain emotional state and in that state trying to imagine being in a different emotional state. His example is that of a man who imagines being sad and then tries to form a mental picture of himself being in a good mood. It does not work. And that it does not work is at least partly due to our being unable to combine the imagined physical symptoms and feelings going with one emotion with the symptoms and feelings of the other. But as the whole experiment is not a real one but takes place entirely in the imagination, it is not due to any really felt physical sensations that the combination of those two states appears impossible. It looks more like a formal or gestalt incompatibility and reminds one of our incapacity to see a picture or hear a tune in two different ways at the same time.

This part of Wittgenstein's remark concerns imagination. But he goes on to real cases and observes that someone who is in a state of sadness cannot convincingly laugh, even if what he is confronted with is exceedingly funny. If he were capable of laughing, we should think that something was wrong with him, that his mind had suffered from the terrible event that brought on his sadness. This, however, has nothing to do with the physical feelings which James calls symptoms of our emotions. It is connected with what we regard as our natural ways of expressing our emotions. And some of these expressions exhibit a pattern in time which is incompatible with interruptions of a certain type. Of course, a great many emotions are quite compatible with other ones. Thus there is nothing strange about laughing at a joke when one is in a generally hopeful mood. But there are other emotions, notably sadness, melancholy, or grief, which form a pattern that is not compatible with interruptions by outbursts of good humour.

A person who is terribly sad can none the less try to show joy or pleasure, for instance because he does not want to disturb others by showing his true feelings. In that case he may, as Wittgenstein points out, feel his sadness even more acutely than before. And that again speaks against the existence of a special logical relation between statements about emotions and statements about the feelings or sensations normally accompanying these emotions. For in cases like that of the sad man trying to laugh at a joke, his attempt at imitating the typical behaviour of a person in high spirits can have the effect that he senses his grief even more sharply than before, even though he feels the muscular sensations normally accompanying laughter. Thus it is, to use Wittgenstein's words, by no means 'clear a priori that whoever imitates joy will feel it'.

However, all these considerations should not make us forget the point from which we started, namely the closeness of the connection between emotion and certain bodily symptoms. Even though we cannot really find anything in the nature of an a priori relation, that connection is confirmed by the incompatibility between what Wittgenstein in the *Philosophical Investigations* calls the *patterns* of our emotions and certain other expressions of emotions, sensations, or feelings. This state of things is emphasized by Wittgenstein in the following remark:

Yet still I mustn't forget that joy goes along with physical well-being, and sadness, or at least depression, often with being physically out of sorts.—If I go for a walk and take pleasure in everything, then it is surely true that this would not happen if I were feeling unwell. But if I now express my joy, saying, e.g., 'How marvellous all of this is!'—did I mean to say that all of these things were producing pleasant physical feelings in me?

In the very case where I'd express my joy like this: 'The trees and the sky and the birds make me feel good all over'—still what's in question here is not causation, nor empirical concomitance, etc. etc. (*RPP* ii. § 322)

The first part of this remark is aimed at making it clear that in talking about, or verbally expressing, a certain emotion we do not *mean* to speak of the physical feelings accompanying the emotion in question, although these feelings are in a certain sense inseparable from the emotion. And it is a sort of corollary of this that expressing a given emotion by mentioning those physical feelings is not meant to be stating a 'causation' or 'empirical concomitance', as Wittgenstein says. Naturally, this is not intended as a denial of the existence of causal relations between what makes me feel a certain emotion and the bodily symptoms accompanying that emotion. But it does bring out that in expressing our emotions by mentioning what may possibly be their causes we still do not make a causal claim; at most we can be said to be trying to make our expressive behaviour specific.

The role of causes is made clearer by the following passage:

Possibly one could be sad because one is crying, but of course one is not sad *that* one is crying. It would after all be possible that people made to cry by application of onions would become sad; that they would either become generally depressed, or would start thinking about certain events, and then grieve over them. But then the *sensations* of crying would not thereby have turned into a part of the 'feeling' of grief. (*RPP* ii. § 323)

The causal story told by Wittgenstein is this. People are made to cry by some artificial means; the crying causes them to become depressed or to think of sad events and thus to come to feel sad. The sensation of crying, which may be indistinguishable from that felt in normal situations of sadness, is here clearly separated from the emotion of feeling sad. And it becomes increasingly clear that what James calls the bodily symptoms of an emotion are not part of the emotion itself. They are closely related to the emotion but not an essential ingredient of it.

William James was led to the conclusion that the physical feelings accompanying an emotion count as its essential component by starting, so to speak, from the inside. His most convincing argument is his thought experiment, in which we try in our imagination to subtract the physical feelings from the emotion and do not succeed. But that still does not show that these feelings are particularly characteristic of our emotions. What is really characteristic of them may become clearer by changing our perspective and looking at the emotions not so much from the inside but from the outside, that is, from the point of view of someone who tries to understand how another person feels by observing his behaviour, his expressions, his gestures, his utterances.

Some things are obvious. We judge that somebody is in a certain emotional state because his behaviour, or part of his behaviour, is a natural expression of a certain emotion. These natural expressions are often directly connected with the bodily symptoms William James talks about: the crying, the trembling, the raised voice, and the facial expression. But oddly enough, these phenomena now seem to be of much greater relevance when looked at from the outside. After all, they are often our only criteria for telling what state another person is in. They are the basis on which we judge whether someone is lying or telling the truth about himself.

It is as seen from the outside that these natural expressions can be useful for understanding and predicting other people's behaviour. Now it cannot be denied that I can sometimes look at my own behaviour as it were from the outside and on the basis of that predict my future states of mind. But this would still be an exception. And equally rare or even rarer would be the type of case in which through noticing certain physical feelings I get clearer about my emotional state.

But the real point I want to make is this. Natural expressions like groaning, crying, trembling, and so on are still only very rough indications of what another person may feel. Taken by itself, weeping does not tell you whether the person concerned is crying from joy or grief, jealousy or relief. And the same goes for the other natural expressions, like groaning, trembling, blushing, etc. In order to understand what they express we need to know more, either about the history of the person in question or about his present state. Knowing more about his history and telling on the basis of that and the natural expression observed would amount to telling a plausible causal story. But if this type of knowledge is unavailable or insufficient we shall have to know more about the other person's present state. One way of finding out about that is by looking at the finer shades of his behaviour, at additional gestures, and especially at the peculiar *tone* in which he utters his expressions.

This point is of the greatest importance, for only now are we approaching what is really specific and characteristic of certain emotions. It is the nuances, the shades and colourings of my expressions which make it possible for others to tell what I feel. An inkling of this is given by the following passage from the *Philosophical Investigations* (II. ix, pp. 187–8):

I say 'I am afraid'; someone else asks me: 'What was that? A cry of fear; or do you want to tell me how you feel; or is it a reflection on your present state?'—Could I always give a clear answer? Could I never give him one?
We can imagine all sorts of things here, for example:
'No, no! I am afraid!'
'I am afraid. I am sorry to have to confess it.'
'I am still a bit afraid, though I won't confess it to myself.'
'I torment myself with all sorts of fears.'
'Now, just when I should be fearless, I am afraid!'
To each of these sentences a special tone of voice is appropriate, and a different context.

The specific tone of our expressions allows other people to understand how we really feel. And it is this tone which is so difficult to imitate when you try to feign or to play-act a certain emotion. It is the existence of a certain tone of expression which enables us to make relatively fine distinctions between types of emotions and feelings, and it is the specificity of the tone which accounts for cultural variations in the expression of emotion. Many feelings can be distinguished from others only because there is a tone going with them. As an example Wittgenstein mentions the feeling of conviction and writes:

One speaks of a feeling of conviction because there is a *tone* of conviction. For the characteristic mark of all 'feelings' is that there is expression of them, i.e. facial expression, gestures, of feeling. (*RPP* ii. § 320)

I think, however, that there are at least two further outstanding features of our expressions of emotions which render them specific and help us to understand them. The first of these features is connected with what Wittgenstein likes to call the pattern of a certain emotion, for instance when he writes in the *Philosophical Investigations* (II. i, p. 174):

'Grief' describes a pattern which recurs, with different variations, in the weave of our life. If a man's bodily expression of sorrow and of joy alternated, say with the ticking of a clock, here we should not have the characteristic formation of the pattern of sorrow or of the pattern of joy.

The expressions of our emotions follow a certain pattern in the sense of having a kind of form or rhythm which can sometimes be imitated in another medium. An example would be music, where we sometimes speak of sad or joyful, melancholic or boisterous tunes, or movements, or even entire pieces. And this possibility is surely due to the fact that something of the rhythm or pattern—and certainly also something of the tone—of these emotions or feelings can be expressed by musical means.

The third and last feature of the expression of emotions I want to mention is related to what was said about the quotation from Goethe's *Faust* concerning Sorge, or care. Here the point is that there are words or phrases by means of which one can contrive to describe the exact characteristics of a certain emotion, although these expressions are descriptive neither of the cause nor of the object of these emotions. Goethe's poetic evocation of Sorge is a particularly accomplished description; but there are many more conventional, even hackneyed, phrases which serve to bring out the specific characteristics of our emotions. Thus we often use colour words to describe what we feel, for instance blue, green, grey, black, and yellow. But there are many more expressions—and sometimes quotations from poetry or song—which serve the same purpose.

These three features—tone, pattern, descriptive phrase—are not merely means of telling how another person feels. They have a lot to do with the perception of our own feelings. The rhythm or pattern, the expressive tone, and the visual or tactile impression corresponding to certain descriptive phrases are *felt* by the person who is in a certain emotional state. I think one could repeat William James's thought experiment and ask whether it would be possible to subtract the typical greyness, the subdued tone, and the slow rhythm from our emotion of melancholy and still retain an idea of what the feeling is like. And the answer, I suspect, would again have to be that an emotion without those ingredients would be a 'nonentity'.

9

Moore's Paradox: Belief, Supposition, Assertion

> All that hangs together with this, that one can say 'I believe he believes . . . ', 'I believe I believed . . . ', but not 'I believe I believe . . . '.
>
> *(RPP* ii. § 282)

WITTGENSTEIN'S discussion of Moore's paradox in the Second Part of the *Philosophical Investigations* (II. x, pp. 190–2) is well known. The remarks published in that book are mostly taken from the remarks on the philosophy of psychology, but in these manuscripts the paradox is discussed at much greater length. In the version reproduced in the *Philosophical Investigations* the selected remarks are arranged in a different order and yield a chain of arguments which it is not easy to reconstruct.[1] In the manuscripts, on the other hand, the thoughts are noted down in an unordered sequence, just as they came to Wittgenstein's mind, but the investigation goes into far more details than in the *Philosophical Investigations*. In this chapter I shall leave aside the—possibly more cogent—later version and try to follow the thread of the thoughts recorded in Wittgenstein's manuscripts.

Probably the first testimony of Wittgenstein's struggle with the paradox is a letter from the end of October 1944 to Moore, in which Wittgenstein praises a paper given by Moore the day before at the Moral Sciences Club. In this unpublished paper Moore deals, as we can gather from Wittgenstein's letter, with sentences of the type 'It is raining but I do not believe it'. In his letter Wittgenstein does not yet speak of a 'paradox' but of an 'absurdity'. He criticizes Moore for saying that a sentence like 'There is a fire in this room and I

---

[1] A reconstruction is attempted in my article ' "Es regnet, aber ich glaube es nicht." Zu *Philosophische Untersuchungen* II. x', *Teoria* (1985).

don't believe there is' is 'an absurdity *for psychological* reasons'.
And Wittgenstein's reason for his criticism is the following: 'If I ask
someone "Is there a fire in the next room?" and he answers "I
believe there is" I can't say: "Don't be irrelevant. I asked you about
the fire, not about your state of mind!"' Thus Wittgenstein's first
commentary concerns our use of the word 'believe', and he takes
exception to the view that by using the locution 'I believe . . .' a
speaker says something about his own state of mind.

   Wittgenstein's second commentary concerns the logical features
of absurd sentences of that type. He says that such a sentence 'is in
fact something *similar* to a contradiction, though it isn't one'. And
he continues:

By the way, don't be shocked at my saying it's something 'similar' to a
contradiction. This means roughly: it plays a similar role in logic. You have
said something about the *logic* of assertion. Viz.: It makes sense to say 'Let's
suppose: p is the case and I don't believe that p is the case', whereas it makes
no sense to assert '⊢—p is the case and I don't believe that p is the case'.
This *assertion* has to be ruled out and *is* ruled out by 'common sense', just as
a contradiction is. And this just shows that logic isn't as simple as logicians
think it is. In particular: that contradiction isn't the *unique* thing people
think it is. It isn't the *only* logically inadmissible form and it is, under
certain circumstances, admissible.[2]

Thus Wittgenstein holds the following: (1) Sentences of that absurd
type are similar to contradictions of the propositional calculus
(*p* & –*p*). (2) Their assertion makes no sense and (3) is therefore to
be excluded from usage. (4) The problem of these absurd sentences
shows that logic is a more comprehensive and more complex
business than logicians dream of. (5) Even for those absurd
sentences (as well as for contradictions) an occasional use may be
found.[3] All these considerations recur in the manuscripts and are
there supplemented by further ideas, examples, and arguments. But

   [2] Letter to G. E. Moore, M. 42. About the history of the paradox, cf. the editors'
note in Wittgenstein, *Letters to Russell, Keynes and Moore* (Oxford, 1974), 177–8.
The paradox is foreshadowed in Moore's *Ethics* (London, 1912), 125. A well-known
early discussion is to be found in J. L. Austin's 'The Meaning of a Word' (1940), in
Philosophical Papers (Oxford, 1970).
   [3] Of course, thesis (5) is not meant to contradict thesis (3). Wittgenstein holds that
it is the absurdity in the form given it by Moore—i.e. in the form of a simple
assertion—which is to be excluded from language, while other forms of using the
same sentence are conceivable which at a pinch could be given a sense.

before going into these, it will be useful to have a look at the general problem raised by Moore's paradox.

At first glance the sentence 'It is raining but I do not believe it' appears absurd, even self-contradictory. But if you look at it more closely, it becomes clear that it is not contradictory in the sense of formal logic, for (1) that it is raining and (2) that I do not believe it are, from a logical point of view, completely independent states of affairs, just as in the case of the individual sentences 'My club has won the match' and 'I do not believe that my club has won the match'. If the logical product of the two statements is false, then it is—in contrast with the sentence 'My club has won the match and my club has not won the match'—contingently false and not necessarily so, that is, it is not false because of the form of the statement.

At the same time it is difficult to believe that rejecting 'It is raining but I do not believe it' depends on knowing certain facts. If one hears a sentence of this kind, one will react by saying: 'No, this will not do; and in order to see this, you will not have to know if it is really raining or if you really do not believe it.' May we thus say that the sentence is senseless or nonsensical? But that too seems to be excluded, because the two constituent sentences are, each taken by itself, paradigms of meaningful sentences, and who would wish to deny that a conjunction of two meaningful sentences will also be meaningful?

It appears that there must be something in this specific combination which prompts us from the very beginning to reject that sentence. And it also appears that here we are, as Wittgenstein says, dealing with something 'similar' to a standard contradiction, as our disapproval has nothing to do with empirical knowledge. But why do we take exception to such sentences without having the feeling that we should first have a closer look at their contents? As it cannot be due to anything belonging to formal logic, the assumption suggests itself that our use of the expression 'I believe' is the responsible factor, since we feel that we want to reject *all* assertoric utterances of the form '*p* and I do not believe that *p*'.

Wittgenstein's first full discussion of the problems surrounding Moore's paradox dates from 3. 10. to 7. 10. 46 (*RPP* i. §§ 470–504). In these remarks Wittgenstein repeats the warning pronounced in his letter to Moore that it must not be thought that the absurdity or paradoxicality of a 'Moorean' sentence like 'It is raining but I do not believe it' is due to psychological reasons: 'It would be asking for trouble to take Moore's paradox for something that can only occur in the mental sphere.' (*RPP* i. § 471)

But here one would like to ask why it might with respect to Moore's paradox appear tempting to call '"I believe . . ." a description of my mental state' (*RPP* i. § 470). The temptation to speak of a description of a mental state in this context is due to the fact that one wishes to find a close connection between the parts of Moorean sentences in order to explain what is obviously paradoxical about them. Even though Moorean sentences are not, from a logical point of view, of the form p & $-p$, our immediate rejection of such sentences seems none the less somehow to be based on our impression that the same 'content' occurs here in a positive and there in a negative context. One is tempted to say that it is not possible simultaneously to entertain one and the same content both positively and negatively conceived.

It must also be remembered that we often seem to use the assertion 'p' (or '⊢—p') in a similar way to the statement 'I believe that p' (cf. *LPP*, 65–6). If someone asserts 'p', we assume that he believes 'p'. And the picture which therefore suggests itself is the following. I am looking out of my window and notice that it is raining; thus I may assert that it is raining. As I have seen that it is raining, I believe that it is raining; consequently I may say that I believe it. I regard myself as a kind of instrument for recording certain facts, and what has been recorded is now contained in my belief:

One would like to say this: If instead of '⊢—p' I use the statement 'I believe p', then this is similar to employing a photograph as a testimony of a certain matter of fact. After all, I do say: 'It gives me that impression.' Thus, instead of describing reality, I describe the effect it makes on me as an instrument. (MS 132, 4. 10. 46)

This image is neither unnatural nor far-fetched. From caricatures or comic strips we all know representations of belief or conviction which depict the relevant state of affairs as something located in the head of the drawn figure (cf. *RPP* i. § 480). If one now takes the statement 'I believe that p' as a *description* of such a state of affairs—that is, of a situation where I am having a picture of a certain fact in my mind—it becomes easy to explain the obvious absurdity of Moorean sentences. That which justifies my assertion '*p*' is the same thing as that on which a description of my belief is based, namely the state of affairs I have in my mind, for example the state of affairs that it is raining. And as it is the same state of affairs in both cases, I cannot at the same time assert and doubt its obtaining. In other words, if I regard the statement 'I believe that *p*' as a description of a mental state and that description as containing a description of a certain state of affairs *x*, then I shall evidently land myself in an absurdity if the described state of affairs *x* does not agree with what I am asserting at the same time. For if I proceed in such a way and compare my state of belief to a photograph, then its ' "description is indirectly an assertion of the state of affairs that is believed".—As, in certain circumstances, I describe a photograph in order to describe what the photograph is a shot of' (*RPP* i. § 481).

In this way the conception of 'I believe . . .' as a description of my mental state yields a certain picture, an explanation of why Moorean sentences immediately appear absurd. In describing my belief '*p*' I am at the same time giving an indirect description of that state of affairs on which the assertion '*p*' rests. But if in my supposed description of that belief I say something which does not agree with the assertion, I am giving two conflicting descriptions of one and the same state of affairs—and that is obviously absurd.

This entire conception, however, is misguided. Some of the reasons for this can be extracted from Wittgenstein's later remarks, but there is one reason which he mentions at once. If belief were something in the nature of a photograph, then it should be possible to take the same attitude towards it as to a photograph. If the comparison with a photograph assimilates belief to a kind of sense impression, it must then be permissible to ask whether the picture given is a good, a reliable, a correct picture.

Belief, however, is different. While it is possible to say that what I believe is either true or false, and while it is also possible to say that what I believe *may* be false or that what I *used* to believe has turned out to be false, I cannot possibly say that what I believe *is* false. I cannot take towards my own belief the same attitude as towards my sense impressions. If I think I see something, I may doubt that things are really that way, and then I may change my point of view, put on my glasses, or ask my neighbour in order to check whether reality corresponds to what I think I see, that is, whether what I think I see is really there to be seen. In the case of belief, on the other hand, nothing of this kind is possible. I cannot 'think I believe' something and then ask my neighbour whether what I think I believe is really there to be believed. It is possible, as Wittgenstein says in a much later remark, to 'mistrust one's own senses, but not one's own belief' (*LW* § 419). That is, the suggested parallel between sense impression and belief is not really tenable. For this reason it is a mistake to think that by describing the supposed mental state of believing one is at the same time giving an indirect description of a state of affairs obtaining in reality.

The tempting aspect of the conception we have just characterized lies in its aim of wanting to explain the paradoxicality of Moorean sentences through the identity of the content of the two constitutive sentences '*It is raining*' and 'I believe that *it is raining*'. A similar idea is, according to Wittgenstein, at the bottom of another conception, which wants to resolve the paradox from the point of view of a 'logic of assertion'. In speaking of such a 'logic of assertion' Wittgenstein is of course thinking of Frege's use of the assertion sign, which he already disapproved of at the time of the *Tractatus* and which he also criticized in Part I of the *Philosophical Investigations*. In neither of these cases nor in his remarks on the philosophy of psychology does Wittgenstein aim at a true interpretation of Frege's theory; what he is interested in is the picture which holds us captive when we find it impossible to free ourselves from the model suggested by the use of the assertion sign.

Roughly speaking, this model is the following. The 'horizontal' (——p) indicates that we are dealing with a judgeable content, a Fregean 'thought', a name of the True or the False. But it does not say anything about whether we regard this thought as true or false. No assertion is made by '——p'; the thought is merely presented. That the thought is taken to be true, or that it is judged to be true, is marked by adding the assertion sign or judgement stroke ($\vdash$—p). 'This separation of the act from the subject-matter of judgment seems to be indispensable; for otherwise we could not express a mere supposition [*Annahme*]—the putting of a case without a simultaneous judgment as to its arising or not.'[4] Thus the symbol '——p' stands for a 'Fregean supposition [*Annahme*]'. This sort of supposition is mentioned by Wittgenstein on various occasions, and

---

[4] G. Frege, 'Function and Concept', in P. Geach and M. Black (edd.), *Philosophical Writings of Gottlob Frege* (Oxford, 1970), 21–2.

several commentators have found his formulation puzzling.[5] In the *Philosophical Investigations*, for example, Wittgenstein writes:

> Imagine a picture representing a boxer in a particular stance. Now this picture can be used to tell someone how he should stand, should hold himself; or how he should not hold himself; or how a particular man did stand in such-and-such a place; and so on. One might (using the language of chemistry) call this picture a proposition-radical [*Satzradikal*]. This will be how Frege thought of the 'assumption' [*Annahme*]. (*PI* I, p. 11)

Like the conception criticized above, the idea of a sentence radical comes from striving to isolate a common, re-identifiable content in diverse sentences and kinds of sentences. This idea plays a great role in recent speech-act theories, which try to keep the propositional content—the radical of the sentence—from its illocutionary force,[6] for instance the force of an assertion, question, or desire, in accordance with the Fregean model. Following this model one writes for example '⊢—p' for the assertion that p is the case, '!—p' for the request or desire that p be the case, '?—p' for the question whether p is the case, and so on. In the case of 'p but I do not believe it' this will not help us, however, for since 'I believe' forms part of the thought we cannot analyse 'I believe p' into an illocutionary element plus 'p'. It is true that 'I believe it is raining' can be used to say much the same thing as the simple assertion 'It is raining', but it is none the less impossible to eliminate 'I believe' without destroying the sense of the sentence.

All the same, we cannot simply ignore the fact that the sentences 'It is raining' and 'I believe that it is raining' contain the same words.

---

[5] Cf. G. E. M. Anscombe, *An Introduction to Wittgenstein's Tractatus* (London, 1971), 105–6, and M. Dummett, *Frege: Philosophy of Language* (London, 1973), 326. Both Anscombe and Dummett are right in pointing out that 'Annahme' was not a technical term for Frege. But it is not clear that Wittgenstein misunderstood Frege merely because he introduced his own terminology, which is after all based on Frege's text, for speaking of the Fregean model. At any rate, Wittgenstein was much more concerned about a general account and criticism of the ideas lying at the bottom of this model than about an accurate description and criticism of Frege's theory.

[6] The expression is J. L. Austin's (cf. *How to Do Things With Words* (Oxford, 1962), Lecture VIII), but the idea is clearly formulated in Frege, who discusses it using the example of assertion and question: 'An interrogative sentence and an indicative one contain the same thought; but the indicative contains something else as well, namely, the assertion. The interrogative sentence contains something more too, namely a request. Therefore two things must be distinguished in an indicative sentence: the content, which it has in common with the corresponding sentence-question, and the assertion.' G. Frege, 'The Thought: A Logical Inquiry', in P. F. Strawson (ed.), *Philosophical Logic* (Oxford, 1967), 62.

After all, it is for this reason that we find Moorean sentences puzzling but not, for example, a sentence like 'It is raining but I do not believe that my club has won the match' (at any rate, they are not puzzling in the same way). Accordingly, Wittgenstein writes in a suppressed remark:

It is as if one could say that the sense of the sentence radicals 'that it is raining' and 'that I believe it is raining' have a facet in common. So that, if each of them is prefixed by the assertion sign 'It is true', the sense of both assertions is the same (or roughly the same); while the remaining facets diverge. If those radicals are for example prefixed by the opening phrase 'Suppose' or if they are turned into reports in the past tense, then these sentences do not have the same sense any more. (MS 132, 6. 10. 46)

The ways in which the 'remaining facets' of the sense of the two sentence radicals diverge become clear as soon as one considers the asymmetries in our use of 'believe' between the different grammatical persons as well as between the present tense and the past tense of the first person singular. 'It rained but I did not believe it' is a perfectly straightforward sentence which may be either true or false, whereas the corresponding formulation in the present tense is, as we have seen, evidently paradoxical. And 'It is raining but he does not believe it' is also quite a normal sentence.

That we marvel at these asymmetries is due to the fact that we expect a word to have a uniform sense, a uniform use. We should like to say: 'But surely "I believed" in the past tense must mean exactly the same as "I believe" in the present tense!' But this expectation is an illusion; it is a deceptive result of our striving for generality and our 'urge for a simple rule' (MS 132, 3. 10. 46). That expectation is equally unjustified as this one: 'Surely $\sqrt{-1}$ must mean just the same for -1 as $\sqrt{1}$ does for 1!' (*RPP* i. § 476) Just as we cannot apply the usual operation of root extraction to -1, so we are not at liberty to use or understand 'believe' in the first person present tense in the same way as we do in the past tense. Therefore we should not be too surprised if 'It is raining and I do not believe it' were just as much to be excluded from language as '$\sqrt{-1}$' is to be excluded from mathematics.

The asymmetry between the two sentence radicals 'that it is raining' and 'that I believe it is raining' becomes particularly striking if they are prefixed by 'Suppose' or 'Let us suppose'. In 'Let us suppose it is raining' a supposition is made about the external world, whereas in 'Let us suppose that I believe it is raining' a supposition is made about *myself*. Whether or not the first supposition is true depends on the weather. The second supposition, on the other hand, has nothing to do with the weather; whether or not it is true depends on what the person in question is thinking, and it is verified or falsified through his statements and actions. 'And here there comes into view what is *subjective* about the psychological'—as Wittgenstein remarks apropos of the locution 'I believe I remember' (*RPP* i. § 107). It comes into view through the unexpected appearance of blatant asymmetries in our use of linguistic expressions which defy all attempts at systematization.

One striking aspect of the asymmetry which becomes evident through prefixing 'Suppose' to various sentence radicals lies in this, that it confounds several of our expectations. There are a large number of contexts where asserting 'p' amounts to more or less the same thing as asserting 'I believe that p'; that is, in many contexts I commit myself to a certain opinion both by making the simple assertion and by asserting 'I believe . . . '. Schematically this can be represented in the following way (where B_I stands for 'I believe'):

$$\vdash p \text{ similar to} \vdash B_I p$$

In this context 'B_I' does not have a particularly important function; occasionally one may even leave it out. But matters are completely different if we are dealing with a supposition. 'Suppose p' and 'Suppose I believe that p' are entirely different kinds of statement. Schematically:

$$-p \text{ not similar to} -B_I p$$

Here it becomes clear why Wittgenstein is so suspicious of the Fregean notation. The symbol '$\vdash$', which is composed of '$-$' and '$\vert$', suggests that the 'content'—what is indicated by the horizontal and the expression following it—is the same in both cases (those of assertion and supposition) because the vertical stroke is something that is *added* to the horizontal stroke. But as we have seen, matters do not agree with what this notation suggests: 'B_I', which in the case of assertion appears quite irrelevant, leads to a complete change of sense in the case of supposition. Thus we must reject the idea suggested by the symbol '⊢' that there is a continuous advance from a 'mere supposition, the putting of a case', to an assertion.

These are the considerations, I think, which led Wittgenstein to the following remark, which would otherwise remain extremely puzzling: 'Moore's paradox may be expressed like this: "I believe p" says roughly the same as "⊢ p"; but "Suppose I believe that p . . ." does not say roughly the same as "Suppose p . . ."' (*RPP* i. § 478). By this Wittgenstein means, if my interpretation is correct, that the expectations aroused by the model 'supposition $\rightarrow$ assertion' are frustrated by Moore's paradox.

What chiefly misleads us is, on the one hand, the concentration on what happens in my own mind—the idea that by using the word 'believe' we refer to a psychological process—and, on the other hand, a too restricted view of the logic of our statements,[7] as it comes to the fore in the conception inspired by Frege's assertion sign. But Wittgenstein does not regard these two misleading ideas as expressions of two completely different tendencies; he regards them as connected elements which support each other. He writes:

The report is a language game with these words. It would produce confusion if we were to say: the words of the report—the reported sentence—have a definite sense, and the reporting—the 'assertion'—adds another one to it. As if the sentence, spoken by a gramophone, belonged to pure logic; as if here it had the purely logical sense; as if here we had before us the object which logicians get hold of and consider—while the sentence as asserted, reported, is what is *in commerce*. As one may say: the botanist considers a rose *as a plant*, not as an ornament for a dress or room or as a delicate attention. The sentence, I want to say, has no sense outside the language game. This hangs together with its not being a kind of *name*. In which case one could say ' "I believe . . ."—*that's* how it is' pointing (inwardly, for instance) at what gives the sentence its meaning. (*RPP* i. § 488)

The first error pointed out by Wittgenstein is the idea that a 'logician' could in a sentence in use discover an element which as it

---

[7] Cf. MS 132, 5. 10. 46: 'Is that report ["p, and I do not believe it"] a *contradiction*, then? If what is called a contradiction is something of the form p & $-p$, then the report is not one. And yet you would tell someone who made such a report that he had contradicted himself! This indicates grave gaps in logic. It indicates what is indicated by so many things, viz. that what we usually call "logic" is only to be applied to a tiny part of the game with language. Which is another reason why logic is just as uninteresting as it should apparently be interesting.'

were represents the 'pure' sense of that sentence while through its use (as an assertion, for instance) it is given an additional sense, which is not so pure. But anyone who really wishes to understand the sense of a sentence must not behave like a botanist, who is not concerned about the possible uses of a plant. For a sentence does not have a sense independently of its uses in language games—this is one of the fundamental claims of Wittgenstein's later philosophy.

This claim is to be taken seriously and must not, if one wishes to do justice to Wittgenstein, be set aside as an exaggerated *bon mot*. The whole discussion of Moore's paradox is aimed at confirming this claim, for Wittgenstein wants to show that the misunderstandings arising in this case (as in many other cases) are engendered by the idea that it is possible to give a sentence sense without taking into account its use in a language game, that is, without characterizing the linguistic and non-linguistic context and specifying the point of an utterance of that sentence.

If one proceeded like a botanist, who may 'construct' an ideal rose while disregarding all possible uses of the plant, one would assume that there are ideal sentence radicals of the type 'that it is raining' and 'that X believes it is raining' with eternally constant meanings, which in their turn are uniformly and continuously connected with the uses of the relevant expressions in all grammatical persons and in all tenses. But then it would be impossible to find an explanation for the similarities and asymmetries of the uses of those expressions which were pointed out above. Moreover, together with the idea of an identical 'content'—which is now asserted, now supposed, now desired, now asked for—the model of a uniform, constant sentence meaning tempts us into assimilating the relevant expressions (sentence radicals) to names which behave like labels in directly indicating the designated objects. In this way Frege was tempted to conceive of sentences as names of truth values, and such an analysis could in a similar fashion lead to the mistaken conception that a sentence of the type 'I believe . . . ' stood for a mental state or process of believing.

Wittgenstein's point is that this rigid 'logical' model of supposition plus assertion, which is inspired by Frege's conception, will support a 'mentalist' approach. For it is associated with the assumption of a content or sentence radical common to different sentences, and this assumption will lead us to look for *one* kind of state of affairs corresponding to that sentence radical. As soon as this tendency joins forces with the insight that there is an irreducibly subjective, speaker-dependent element in 'I believe . . .' if prefixed by 'Suppose . . . ', we shall be tempted to identify the state of affairs which is being looked for with an inner state or process. Conversely, through concentration on an inner state or process one is apt to be induced into striving for a uniform analysis on the model 'supposition → assertion', as it appears desirable to have an identical form of designation corresponding to a certain kind of state or process. The idea of a corresponding sentence radical of the type 'that I believe . . .' is extremely convenient for someone who assumes that there is an identifiable inner state or process of believing.

As a remedy against both tendencies Wittgenstein recommends an investigation of the language games which are played with the expressions concerned:

If you consider the *language game* with the assertion 'He is going to come', you won't hit on the idea of analysing the assertion into a Fregean supposition (a content, as it were) and the asserting of this content. Anyway, it is again that notion of a process in the mind which suggests the idea of such a composition and analysis. (MS 132, 6. 10. 46)

The situation which Wittgenstein alludes to is one in which I am wondering if a certain person X is going to come, whereupon someone else remarks, 'Yes, he is going to come.' In this situation he might just as well have said, 'I believe he is going to come'—this would hardly have changed either my reactions to his remark or their consequences. If a Moorean sentence ('He is going to come but I do not believe it') or the insights gained through investigating Moore's paradox into the asymmetries of our use of 'believe' (as regards present and past tense as well as the formulation of a supposition) are brought into one's consideration of this situation, then one might feel an urge to find a uniform analysis of both sentences in order to give an explanation of the sameness or similarity of their meanings. If, on the other hand, one simply sticks to looking at the language game, that is, at the moves which can be made by means of the expressions 'He is going to come' and 'I believe he is going to come', one will find that there are situations where there is no considerable difference between these two forms of expression, whereas our reactions and their consequences, and hence the meanings of those expressions, will diverge a great deal if the linguistic and non-linguistic contexts are modified.

Why there is sameness or similarity of meaning in such a situation can be elucidated satisfactorily if one focuses attention on the function of those expressions in various language games and *puts up* with divergences and asymmetries without wanting to impose a uniform analysis on all their uses. In this way one may, for example, point out that in the situation described the speaker does not use the sentence 'I believe he is going to come' to say something about himself and that in this situation his hearer or hearers will react to an utterance of this sentence more or less the same way as to an utterance of the words 'He is going to come', whereas 'I wish I believed that he is going to come' or 'Suppose I believe he is going to come' are both in point of speaker's intention and of hearer's reaction quite different from 'I wish that he were going to come' or 'Suppose he is going to come'. One might put it by saying that at a certain point the language games of assertion and belief intersect and then proceed to diverge.[8] However, the fact that these games intersect at one point is no compelling reason for wanting to get all uses of 'believe' under *one* umbrella.

The extent to which the various uses of 'believe' diverge as well as the heterogeneity of these uses become clear if one confronts the standard use of 'I believe that . . . ' with the use of 'believe' in the third person. If the other person says, 'I believe it is raining', I can draw certain inferences from his utterance as to his future behaviour, for instance that he will stay at home or that he will take his umbrella along or something of that kind. Corresponding to these are the inferences that can be drawn from my use of the sentence 'He believes it is raining'; thus such a statement may for example be regarded as giving a motive for his actions. But in the

---

[8] Cf. MS 132, 6. 10. 46: 'It is part of the essence of what is called "assertion" as well as part of the essence of what is called "believing" that the statement "I believe *p*" amounts to the same thing as the assertion "⊢——". / One might also say: it is part of the language game of asserting and part of the language game with the word "believe".' This quotation clearly confirms the view, presented in Ch. 2, above, that very different kinds of thing are called language games by Wittgenstein: the language game of assertion is to be described in a completely different way and with completely different means from the language game with the word 'believe'. A description of the latter must primarily refer to the use of the word 'believe', while the language game of assertion is to a larger extent to be accounted for by means of specifying a context, a speaker's behaviour, the consequences of his utterance, and his tone.

case of *my* utterance of 'I believe it is raining' things are completely different:

I do not draw from what I am saying any inference as to what I am likely to do. If I do so nevertheless, one would say that I am as it were speaking like a super-ego, that I have a split personality, or something of that kind. But that is not an *explanation* of my way of talking; it merely expresses that this is the way one normally talks about another person, not about oneself.[9]

Wittgenstein does not emphasize this asymmetry between first and third person—between my utterance and the utterance of another person—because I know more about my own mental life than about the other; he emphasizes it to point out that the ways we react to these utterances, which sound the same but are made by different people or differ as to the grammatical person, are completely different. If I wanted to take the same attitude towards my own utterance as to that of another person, I should have to behave like a schizophrenic, that is, I should have to react to my own utterance as if a different person were speaking through my mouth (cf. *PI* II. x, p. 192).

At this point of Wittgenstein's considerations we again notice how those two tendencies of concentrating on inner processes and of striving for a uniform explanation of the logic of our concepts work together and are for this reason attacked by Wittgenstein in the same breath. In order to avoid having to admit to a hiatus in the logic of 'believe' the advocate of uniformity tries to reduce the differences between first and third person to differences in our possibilities of coming to know something (and not, for instance, to differences between several meanings of one and the same word). The advocate of uniformity thinks that in my own case I simply know better. I need not pay attention to my own utterances to find out what I am going to do; to find that out it is enough to glance into my mind. And this has just as little to do with the meaning of 'believe' as the several points of view or the various possibilities of verification of a group of observers have with the meaning of 'see'.

Thus the advocate of a uniform explanation of meaning, through his striving for that aim, is tempted to assimilate observation of self

---

[9] MS 133, p. 129. Cf. *RPP* i. § 708: 'My super-ego might say of my ego: "It is raining, and the ego believes so", and might go on, "So I shall probably take an umbrella with me." And now how does this game go on?'—For comparisons between the first and the third persons, cf. also MS 133, pp. 118 ff. (Feb. 1947): *RPP* i. §§ 700 ff.; and MS 134, 4. 3. 47: *RPP* i. §§ 808 ff.

and observation of others and to conceive of them as varieties of one and the same species (verification) for the sake of preserving a single sense of 'believe'. In this way he is led to concentrate on believing as an inner state or process which in the case of other people I find out about with more or less difficulty while in my own case I do so immediately and without any doubt.

This understanding of the expression 'believe' could be defended only if all sentences with 'I believe . . .' were used as statements about the speaker. But as we have already seen, this is not at all the case, for the intention of the speaker is usually directed to the believed state of affairs. The hearer will normally understand such sentences as statements about certain states of affairs to which the speaker is committing himself, not as statements about the speaker himself, like 'I do not feel well', 'I am mortified', and so forth.[10]

Consideration of the language games with the word 'believe' shows that I do not take the same attitude towards other people's utterances of 'I believe . . .' as I do towards my own. In the case of another person's utterance I may find it useful to check and to find out what it is that he believes and whether he is really convinced of it. It is really possible for me to verify whether he does believe, and the 'question about "verification" is a question about the grammar of the expression, about the rules which guide the use of the expression' (MS 133, p. 160). In my own case there is *no* question about verification; therefore the parallel between my own utterance and that of other people suggested by the advocate of a uniform explanation of meaning does not exist. In Wittgenstein's view this lack of the possibility of verification constitutes a crucial 'grammatical' difference, and hence a difference which determines the meaning of the word 'believe'. Thus striving for a uniform explanation of meaning leads to an erroneous understanding of meaning and, as has already been pointed out, to an unnecessary appeal to inner states or processes.

To this the advocate of uniformity may reply: 'But why is the use of the verb "believe", its grammar, put together in such a queer

---

[10] Cf. *RPP* i. § 750: 'So is each judgment a judgment about the one who is judging? No, it is not, inasmuch as I don't want the main consequences that are drawn to be ones about *myself*, I want them rather to be about the subject matter of the judgment. If I say "It's raining", I don't in general want to be answered: "So *that's* how it seems to *you*." "We're talking about the weather," I might say, "not about me."'

way?' And the right answer to that is: 'Well, it isn't *queerly* put together. It's only queer if one compares it with, say, the verb "eat"' (*RPP* i. § 751). The advocate of uniformity makes the mistake of expecting all expressions to behave in the same uniform manner and, if he encounters unexpected forms of behaviour, to avoid facing up to undesirable characteristics of our use of linguistic expressions by side-stepping and appealing to misleading similarities. He is tempted by surface analogies to assume that there are corresponding analogies of function and meaning. And he tends to overlook that surface analogies may hide completely different ways of functioning, as in the following image from the *Philosophical Investigations*:

It is like looking into the cabin of a locomotive. We see handles all looking more or less alike. (Naturally, since they are all supposed to be handled.) But one is the handle of a crank which can be moved continuously (it regulates the opening of a valve); another is the handle of a switch, which has only two effective positions, it is either off or on; a third is the handle of a brake-lever, the harder one pulls on it, the harder it brakes; a fourth, the handle of a pump: it has an effect only so long as it is moved to and fro. (*PI* § 12)

The extent to which the meaning of our expressions depends on their use, that is, on their roles in various language games, shows itself as soon as one tries to find out which expressions may replace others and may hence be used interchangeably. There are, as we have seen, some contexts where there is no noticeable difference between a straightforward assertion of '*p*' and an assertion of 'I believe that *p*'. Thus saying, 'He is going to come' will in most contexts amount to the same thing as saying, 'I believe he is going to come.' In both cases I commit myself to the view that he is going to come—Wittgenstein says I accept as it were a bet on his going to come.[11]

The case is different if we use the words 'I believe . . . ' to express that we are not quite sure of what we are saying. In such a case the words 'I believe . . . ' may be substituted by 'It may . . . ' or the like:

[11] MS 133, p. 120. Presumably Wittgenstein also cites the comparison with a bet (cf. *LPP* 194) to show, by looking at the function of the relevant expressions in their respective language games, why Moorean sentences are absurd. 'I bet that *p* but I do not believe it' is evidently not self-contradictory but unreasonable. If someone said something of that kind, we should think that he did not understand what he was saying.

For consider this fact: the words "I believe it is raining" and "It may be raining" may say the *same*: *inasmuch*, that is, as in some contexts it makes no difference which of the two sentences we use. (And rid yourself of the idea that one of them is accompanied by a different mental process from the other.) The two sentences may say the same thing, although there is an 'I believe . . .' and 'He believes . . .' etc. that corresponds to the first and not to the second. For a different *concept* is used in the construction of the first. That is: in order to say that perhaps it is raining we do *not* need the concept 'believe', although we may use it for that purpose. (*RPP* i. § 821)

That is, we can make the move in the language game made with 'I believe . . .' by means of a formulation which does not tempt us as easily to think that we are here talking about a mental process.

But substitution of 'I believe . . .' by 'It may . . .' not only has the advantage of deflecting our attention from the alleged mental process, it also enables us to reformulate the relevant Moorean sentence in a new idiom. Thus 'It may be raining but it is not raining' (and even 'It may be raining and it is raining') simply serve no purpose. In this case, however, we are not so tempted to look for an explanation which appeals to a supposed sameness of 'content' or to the incompatibility of conflicting mental processes. In this new case of a paradoxical formulation we find it easier to point out that the absurdity of such utterances is due to their unusability in a language game.

This, however, should not prevent us from accepting the insight that this is really a point of intersection between our uses of the concepts 'believe' and 'it may': in this sense—that is, in this context and used with this intention—they are interchangeable.[12] This means that we should draw the consequence and assign this facet of meaning to the *concept* 'believe', just as we also assign to it the reference to the speaker in sentences like 'Suppose I believe . . .'. The fact that on some occasions this reference is brought into play while on other occasions it remains absent may render this concept difficult to learn, but it is not for this reason an 'odd' one. The

[12] Wittgenstein points out that 'It may . . .' (and consequently 'I believe . . .') may in some cases be replaced by 'It seems . . .'. But in contrast with the other two expressions 'It seems . . .' does not lead to Moore's paradox. 'It seems to be raining and it is (not)' makes just as much sense as 'It seems to be raining and I (do not) believe it' (cf. *RPP* i. § 822). So here we have got a third concept which in one of its uses agrees with the other two while it diverges from them in other respects.

crucial point is that we do not really expect to be able to treat all concepts alike. It is a superstition to think that a word must have the same meaning in all its uses. And it is no less mistaken to hold that two words which diverge in some uses must be different in all cases.

This consideration may serve to explain the point of a remark from the *Philosophical Investigations* which is particularly difficult to grasp: 'Don't regard a hesitant assertion as an assertion of hesitancy' (*PI* II. x, p. 192). A hesitant assertion would be a statement like 'It may be raining' or (in same cases) 'I believe it is raining'. To understand (or misunderstand) such a statement as an assertion of hesitancy is a reading which is suggested if one conceives of it as saying something about the speaker or his mental processes. This kind of misunderstanding can be avoided if one pays attention to the ways these expressions are used in their respective language games and if one refrains from attempting to give nothing but uniform explanations of words like 'believe'.

In the third of his extensive discussions of Moore's paradox Wittgenstein returns to some of the subjects mentioned above.[13] After investigating some expressions which, in spite of numerous divergences, can function the same way in certain contexts, he turns to considering the possibility of using one and the same expression in different ways, thus giving it different senses. It is not at all difficult, for instance, to imagine a situation where the sentence 'It is raining' is uttered, not as an assertion, but as a supposition and where this is not made explicit by such a locution as 'Suppose . . .'. In a suppressed remark Wittgenstein writes:

It is quite possible that a sentence, e.g. 'It is raining', is at one time uttered as an assertion, at another time as a supposition (even if it is not prefixed by 'Suppose')—what renders it the one, what the other?—On the one hand I want to answer: the game in which it is used. On the other hand: the intention with which it is uttered. How do these two tally with each other? (MS 136, 10. 1. 48)

One consequence of this possibility of using 'It is raining' as a supposition without additional qualifications is that one might thereby produce a meaningful utterance of the sentence 'It is raining but I do not believe it'; for if we are dealing with a supposition, that sentence loses its paradoxical character and might really be used under certain conditions. In such a case it might mean something like 'Provided it is raining but I do not believe it' (cf. *RPP* ii. § 280).

Wittgenstein says that how the sentence 'It is raining' is to be understood is also dependent on how it is 'meant'. What does that amount to? We must not believe that this kind of meaning could be explicated by indicating an inner act of intending, even if Wittgenstein in no way denies the possibility that while uttering that sentence as a supposition all kinds of things may be going on in our minds. In order to explain the way the sentence is meant I shall have to explain its function in the language game concerned, and hence the language game itself: ' "I intended the sentence as a supposition"—how do I explain that?—I intended that game. I can only explain even the fact that I intended this movement as the opening of a chess match by explaining the game of chess' (MS 136, 10. 1. 48). If I advance a pawn on the chess-board and someone asks me what I am doing this for, I may answer by saying that this move was meant to be the opening of a chess match. If the person who has asked the question knows how the game of chess is played, my explanation will be sufficient. If he does not know that, I cannot help him by telling him something about my intention or even about the mental process of intending this or that. In order to make him understand my intention I shall have to explain the game of chess to him. And if he eventually grasps what I intended, he will have understood it without my having made any reference to mental processes.

The same applies to the game of supposition. If my interlocutor does not understand the statement that I meant the sentence 'It is raining' as a supposition (so that I might, for example, proceed by saying 'and I do not believe it'), then he will not be helped by a description of my mental states; I shall rather have to explain to him how the language game of supposition works, which does not necessarily require teaching him all the details of our use of the word 'suppose'. He will have to learn what is involved in making a supposition, for instance that the conclusions drawn from a supposition are to be treated differently from the conclusions drawn from a statement. And he will also have to learn the *point* of making suppositions. Thus he may, for instance, be told that they serve to review possible courses of action in the past or in the future, which may then help to organize our own future actions. And he will also have to learn what the consequences of suppositions are and how one reacts to them. Our mental states and processes are never mentioned in these cases—they simply have no role to play here.

Wittgenstein tries again and again to show how the meaning of linguistic expressions depends on their use in language games, and it is for this reason that in his investigations of 'grammatical' peculiarities he takes great pains to specify the respective contexts of the various language games as accurately as possible. This is why he does not like to speak of a language game of assertion but prefers to describe games of reporting, for instance, as this specification makes it clearer what the point of the speaker's assertion may be. Wittgenstein implies that the language game of reporting is relatively uncomplicated and well entrenched in our natural kinds of behaviour. The report 'I believe . . .' is a straightforward way of saying what I think, whereas a supposition beginning with 'I believe . . .' or 'Suppose I believe . . .' tends to involve a much more complicated context—one might wish to say: a theoretical context.

It is not difficult to imagine how a report of the type 'I believe . . .' may be replaced by more primitive forms of expression, for instance by pictures, gestures plus ejaculations, etc., just as the statement 'I am in pain' may be replaced by a groan.[14] Supposing, on the other hand, is a game which presupposes so much and whose playing depends on so many details that it is quite inconceivable that an explicit supposition or a statement which by its tone or verbal context is marked as a supposition might be replaced by pictures, gestures, or similar devices. Such pictures or gestures could be used as auxiliary means of formulating a supposition; but it would not be feasible to replace the essentially linguistic element of a supposition by such means.

The real extent of the complexity of the game of supposition becomes visible as soon as we compare it with the model 'supposition of a content → assertion of a content', which was inspired by Frege's assertion sign. Only through such a comparison will it become clear what Wittgenstein means by the following

---

[14] 'Why is the report "I believe it is raining" similar to this one: "It is raining", whereas the supposition that I believe it is raining is completely dissimilar from the supposition that it is raining? Well, the report "I believe . . ." is an utterance of the belief, but the supposition is not an utterance. As a groan may replace the report "I am in pain" but not the supposition' (MS 136, 10. 1. 48; cf. *RPP* i. § 281).

remark: 'In the *supposition* the line is already different from what you think' (*RPP* ii. § 416). What is meant by the 'line' is the line associated with the concept 'believe' and leading from supposition to assertion. And the word 'already' suggests that Wittgenstein is here thinking of the 'Fregean' model, according to which we *advance* from the supposition (first step) of a content to its assertion (second step).[15] Evidently this model has been derived from simple assertoric statements and appears to be quite appropriate to them. Here the move from supposing that it is raining to recognizing and asserting its truth appears just as correct as its representation by '——It is raining / ⊢——It is raining' seems adequate. A disturbing element comes into play only if we think of verbs like 'believe'. The supposition '(Suppose) it is raining and I do not believe it' is a meaningful sentence, whereas the assertion '(It is true that) it is raining and I do not believe it' does not make sense; we do not know how to make any use of it. Here the normal line, which leads from a meaningfully supposed content to a meaningful (true or false) assertion of this content, is interrupted. As we see, not every content which may meaningfully be supposed will also count as a meaningfully assertable content.

If one does not have a clear and conspicuous view of the various uses of the word 'believe' and if one has not understood the consequences it may have in the language game, one will easily be misled by the model 'supposition → assertion'. Only if one has grasped that 'believe' occurs not only in simple statements but may also be used in expressions such as 'I believe it but I am not sure', 'I believe it but it may turn out to be different', etc., will one understand that the supposition 'I believe . . .' does not have a clearly circumscribed content, that the line does not always run straightforwardly from a supposition to an assertion. This is why Wittgenstein continues in the following way:

I should like to say: When you say 'Suppose I believe that' you are presupposing the whole grammar of the word 'to believe'. You are not supposing something given to you unambiguously through a picture, so to

---

[15] This interpretation is confirmed by the following suppressed remark which precedes *RPP* ii. § 416 in the manuscript: 'That is our concept of "believe"—*this* is the way we continue the line from supposition to assertion. Now we try out another continuation, we modify the line of the concept, and we say, "This is not the same at all any more!". That is: now the word "believe" will no longer fit even *that* part of the line which we have left unchanged.' (MS 137, 3. 2. 48)

speak, so that you can tack on to this supposition some assertion other than the ordinary one. *You would not know at all* what you were supposing here, if you were not already familiar with the use of 'believe'. (*RPP* ii. §416)

The idea of a content common to assertion and supposition tempts us into looking for a correspondence between the state of affairs mentioned in the assertion and the state of affairs which according to the supposition has been picked out by a belief, and it tempts us into looking for this by way of 'imagining what is going on when one believes something': 'Thus I imagine that I am directing my gaze into myself to discover there the belief in that state of affairs.' But to the formulation 'imagining what is going on when one believes something' Wittgenstein adds the parenthetical remark: 'Of course, all this is only a misunderstanding' (MS 137, 3. 2. 48). The misunderstanding arises because we are looking for a parallel where there is none to be found. The picture we have in mind is that of advancing from the supposition that it is raining to the assertion 'It is raining', and we think that everything must be similar if we start from the supposition 'I believe it is raining'. But, as we have seen, this is not so, for here there is an 'invisible use showing its face', for example, if we stumble into Moore's paradox and do not know how to go on. We are fettered by the picture of a common content and, as we have not got a sufficiently far-ranging overview, we have not taken into account the possibility that certain peculiarities of the use of words like 'believe' may fool us. Wittgenstein's examples, however, show that 'it is not the picture which matters but its use' (MS 137, 2. 2. 48), and if we consider the use of the picture of a speaker who believes it is raining, it becomes clear that an apparently inconspicuous modification, such as the addition of a tiny word or phrase, may transform the sense of the picture completely.

For Wittgenstein, Moore's paradox is not just a problem which arises within a certain theory and which ought to stimulate us to correct the theory so that the paradox cannot be formulated. Paradoxical sentences of the Moorean kind may simply be ruled out because, as Wittgenstein maintains, they do not have a use. But the possibility of formulating them should teach us the importance of arriving at an overview of the grammar of our expressions, even if they appear harmless. To arrive at an overview of the grammar of a concept is tantamount to understanding that concept, and this requires scrutinizing all kinds of possibilities for using it in our language games. Such a scrutiny will always involve a specification of the linguistic and non-linguistic context, of the consequences of using the concept, of the evident and identifiable intentions of the speaker, as well as of the characteristic reactions of the audience. For Wittgenstein, all of this is part of what he calls the 'logic' of our language. As he emphasizes in the letter to Moore quoted at the beginning of this chapter, this 'logic' is much more comprehensive than formal logic, which Wittgenstein likes to style 'Aristotelian' logic. In a suppressed remark he gives the following summary:

At first glance Moore's paradox seems to be just a contradiction; but then it is clear that it cannot be one, for the one sentence is a sentence about the weather, say, while the other is about *me*. Thus it now seems as if the paradox were merely a psychological incongruity, similar, for instance, to the case where someone says: 'The apple tastes fine but I do not like it.' But this is not the way things are in that first case.—It is as if logic could not concern it or—what a shocking thought!—as if there would have to be a logic of assertion besides the logic of propositions. There would have to be an extension of logic containing rules which, while they admit the supposition $p \cdot -q$, do not under certain circumstances allow the assertion. And where will that lead to! For one imagines a logic of the Aristotelian type, only more complicated still. And it is nevertheless difficult to imagine how such a logic may be delimited, how it may have the clear, simple outlines of the Aristotelian one. (MS 136, 11. 1. 48)

Wittgenstein does not want to recommend a new kind of formal logic, which might in addition to 'Aristotelian' logic also comprise a logic of assertion. The philosophical problems arising from 'absurd' sentences of the kind indicated by Moore's paradox need a different, a more complex and more comprehensive treatment, which, while it may sacrifice the uniformity and simplicity of the earlier analysis, throws into relief the physiognomy of the use of the relevant concepts. To be sure, such a procedure, which, instead of trying to explain away the striking differences between various uses of 'believe', makes them stand out more clearly, may have to put up with the objection that a physiognomy which has been reconstructed in this way does not display the regularity of the features we are used to. But the right reply to this is that, if one really wants to come to know a phenomenon, one will have to look at it from *all* sides, and that one must not then be surprised if unsuspected anomalies confound fondly held prejudices, for 'what can be more different than the profile and the front view of a face' (*RPP* i. § 45)?

10

Epilogue: Ultimate Questions

> The brain looks like a writing, inviting us to read it, and yet it isn't a writing.
>
> (*LW* § 806)

Much has been written within philosophical psychology to defend or refute some position on the so-called mind–body problem. But it quite frequently happens that even authors who do not take a stance on this problem are regarded as belonging to one of the parties in this dispute. It seems that every author writing about psychological concepts must count as a dualist or a materialist, as a defender of interactionism or of behaviourism, as an advocate of psychophysical parallelism or of functionalism. In view of all this zeal for classification Wittgenstein's attitude presents a kind of scandal. In the *Philosophical Investigations* he mentions behaviourism, but only to indicate the origins of a misleading way of looking at things (*PI* §§ 307–8). In another passage he speaks of the 'prejudice in favour of psycho-physical parallelism', but again only to underline the 'grammatical' misunderstandings at the bottom of this prejudice (*RPP* i. § 906; *Zettel* § 611). Evidently Wittgenstein wants to have nothing to do with the traditional ways of discussing the mind–body problem; it even appears that he regards this whole question as misguided.

In spite of this Wittgenstein has been classified as belonging to one party or another; in most cases people have preferred to call him a kind of behaviourist. A well-known thesis is that defended by Chihara and Fodor, according to which Wittgenstein is to be counted as an advocate of 'logical behaviourism'. Even though these authors are aware of the fact that the label 'behaviourist' is hard to defend if applied to a philosopher who, precisely in contrast with classical behaviourism, sets great store by an analysis of our everyday concepts for psychological phenomena, they try to justify their claim by affirming that Wittgenstein holds the same view as C. F. Hull, for instance, according to which it is a condition for the coherent use of mental predicates that they be connected with behavioural predicates not only in an empirical but also in a 'logical' way.[1] Of course, in this highly general formulation that claim amounts to no more than saying that there have to be conceptual connections between mental and behavioural predicates. That is a statement which very few people would want to reject and which surely cannot be a reason for calling someone a logical behaviourist. Chihara and Fodor try to put their thesis more specifically and to justify it by ascribing to Wittgenstein an extreme form of 'operationalism'; but this idea is based on a number of misunderstandings whose discussion would lead us too far afield.

Wittgenstein's opinion of behaviourism is indicated by the following passage:

Then is it misleading to speak of man's soul, or of his spirit? So little misleading, that it is quite intelligible if I say 'My soul is tired, not just my mind'. But don't you at least say that everything that can be expressed by means of the word 'soul', can also be expressed somehow by means of words for the corporeal? I do not say that. But even if it were so—what would it amount to? For the words, and also what we point to in explaining them, are nothing but instruments, and what matters now is their use. (*RPP* i. § 586)

Here (1) Wittgenstein mentions an example of a non-metaphorical use of the word 'soul' which at the same time does not imply any ontological commitment. (2) To the relevant question he replies that he does not believe that a 'mentalistic' language can be replaced by a 'physicalistic' one. (3) As words do not by themselves designate anything specific but only gain meaning and reference by being used in a linguistic community, even the existence of a language without explicit expressions for psychological phenomena would not demonstrate that this language was not used to speak of something psychological. In order to see this it will suffice to extend Wittgenstein's fiction of a 'soulless tribe' (cf. *RPP* i. § § 93 ff.) and suppose that the members of this tribe are not taught any explicitly psychological expressions and that the use of such expressions in communicating with them is not allowed. They will none the less be able to communicate and to pursue all kinds of activities. It is an idle question to ask whether by using such phrases as 'I am wounded', 'I

[1] J. A. Fodor, *Representations* (Cambridge, Mass., 1981), 318–19 n. 1.

am sweating', 'My feet start twitching' they really want to say 'I am in pain', 'I am afraid', 'I feel a certain rhythm'. The crucial point is how they react to such expressions and what use they make of them in performing various actions and respecting certain customs. The lesson we should learn from this consideration is of course this, that our own psychological expressions are themselves not primarily used to make statements about mental states or processes. In speaking of my being afraid I do not normally mean to describe it; I mean to be consoled, for instance. But even if a behaviourist succeeded in replacing our entire psychological vocabulary with some usable set of terms for corporeal things, this would in Wittgenstein's view say nothing very interesting about our psychological concepts; for what is meant by them must show itself in our language games, that is, in our actions.

A serious objection to a behaviourist's or physicalist's attempt to reduce our psychological language would concern the way that would restrict the richness of our ways of speaking. Alluding to Nietzsche's *Zarathustra*,[2] Wittgenstein wonders: 'Am I saying something like, "and the soul itself is merely something about the body"? No. (I am not that hard up for categories.)' (*RPP* ii. § 690). Wittgenstein does not wish to object to the physicalist that he is somehow wrong about matters of fact; he complains about the expressive poverty of the intended language. Wittgenstein sees no philosophical relevance in the physicalist's way of putting his questions but merely a deplorable tendency towards simplification.

But not only behaviourism has been ascribed to Wittgenstein. In a review of the *Remarks on the Philosophy of Psychology* Ian Hacking compares Wittgenstein to Descartes, finds a number of similarities, and goes so far as to call Wittgenstein a dualist.[3] But of course he has to admit that there are a number of differences between Wittgenstein and Descartes: (1) In contrast with Descartes, Wittgenstein does not teach the existence of two substances; he simply does not discuss the Cartesian question of substances. (2) While Descartes assumes that we can be absolutely certain of our own thoughts,

---

[2] Nietzsche, *Thus Spoke Zarathustra* (Harmondsworth, 1961), 61: 'But the awakened, the enlightened man says: I am body entirely, and nothing beside; and soul is only a word for something in the body.'

[3] I. Hacking, 'Wittgenstein the Psychologist', *New York Review of Books*, 29 5 (1982).

Wittgenstein argues that intersubjective, public matters are the only ones of which it can be said that we know them. Time and again he characterizes the method of starting from the ego as mistaken, misleading, and useless. (3) Whereas Descartes employs an extremely comprehensive concept of thinking,[4] Wittgenstein feels incapable of devising a general concept for the content of consciousness or the like. Even his modest attempt at a classification of psychological concepts from a relatively general point of view remains, as we have seen, sketchy and incomplete.

One would think that such clear and important differences between two philosophers should suffice to reject any claim as to their kinship. Nevertheless, Hacking writes:

> [I]n many essentials, [Wittgenstein] is just as much a dualist as Descartes. Both hold that psychology requires forms of description and methodology quite different from those called for in natural science. Reflection on thinking is not remotely like the study of the inhuman world of spatial, mechanical objects. . . . There is a whole domain of descriptions about how one feels thirsty, sees trees, grieves, and so forth, where one would be making some sort of conceptual error to ask for explanations of a materialistic sort. This is the important sense in which Wittgenstein and Descartes are equally dualistic.[5]

In this passage Hacking mentions at least two 'dualistic' aspects: first, the incompatibility of psychology with natural science; and, secondly, the contrast between a materialistic or physicalistic explanation, on the one hand, and a helpful description of psychological phenomena, on the other. As far as the second point is concerned, Hacking is probably right, for Wittgenstein does emphasize that physicalistic explanations are incapable of yielding satisfactory answers to our conceptual questions regarding memory, vision, emotion, and so forth. The first point, however, is not well taken. According to Wittgenstein, it is not only the philosophy of *psychology* which is completely different from natural science but philosophy in general. As long as we are dealing with *conceptual* questions concerning psychology, we are not doing science, any

---

[4] Cf. B. Williams, *Descartes* (Harmondsworth, 1978), 78: 'For Descartes, however, a *cogitatio* or *pensée* is any sort of conscious state or activity whatsoever; it can as well be a sensation (at least, in its purely psychological aspect) or an act of will, as judgement or belief or intellectual questioning.'

[5] Hacking, 'Wittgenstein the Psychologist', 42 and 44.

more than in discussing conceptual problems of mathematics, anthropology, art, or physics. Thus it is not the subject-matter of an investigation on which the difference depends; for Wittgenstein, a philosophical investigation is basically and essentially different from any kind of scientific procedure (and in this there may lie another difference between Wittgenstein and Descartes).

What remains of Hacking's thesis that there is a similarity between Descartes and Wittgenstein? As far as I can see, all that remains is a vague agreement as regards certain differences between scientific explanations and a philosophical elucidation of psychological concepts. Is that enough, however, to call Wittgenstein a dualist? I think not. To be sure, Wittgenstein explicitly says that a certain form of dualism is at least not senseless:

How about religion's teaching that the soul can exist when the body has disintegrated? Do I understand what it teaches? Of course I understand it—I can imagine a lot here. (Pictures of these things have been painted too. And why should such a picture be only the incomplete reproduction of the spoken thought? Why should it not perform the *same* service as our sentences? And this service is the point.) (*RPP* i. § 265)

No doubt, we *understand* the last pictures of Wilhelm Busch's series of cartoons *Die fromme Helene*.[6] And generations of adults have explained the *sense* of these pictures to generations of children. But this does not suffice to show the alleged truth of dualism.

There is in fact a number of remarks by Wittgenstein which may at first blush make him appear a kind of dualist. But if one looks more closely at these passages, it soon turns out that the function of these remarks is essentially critical and that they are by no means intended to lay the foundations of a dualistic or somehow mentalistic position. Wittgenstein writes:

No supposition seems to me more natural than that there is no process in the brain correlated with associating or with thinking; so that it would be impossible to read off thought-processes from brain-processes. I mean this: if I talk or write there is, I assume, a system of impulses going out from my brain and correlated with my spoken or written thoughts. But why should the *system* continue further in the direction of the centre? Why should this

---

[6] The illustrator and poet Wilhelm Busch (1832–1908) was widely known in German-speaking countries for his works *Max und Moritz*, *Maler Klecksel*, *Die fromme Helene*, etc., which Wittgenstein liked and admired. The last pictures of *Die fromme Helene* represent the heroine's soul as a separate entity from her body.

order not proceed, so to speak, out of chaos? The case would be like the following—certain kinds of plants multiply by seed, so that a seed always produces a plant of the same kind as that from which it was produced—but *nothing* in the seed corresponds to the plant which comes from it; so that it is impossible to infer the properties or structure of the plant from those of the seed that it comes out of—this can only be done from the *history* of the seed. So an organism might come into being even out of something quite amorphous, as it were causelessly; and there is no reason why this should not really hold for our thoughts, and hence for our talking and writing. (*RPP* i. § 903; cf. *LPP* 90)

The central idea of this remark is that there is no reason to think that something in the structure of the organism, of its nervous system, must correspond to the structure of certain psychological phenomena. Suppose there is someone who feels the 'switch' from one aspect to the other every time he looks at the duck-rabbit picture, and suppose that every time he feels this 'switch' something happens in his brain. We may even assume that there is a correlation between where he feels the 'switch' and where the physical event occurs in his nervous system—but as a physiological *explanation* it would not suffice. For it is quite possible that at one time the relevant neural occurrence exhibits properties A, B, C, at another time properties C, D, E, and every time more or less different ones. In this case there would be no recurrent regular structure corresponding to the occurrence which is to be explained, namely the feeling of a 'switch'. This would be analogous to the case of the seed, where I know that seeds from a given tree have always produced trees of the same kind, but where it is not in the nature of things for these seeds to display properties which somehow correspond to properties of the resulting trees. Thus our knowledge is 'historical' in the sense that only the fact that the seed actually came from and has produced a tree of type X permits us to say that it is a seed for that kind of tree. And it is in analogy with this that we may claim that there are no conceptual reasons for believing that there is any structural correspondence between a brain process and a psychological phenomenon.

But even if there are no structurally relevant correlates to be found in the nervous system, this would not mean that there can be no lawlike regularities between psychological states and processes. It is quite conceivable that the feeling of a 'switch', for instance, will always cause a certain satisfaction or that certain sensations of 'vacuousness' will again and again lead to a desire for shelter. If one examined a number of cases, one would find many lawlike regularities of this kind, such as correlations between sensations of taste and smell and certain images. Here one might speak of a 'causality between psychological phenomena' (*RPP* i. § 906), for: 'Why should there not be a psychological lawlikeness to which *no* physiological lawlikeness corresponds? If this upsets our concepts of causality then it is high time they were upset' (*RPP* i. § 905).

With these remarks Wittgenstein turns against the idea that there *must* be a physiological or a somehow materialistic explanation of psychological processes. There is *nothing* which speaks against the possibility of lawlike psychological regularities without corresponding correlates in the nervous system. Is this, however, an argument for mentalism? Certainly not. Moreover, Wittgenstein argues against the necessity of those 'inner representations' of which most mentalists have grown so fond:

Imagine the following phenomenon. If I want someone to remember a text that I recite to him, so that he can repeat it to me later, I have to give him paper and pencil; while I am speaking he makes lines, marks, on the paper; if he has to reproduce the text later he follows those marks with his eyes and recites the text. But I assume that what he has jotted down is not *writing*, it is not connected by rules with the words of the text; yet without these jottings he is unable to reproduce the text; and if anything in it is altered, if part of it is destroyed, he gets stuck in his 'reading' or recites the text uncertainly or carelessly, or cannot find the words at all.—This *can* be imagined!—What I called jottings would not be a *rendering* of the text, not a translation, so to speak, in another symbolism. The text would not be *set down* in the jottings. And why should it be set down in our nervous system? (*RPP* i. § 908)

Here certain occurrences in the nervous system are compared to a kind of doodle or scratches which look like writing but are not writing (nor are they cryptograms or codes). While there is a dependence between those scratches and my acts of remembering things, what I remember is in no way *read off* those scratches—they lack all regularity. This possibility can be generalized and applied to all forms of representation: according to Wittgenstein, it is nothing but wishful thinking which makes us believe that there must be a rule-guided or at least a regular mediation between certain experiences and certain forms of expression. The notion of lawlike regularities between types of experience and types of expression is independent of the idea of lawlike connections established by representations.[7]

In sum, Wittgenstein does not really take a stand on the traditional mind–body problem. He explicitly says that he is not a behaviourist, and many things he says are indeed incompatible with classical or 'logical' behaviourism. And it is obvious that he is not at all in sympathy with most mentalistic positions. But it should be equally clear that, for Wittgenstein, many of the questions that have arisen in the context of discussions of the mind–body problem are just confused or, at best, unanswerable.

[7] D. C. Dennett for example claims: '[T]he only psychology that could possibly succeed in explaining the complexities of human activity must posit internal representations. This premiss has been deemed obvious by just about everyone except the radical behaviourists' ('Artificial Intelligence as Philosophy and as Psychology', in *Brainstorms* (Brighton, 1981), 119). The fact that this premiss seems self-evident to many authors is not a good reason for accepting its truth, especially in view of the further fact that the only convincing argument mentioned by Dennett in this context is an argument *against* this premiss, viz. what he calls 'Hume's problem': 'On the one hand, how could *any* theory of psychology make sense of representations that *understand themselves*, and on the other, how could *any* theory of psychology avoid regress or circularity if it posits at least one representation-understander in addition to the representations?' (ibid. 122–3).

Appendix

German Originals for Manuscript Quotations

These manuscripts are held in the Wren Library, Trinity College, Cambridge.

p. 19. Man muß eben den Begriff 'sehen' nehmen, wie man ihn findet; ihn nicht verfeinern wollen. . . . Weil es nicht unsre Aufgabe ist, ihn zu ändern, einen für irgendwelche Zwecke geeigneteren einzuführen (wie es die Wissenschaft macht), sondern ihn zu verstehen; d. h., uns von ihm nicht ein falsches Bild zu machen. (MS 137, 9. 2. 48)

p. 20. Wir dürfen nicht vergessen: auch unsere feineren, mehr philosophischen Bedenken haben eine instinktive Grundlage. Z. B. das 'Man kann nie wissen . . .' Das Zugänglichbleiben für weitere Argumente. Leute, denen man das nicht beibringen könnte, kämen uns geistig minderwertig vor. *Noch* unfähig, einen gewissen Begriff zu bilden. (MS 137, 30. 6. 48)

p. 22. Der Begriff ist ja nicht nur die Art und Weise, wie wir über die Sache *denken*.
Er ist nicht nur eine Art der Einteilung, ein Gesichtspunkt des Ordnens. Er ist ein Teil unsres Handelns. (MS 137, 1. 7. 48)

p. 24 n. 2. Betrachte die Furcht, die Freude, das Denken, etc., der Menschen! / Aber wie kommt es, daß ich hier 'etc.' sagen kann? (MS 135, 11. 12. 47)

p. 25. Ich gehe das Problem aber noch nicht ganz richtig an. Es ist, als *wollte* ich ein impressionistisches Bild malen, wäre aber noch zu befangen in der alten Malweise und malte daher trotz allen Bemühens immer noch, was man *nicht* sieht. Ich trachte z. B. weit mehr in's Detail zu gehen, als ich müßte und sollte. (MS 135, 16. 12. 47)

pp. 38–9. Das, was ich wirklich von ihr [der musikalischen Phrase] sage, oder meine Gebärde, sind offenbar ganz ungenügend. Sie mögen, wenn sie von der Musik begleitet sind, passend erscheinen, würden aber niemand, der die Musik nicht kennt, eine Ahnung von ihrem Charakter geben. (MS 130, p. 57)

p. 39. . . . der Ernst, die Bedeutsamkeit dieser Gebärde . . . Meine Erklärung wird am Schluß darin bestehen, daß ich die Töne mit einer Gebärde und Miene *begleite*. Und diese Erklärung befriedigt mich. (MS 130, pp. 60–1)

p. 39. Es ließe sich vielleicht in einem Gedicht eine Wendung finden, die diesem Ausdruck der Tonsprache entspricht. Und das gäbe mir gewiß große Befriedigung. (MS 130, p. 62)

p. 44. Wie ist es aber, wenn jemand einen Satz in sehr ausdrucksvoller Weise sagt. Wenn etwa jemand eine gewisse Phrase in einem Ton und mit einer Miene ausspricht, wie sie nur ein Amerikaner aussprechen kann. Könnte ich *hier* den Ausdruck auf andere Weise wiedergeben? (MS 130, pp. 57–8)

p. 44–5. Aber es ist doch ein ganz bestimmter Ausdruck! Er drückt doch etwas ganz Bestimmtes aus!—Aber was er ausdrückt, ist nun nicht dadurch erklärt, daß wir ihn durch das und das ersetzen können, sondern durch seine *Umgebung*. In ihr nämlich erscheint, was er sagt, *ausdrucksvoll*. Denn was uns ausdrucksvoll erscheint, würde Einer der sozusagen die Implikationen nicht kennt, nicht ausdrucksvoll nennen. (MS 130, p. 58)

p. 49 n. 12. Wer 'Rot' erklärt, zeigt denn der auf einen Erlebnisinhalt? (MS 133, 4. 11. 46)

p. 75. Und der Vergleich mit dem *Sehen* ist eben gefährlich. Und *das* müßte ich daraus lernen. Ja, es sind hier Analogien, aber auch begriffliche Verschiedenheiten. (MS 135, 20. 7. 47)

p. 138. Man will nun so sagen: Wenn ich die Aussage 'Ich glaube p' statt '⊢—' verwende, so ist das ähnlich, wie wenn ich eine Photographie als Zeugnis eines bestimmten Tatbestandes verwende. Ich sage ja: 'Es macht auf mich den Eindruck'. Statt also die Wirklichkeit zu beschreiben, beschreibe ich die Wirkung, die sie auf mich, als Instrument, hat. (MS 132, 4. 10, 46)

p. 142 Es ist, als könnte man sagen, daß der Sinn des Satzradikals 'daß es regnet' und 'daß ich glaube, es regnet' eine Facette miteinander gemein haben. So daß, wenn man vor jedes der beiden das Zeichen der Behauptung 'Es ist wahr' setzt, der Sinn der beiden Behauptungen der gleiche (oder ungefähr der gleiche) ist; während die übrigen Facetten auseinandergehen //divergieren//. Wenn man z. B. vor jene Radikale den Satzanfang 'Angenommen' setzt oder einen Bericht in der Vergangenheitsform aus ihnen macht, so haben die Sätze nun nicht mehr den gleichen Sinn. (MS 132, 6. 10. 46)

p. 142. Das *Bedürfnis* nach einer einfachen Regel. (MS 132, 3. 10. 46)

p. 144 n. 7. Ist nun aber jene Meldung ein *Widerspruch*? Nennt man Widerspruch, was ich Kontradiktion nenne, //etwas von der Form p & –p// so ist die Meldung keiner. Und doch würde man Einem, der sie erstattete, sagen, er widerspräche sich selbst! Das weist auf schwere Lücken in der Logik hin. Es weist darauf hin—worauf so vieles hinweist—, daß, was wir für gewöhnlich 'Logik' nennen, nur auf einen winzigen Teil des Spiels mit der Sprache anzuwenden ist. Daher ja auch die Logik so uninteressant ist, wie sie dem Anschein nach interessant sein sollte. (MS 132, 5. 10. 46)

p. 146. Wenn man das *Sprachspiel* mit der Behauptung 'Er wird kommen' betrachtet, so fällt es einem nicht ein, die Behauptung in eine Fregesche Annahme (einen Inhalt sozusagen) und das Behaupten des Inhalts zu zerlegen. Es ist überhaupt wieder die Vorstellung von einem Vorgang im Geiste, die die Idee einer solchen Zusammensetzung und Analyse nahelegt. (MS 132, 6. 10. 46)

p. 147 n. 8. Es liegt im Wesen dessen, was man 'Behauptung' nennt, und im Wesen dessen, was man 'glauben' nennt, daß die Aussage 'Ich glaube p' der Behauptung '$\vdash$p' gleichkommt. / Man könnte auch sagen: es liegt im Sprachspiel des Behauptens und im Sprachspiel mit dem Worte 'glauben'. (MS 132, 6. 10. 46)

p. 148. Ich schließe nicht aus dem, was ich sage, darauf, was ich wahrscheinlich tun werde. Tue ich dies dennoch, so wird man sagen, ich spreche gleichsam wie ein Überich, ich habe eine geteilte Persönlichkeit, oder dergl. Aber das ist nicht eine *Erklärung* meiner Redeweise, sondern nur der Ausdruck dafür, daß man so für gewöhnlich nur über den Andern, nicht über sich selbst spricht. (MS 133, p. 129)

p. 149. Die Frage nach der 'Verifikation' ist eine Frage nach der Grammatik des Ausdrucks, nach [den] Regeln, . . . die den Gebrauch des Ausdrucks leiten. (MS 133, p. 160)

p. 152. Ein Satz, z. B. 'Es regnet', kann sehr wohl einmal als Behauptung, einmal als Annahme ausgesprochen werden (auch wenn ihm kein 'Angenommen' vorausgeht)—was macht ihn zum einen, was zum andern?— Einerseits möchte ich antworten: Das Spiel, in dem er gebraucht wird. Andererseits: die Intention, mit welcher er ausgesprochen wurde.//wird.// Wie reimen sich diese beiden zusammen? (MS 136, 10.. 1. 48)

p. 153. 'Ich hatte den Satz als Annahme intendiert'—wie erkläre ich das?—Ich hatte dies Spiel intendiert. Ich kann auch, daß ich diese Bewegung als Anfang einer Schachpartie intendierte, nur dadurch erklären, daß ich das Schachspiel erkläre. (MS 136, 10. 1. 48)

p. 154 n. 14. Warum ist die Meldung 'Ich glaube, es regnet' so ähnlich der: 'Es regnet'; dagegen die Annahme, ich glaube, es regnet, ganz unähnlich der Annahme, es regne? Nun, die Meldung 'Ich glaube . . .' ist eine Äußerung des Glaubens, aber die Annahme ist keine Äußerung. Wie ein Stöhnen die Meldung 'Ich habe Schmerzen' ersetzen kann, aber nicht die Annahme. (MS 136, 10. 1. 48)

p. 155 n. 15. *Das* ist unser Begriff vom 'glauben'—*so* setzen wir die Linie von der Annahme zur Behauptung fort. Nun versuchen wir eine andere Fortsetzung, wir verändern die Linie des Begriffs und sagen nun 'Das ist ja gar nicht mehr derselbe!' Das heißt: das Wort 'glauben' paßt nun auch nicht mehr für *den* Teil der Linie, den wir unverändert ließen. (MS 137, 3. 2. 48)

p. 156. Darauf *scheint* eine Antwort möglich, indem ich mir *vorstelle*, wie das ist: zu glauben. (Freilich ist das alles nur Mißverständnis.) Ich richte also meinen Blick in der Vorstellung //Phantasie// in mich, um dort das Glauben an den Sachverhalt zu entdecken. (MS 137, 3. 2. 48)

p. 156. . . . es kommt auf's Bild nicht an, sondern auf seine Verwendung. (MS 137, 2. 2. 48)

p. 157. Das Mooresche Paradox erscheint uns auf den ersten Blick einfach als Widerspruch; dann aber ist es klar, es könne keiner sein, da der eine Satz, sagen wir, vom Wetter handelt, der andere von *mir*. So erscheint es nun, als wäre das Paradox nur eine psychologische Unwahrscheinlichkeit. // Unstimmigkeit.// So etwa, wie wenn Einer sagte 'Der Apfel schmeckt sehr gut, aber ich mag ihn nicht.' Aber so ist es in jenem Fall auch nicht. —Es ist, als könne ihn die Logik nichts angehen, oder als müsse es (zu unserm Schreck) eine Logik der Behauptung außer der Logik der Sätze geben. Es müsse eine Erweiterung der Logik geben mit Regeln, die zwar die Annahme p˙−q gestattet, aber unter gewissen Umständen nicht die Behauptung. Und wo sollte das hinführen! Man stellt sich nämlich eine Logik nach Art der aristotelischen vor, nur noch komplizierter. Und doch ist schwer vorzustellen, wie so eine Logik begrenzt sein, wie sie die klaren, einfachen Konturen der aristotelischen haben kann. (MS 136, 11. 1. 48)

List of Manuscripts

1. MS 130: the first half without dates; the earliest date 26. 5. 46 (*RPP* i. 91), later dates 22. 7. (*RPP* i. § 132) and 28.7. (*RPP* i. § 158); then practically continuously dated until 9. 8. (*RPP* i. § 221); the last 110 pages written in under 20 days.
2. MS 131: continuous dates from 10. 8. 46 (*RPP* i. § 222) to 9. 9. 46 (*RPP* i. § 399); 206 manuscript pages in one month.
3. MS 132: practically continuous dates from 9. 9. 46 (*RPP* i. § 400) to 22. 10. 46 (*RPP* i. § 572); 212 manuscript pages in one month and a half.
4. MS 133: practically continuous dates from 22. 10. 46 (*RPP* i. § 572) to 17. 11. 46 (*RPP* i. § 659); then at first some private and some general entries; only few 'satisfactory' remarks; scattered dates (1. 12., 4. 12., 7. 1. 47, 19. 1. [*RPP* i. § 667]); then undated remarks until 12. 2. (*RPP* i. § 711) and undated continuation until 27. 2. (*RPP* i. § 799); last entries 28. 2. 47 (*RPP* i. § 803). Wittgenstein's work comes to a halt towards the end of 1946; then there is a brief revival at the beginning of November; then there is a pause. A new start at the end of January or the beginning of February 1947. Altogether only 190 manuscript pages in more than four months.
5. MS 134: frequent dates between 28. 2. 47 (*RPP* i. § 803) and 28. 4. 47 (after *RPP* i. § 950). Interruption until 10. 5; then a very few further entries. A new start on 27. 6. (*RPP* i. § 964), but still with many interruptions; the last entry is *RPP* i. § 991 (not dated).
6. MS 135: continuously dated from 12. 7. 47 (*RPP* i. § 992) until 3. 8. 47 (*RPP* i. § 1125): an impressive new start; then presumably revision of the manuscript material written so far. There are a few further entries (*RPP* i. § 1126–37) before and until 9. 11. 47, when TS 229 was completed. The first 140 manuscript pages were written in three weeks. A new start on 8. 12. (*RPP* ii. § 5); the remaining entries are practically continuously dated until 18. 12. 47 (*RPP* ii. § 57).
7. MS 136: continuous dates from 18. 12. 47 (*RPP* ii. § 58) to 25. 12. (*RPP* ii. § 165); then a short interruption. A new start of daily work on 1. 1. 48 (*RPP* ii. § 166); the manuscript ends on 25. 1. with *RPP* ii. § 414; 288 manuscript pages in little more than one month.
8. MS 137: initially continuous, later halting work from 2. 2. (*RPP* ii. § 415) until 25. 3. 48 (*RPP* ii. § 557). Then interruption until 28. 5. (*RPP* ii. § 558); at first Wittgenstein's work proceeds speedily, but slows down rather soon until 25. 8. 48 (*RPP* ii. § 737). Then revision and dictation of TS 232 (until end of October 1948). New start on 22. 10. 48 (*LW* § 1); continuous dates until 9. 1. 49 (*LW* § 694).

9. MS 138: continuous dates from 15. 1. 49 (*LW* § 695) until 3. 3. 49 (*LW* § 964). Then a few further entries during the second half of March (*LW* §§ 965–78); last entry (*LW* § 979) on 20. 5. 49.

Bibliography

AMBROSE A. (ed.), *Wittgenstein's Lectures: Cambridge 1932–1935: From the Notes of Alice Ambrose and Margaret Macdonald* (Oxford: Blackwell, 1979).

ANSCOMBE, G. E. M., *An Introduction to Wittgenstein's Tractatus* (London: Hutchinson, 1971).

AUSTIN, J. L., *How To Do Things with Words* (Oxford: Clarendon Press, 1962).

—— 'The Meaning of a Word', in *Philosophical Papers*² (Oxford: Clarendon Press, 1970), 55–75.

BAKER, G. P., and HACKER, P. M. S., *Wittgenstein: Understanding and Meaning* (Oxford: Blackwell, 1980).

BENJAMIN, W., *One-Way Street and Other Writings*, trans. E. Jephcott and K. Shorter (London: New Left Books, 1979).

BRENTANO, F., *Psychology from an Empirical Standpoint*, ed. Linda L. McAlister (London: Routledge & Kegan Paul, 1973).

BRITTON, K., 'Portrait of a Philosopher', in K. T. Fann (ed.), *Ludwig Wittgenstein: The Man and His Philosophy* (New York: Dell, 1967), 56–63.

COOPE, C., 'Wittgenstein's Theory of Knowledge', in G. Vesey (ed.), *Understanding Wittgenstein* (London: Macmillan, 1974), 246–67.

CORNFORD, F. M., *Plato's Theory of Knowledge* (London: Routledge & Kegan Paul, 1935).

DAVIDSON, D., 'Communication and Convention', in *Inquiries into Truth and Interpretation* (Oxford: Clarendon Press, 1984), 265–80.

—— 'What Metaphors Mean', in *Inquiries into Truth and Interpretation*, 245–64.

DENNETT, D. C., 'Artificial Intelligence as Philosophy and as Psychology', in *Brainstorms: Philosophical Essays on Mind and Psychology* (Brighton: Harvester Press, 1981), 109–26.

—— 'Beyond Belief', in A. Woodfield (ed.), *Thought and Object: Essays on Intentionality* (Oxford: Clarendon Press, 1982), 1–95.

DRURY, M. O'C., 'Conversations with Wittgenstein', in R. Rhees (ed.), *Ludwig Wittgenstein: Personal Recollections* (Oxford: Blackwell, 1981), 112–89.

DUMMETT, M., *Frege: Philosophy of Language* (London: Duckworth, 1973).

EHRENFELS, C. VON, 'On "Gestalt Qualities"', in B. Smith (ed.), *Foundations of Gestalt Theory* (Munich: Philosophia, 1988), 82–117.

FODOR, J. A., *Representations: Philosophical Essays on the Foundations of Cognitive Science* (Cambridge, Mass.: MIT Press, 1981).

—— *The Modularity of Mind* (Cambridge, Mass.: MIT Press, 1983).

FREGE, G., *Grundgesetze der Arithmetik* (Hildesheim: Olms, 1966).

—— 'Function and Concept', in P. Geach and M. Black (edd.), *Philosophical Writings of Gottlob Frege* (Oxford: Blackwell, 1970), 21–41.

—— 'The Thought: A Logical Inquiry', trans. A. M. and M. Quinton, in P. F. Strawson (ed.), *Philosophical Logic* (Oxford: Oxford University Press, 1967), 17–38.

GRILLPARZER, F., *Sämtliche Werke*, iii, ed. P. Frank and K. Pörnbacher (Munich: Hanser, 1964).

HACKING, I., 'Wittgenstein the Psychologist', *New York Review of Books*, 29: 5 (1982), 42–4.

HALLETT, G., *A Companion to Wittgenstein's 'Philosophical Investigations'* (Ithaca, NY: Cornell University Press, 1977).

HUME, D., *A Treatise of Human Nature*, ed. C. A. Selby-Bigge (Oxford: Clarendon Press, 1888).

JAMES, W., *The Principles of Psychology* (New York: Dover, 1950).

KENNY, A., *Wittgenstein* (London: Allen Lane, 1973).

—— 'From the Big Typescript to the Philosophical Grammar', *Acta Philosophica Fennica*, 28 (1976), 41–53.

KÖHLER, W., *Gestalt Psychology: An Introduction to New Concepts in Modern Psychology* (New York: Mentor, 1975).

KRIPKE, S., *Wittgenstein on Rules and Private Language* (Oxford: Blackwell, 1982).

LEE, D. (ed.), *Wittgenstein's Lectures: Cambridge 1930–1932: From the Notes of John King and Desmond Lee* (Oxford: Blackwell, 1980).

LOCKE, J., *An Essay Concerning Human Understanding*, ed. J. W. Yolton (London: Dent, 1961).

MACH, E., *Erkenntnis und Irrtum: Skizzen zur Psychologie der Forschung* (Darmstadt: Wissenschaftliche Buchgesellschaft, 1976).

—— *Die Analyse der Empfindungen und das Verhältnis des Physischen zum Psychischen*, ed. G. Wolters (Darmstadt: Wissenschaftliche Buchgesellschaft, 1985).

McGUINNESS, B., '"I Know What I Want"', *Proceedings of the Aristotelian Society* (1957–8), 305–20.

—— *Wittgenstein: A Life*, i. *Young Ludwig 1889–1921* (London: Duckworth, 1988).

MALCOLM, N., *Memory and Mind* (Ithaca, NY: Cornell University Press, 1977).

MANN, T., *Tristan*, trans. H. T. Lowe-Porter (New York: Alfred A. Knopf, 1979).

MAUTHNER, F., *Beiträge zu einer Kritik der Sprache. Zur Sprache und zur Psychologie* (Frankfurt/Berlin/Vienna: Ullstein, 1982).

MOORE, G. E., *Ethics* (London: Oxford University Press, 1912).

—— 'Some Judgements of Perception', in *Philosophical Studies* (London: Routledge & Kegan Paul, 1922), 220–52.

—— 'A Reply to My Critics', in P. A. Schilpp (ed.), *The Philosophy of G. E. Moore* (Chicago: Northwestern University Press, 1942).

—— *Some Main Problems of Philosophy* (London: George Allen & Unwin, 1953).

NIETZSCHE, F., *Thus Spoke Zarathustra*, trans. R. J. Hollingdale (Harmondsworth: Penguin, 1961).

PASSMORE, J., *A Hundred Years of Philosophy* (Harmondsworth: Penguin, 1978).

RHEES, R., 'Wittgenstein's Builders', in *Discussions of Wittgenstein* (London: Routledge & Kegan Paul, 1970), 71–84.

—— Preface, in L. Wittgenstein, *The Blue and Brown Books* (Oxford: Blackwell, 1972), pp. v–xiv.

RUSSELL, B., *The Analysis of Mind* (London: George Allen & Unwin, 1971).

RYLE, G., *The Concept of Mind* (Harmondsworth: Penguin, 1970).

SCHOPENHAUER, A., *Paralipomena*, in *Sämtliche Werke*, ed. V. Löhneysen, v (Stuttgart/Frankfurt: Cotta-Insel, 1965).

SCHULTE, J., 'Bedeutung und Verifikation', *Grazer philosophische Studien* (1982), 241–53.

—— ' "Es regnet, aber ich glaube es nicht": Zu *Philosophische Untersuchungen* II. x', *Teoria* (Pisa, 1985), 187–204.

—— 'World-picture and Mythology', *Inquiry*, 31 (1988), 323–34.

—— *Wittgenstein: Eine Einführung* (Stuttgart: Reclam, 1989).

—— 'Wittgenstein's Notion of Secondary Meaning and Davidson's Account of Metaphor', in J. Brandl and W. L. Gombocz (edd.), *The Mind of Donald Davidson* (Amsterdam: Rodopi, 1989), 141–8.

—— 'Chor und Gesetz: Zur "morphologischen Methode" bei Goethe und Wittgenstein', in *Chord und Gesetz* (Frankfurt: Suhrkamp, 1990), 11–42.

STENIUS, E., *Wittgenstein's Tractatus* (Oxford: Blackwell, 1960).

STICH, S., *From Folk Psychology to Cognitive Science: The Case against Belief* (Cambridge, Mass.: MIT Press, 1983).

WAISMANN, FRIEDRICH, *Ludwig Wittgenstein and the Vienna Circle*, ed. B. McGuinness, trans. J. Schulte and B. McGuinness (Oxford: Blackwell, 1979).

WILLIAMS, B., *Descartes: The Project of Pure Enquiry* (Harmondsworth: Penguin, 1978).

WITTGENSTEIN, L., *Philosophical Investigations*, ed. G. E. M. Anscombe and R. Rhees, trans. G. E. M. Anscombe (Oxford: Blackwell, 1953).

—— *The Blue and Brown Books* (Oxford: Blackwell, 1958).

—— 'Wittgenstein's Notes for Lectures on "Private Experience" and "Sense Data" ', ed. R. Rhees, in *Philosophical Review*, 77 (1968), pp. 275–320.

—— *On Certainty*, ed. G. E. M. Anscombe and G. H. von Wright, trans. D. Paul and G. E. M. Anscombe (Oxford: Blackwell, 1969).

—— *Philosophical Grammar*, ed. R. Rhees, trans. A. Kenny (Oxford: Blackwell, 1974).

—— *Letters to Russell, Keynes and Moore*, ed. G. H. von Wright and B. McGuinness, trans. B. McGuinness (Oxford: Blackwell, 1974).

—— *Philosophical Remarks*, ed. R. Rhees, trans. R. Hargreaves and R. White (Oxford: Blackwell, 1975).

—— *Remarks on the Foundations of Mathematics*, ed. G. H. von Wright, R. Rhees, and G. E. M. Anscombe, trans. G. E. M. Anscombe (Oxford: Blackwell, 1978).

—— *Culture and Value*, ed. G. H. von Wright, trans. P. Winch (Oxford: Blackwell, 1980).

—— *Remarks on the Philosophy of Psychology*, i. ed. G. E. M. Anscombe and G. H. von Wright, trans. G. E. M. Anscombe (Oxford: Blackwell, 1980).

—— *Remarks on the Philosophy of Psychology*, ii. ed. G. H. von Wright and H. Nyman, trans. C. G. Luckhardt and M. A. E. Aue (Oxford: Blackwell, 1980).

——*Zettel*, ed. G. E. M. Anscombe and G. H. von Wright, trans. G. E. M. Anscombe (Oxford: Blackwell, 1981).

—— *Last Writings on the Philosophy of Psychology*, ed. G. H. von Wright and H. Nyman, trans. C. G. Luckhardt and M. A. E. Aue (Oxford: Blackwell, 1982).

—— *Lectures on Philosophical Psychology, 1946–47*, ed. P. T. Geach (Hemel Hempstead: Harvester Wheatsheaf, 1988).

WRIGHT, G. H. VON, 'A Biographical Sketch', in *Wittgenstein* (Oxford: Blackwell, 1982), 13–34.

—— 'The Origin and Composition of the *Philosophical Investigations*', in *Wittgenstein*, 111–36.

—— 'Wittgenstein on Certainty', in *Wittgenstein*, 163–82.

—— 'The Wittgenstein Papers', in *Wittgenstein*, 35–62.

WUNDT, W., *Grundzüge der physiologischen Psychologie*, ii (Leipzig: Wilhelm Engelmann, 1893).

Index

report 144, 154
reproduction 59, 61–3
Rhees, R. 13–14, 67–70, 72
rule 15, 92
Russell, B. 8, 96–7
Ryle, G. 109

Schlick, M. 101
Schopenhauer, A. 98
Schubert, F. 40
Schulte, J. 1, 15, 16, 27, 35, 43, 135
Schumann, R. 42, 44, 68, 69, 72, 73,
   106, 107
science 76–9, 162–3
seeing 75, 84–5, 88–9
seeing-as 54–7, 63–5, 75, 84–5, 89
sensation 31–2, 80
sense datum 85–94, 103
sense impression 55–6
sentence radical
   (*Satzradikal*) 141–3, 145–6
simplicity 13
smell 85, 98
solipsism 93–4
sound 85, 91
specific 44–50, 51–3
speech-act theory 141
spontaneous 44–5, 52–3, 73
Stich, S. 101
subjective 36, 96, 104, 112, 146
supposition 135–58

surface grammar 15
synonym 73

taste 50, 85
teach 13
theory 23, 26, 35
thinking 28, 30
tone 107, 122, 132–4
trace 113–19
training 44
transparent 87

undergoing (*Erfahrung*) 29
understand 40–4
unreality 9
use 11, 14, 70, 145, 156
utterance 56, 61–2, 123, 132

verification 90, 149
vivacity 32
voluntary 109–10, 113

Wagner, R. 38, 51
Waismann, F. 101
Webern, A. von 38
Williams, B. 162
word meaning/sentence
   meaning 71–4
work 1–4
world picture 16
Wright, G. H. von 5–6, 8, 10, 16
Wundt, W. 29